Oxford Modern Britain

Race and Ethnicity in Modern Britain

Second Edition

David Mason

Series Editor: John Scott

OXFORD
UNIVERSITY PRESS

OXFORD
UNIVERSITY PRESS

Great Clarendon Street, Oxford OX2 6DP

Oxford University Press is a department of the University of Oxford.
It furthers the University's objective of excellence in research, scholarship,
and education by publishing worldwide in

Oxford New York

Athens Auckland Bangkok Bogotá Buenos Aires Calcutta
Cape Town Chennai Dar es Salaam Delhi Florence Hong Kong Istanbul
Karachi Kuala Lumpur Madrid Melbourne Mexico City Mumbai
Nairobi Paris São Paulo Singapore Taipei Tokyo Toronto Warsaw

with associated companies in Berlin Ibadan

Oxford is a registered trade mark of Oxford University Press
in the UK and in certain other countries

Published in the United States
by Oxford University Press Inc., New York

First published 1995
Second Edition 2000

British Library Cataloguing in Publication Data
Data available

Library of Congress Cataloging in Publication Data
Data available

ISBN 0-19-874285-1

10 9 8 7 6 5 4 3 2 1

Typeset by RefineCatch Limited, Bungay, Suffolk
Printed in Great Britain
on acid-free paper by
T.J. International Ltd, Padstow, Cornwall

Oxford Modern Britain

Race and Ethnicity in Modern Britain

The *Oxford Modern Britain* series comprises authoritative introductory books on all aspects of the social structure of modern Britain. Lively and accessible, the books will be the first point of reference for anyone interested in the state of contemporary Britain. They will be invaluable to those taking courses in the social sciences.

Also published in this series

Kinship and Friendship in Modern Britain
Graham Allen

Religion in Modern Britain
Steve Bruce

Women and Work in Modern Britain
Rosemary Crompton

Mass Media and Power in Modern Britain
John Eldridge, Jenny Kitzinger, and Kevin Williams

Health and Health Care in Modern Britain
Joan Busfield

Age and Generation in Modern Britain
Jane Pilcher

Youth and Employment in Modern Britain
Kenneth Roberts

Forthcoming titles

Business and Organization in Modern Britain
Stephen Ackroyd

Nations and Nationalism in Modern Britain
Christopher G. A. Bryant

Gender in Modern Britain
Nickie Charles

Voting Behaviour in Modern Britain
Anthony Heath

To the continuing memory of Lillian Rose Mason
1919–1982

Foreword

THE Oxford Modern Britain series is designed to fill a major gap in the available sociological sources on the contemporary world. Each book will provide a comprehensive and authoritative overview of major issues for students at all levels. They are written by acknowledged experts in their fields, and should be standard sources for many years to come.

Each book focuses on contemporary Britain, but the relevant historical background is always included, and a comparative context is provided. No society can be studied in isolation from other societies and the globalized context of the contemporary world, but a detailed understanding of a particular society can both broaden and deepen sociological understanding. These books will be exemplars of empirical study and theoretical understanding.

Books in the series are intended to present information and ideas in a lively and accessible way. They will meet a real need for source books in a wide range of specialized courses, in 'Modern Britain' and 'Comparative Sociology' courses, and in integrated introductory courses. They have been written with the newcomer and general reader in mind, and they meet the genuine need in the informed public for accurate and up-to-date discussion and sources.

John Scott
Series Editor

Acknowledgements

As with the first edition, many people have contributed in some way to the production of this book. Once again I owe a debt to John Scott and the editorial staff at Oxford University Press, Angela Griffin and Ruth Marshall, for their patience as I failed to meet their deadlines.

Thanks are again due to David Owen, of the National Ethnic Minority Data Archive, for permission to reproduce tables from his Census Statistical Papers (these draw on Census data which are Crown Copyright and are made available to the academic community through the ESRC purchase), and to the Policy Studies Institute, for permission to reproduce material from Brown (1984), Brown and Gay (1985), Jones (1993), and Modood (1997b).

In the first edition, I offered my thanks to the many people who had supported and stimulated me over the course of my career. My gratitude to them remains profound. In addition, in the years since the first edition, I have benefited from the advice, friendship, and understanding of my new colleagues at the University of Plymouth. Whilst it is always invidious to single out individuals, I should nevertheless record my debts to Alison Anderson, Lyn Bryant, Joan Chandler, Paul Iganski (now at the University of Sussex), Geoff Payne, and Mary Watkins. Recent graduate students, particularly Andy Smart and Samantha Regan de Bere, have constantly reminded me of why I chose an academic career and have, with their own successes, added those moments of joy and pride which make the hard grind of modern academic life worthwhile. Finally, in my renewed collaboration with Christopher Dandeker, a friend and colleague for a quarter of a century, I have discovered that it is never too late even for a dog as old as me to learn new tricks.

And behind and underpinning everything are those who constantly remind us that there is more to life than writing books and papers, even about topics as important as the subject matter of this volume. To Helen, Alison, Alexandra, and Simon I offer my love and gratitude for everything, but most of all for being there.

Outline Contents

Detailed Contents

List of Tables

Chapter 1

Introduction

THIS new edition has the same broad aims as the first edition. It attempts to provide an introductory overview of those aspects of the life of modern Britain that are commonly captured by the terms race and ethnicity. Questions of terminology are addressed at some length in the next chapter. It is, however, important to note at the outset that the whole argument is predicated on two assumptions. The first is that there are no races, in the biological sense of distinct divisions of the human species. Rather there are social interactions that are constituted by their participants as a particular kind of social relationship: race. The second, is that ethnicity is also a relational concept. That is, the existence of one ethnic group or identity presumes another. Ethnicity, then, is both a matter of how people see themselves and of how they are defined by others.

There are two ways of approaching an introductory text where space is at a premium. The first is to attempt a comprehensive coverage of relevant issues and to accept that the result will be a superficial survey of a wide range of matters. The other is to be more selective and to organize the discussion around some key themes that the reader may subsequently choose to apply to a wider range of questions. I have chosen the latter course. In part I have done so because of a belief that an introductory text does not need to be 'easy'. Indeed, some of the matters I raise are potentially highly complex. However, only by struggling with them can we hope to transcend some of the more simplistic assumptions that have, as we shall see, all too often guided British social policy in this area.

My aim then has been to provide information, without simply producing a list of data. I have tried to raise conceptual issues and highlight recurrent themes in a way that ties the various parts of the book together. I have, moreover, sought to alert the reader to key debates and points of controversy. However, the result does not pretend to be comprehensive. I have been consciously selective and I have no doubt that others will conclude that I have chosen wrongly. Throughout, however, I have been informed by my commitment to a sociological perspective. A key feature of this perspective is that it is relational; that is, it sees the apparently concrete and given features of social life as a product of the actions of human beings relating to one another as individuals and as members of groups.

Moreover, given the close interconnections between sociological and political concerns which characterize the subject-matter of this book, it is important to be clear at the outset about my own intellectual starting-point. This is the strongly held view that the only claim sociology has to the attention of others is that it can make a contribution to the understanding of social life. In my view, this means that we must have something to offer other than simple reproductions, often formulated in arcane language, of everyday arguments and interpretations. The implication of this is that we must proceed with a measure of detachment; respecting the criteria of truth and validity that are widely shared and recognized inside and outside the scientific community. It implies a respect for evidence and a concern with the internal consistency of our arguments. This does not mean that I do not hold strong personal views about the matters that are our concern here. Sometimes they may be apparent to the reader. However, the ultimate aim of this volume is explanatory not polemical (compare the discussion in Genovese, 1968).

Difference versus diversity

Throughout this book I make a distinction between difference and diversity. As we shall see difference, particularly ethnic difference, has typically been seen as a problem in Britain. This is in part because of the tendency to assume that there was some primordial norm of Britishness from which newcomers, such as migrants, initially diverged but towards which they could ultimately be expected to change. The result, as we shall see, is that social policy in Britain has been consistently informed by assimilationist assumptions. These placed the onus for change and adaptation squarely on the shoulders of the excluded and, hence, tended to blame the victims of inequality for their own situations. The other major related characteristic of this conception of difference is that all those who are different can be categorized together. The contrast is between 'them' and 'us'. The implication is that problems will be solved when maximum similarity is achieved with only a rump of cultural difference remaining to provide exotic diversion.

Diversity, by contrast, entails a very different perspective. The concept of diversity entails recognizing that both 'they' and 'we' are categories that are internally differentiated. From this perspective, it is not simply terms like 'immigrant' and 'ethnic minority' that are insensitive to the variety of self-conception and identity. The same is also, in principle, true of the term 'white'. (See the discussion in Chapter 2 below.)

We need, moreover, to be conscious that all social groups are gendered. Ethnic groups contain both women and men. The relations between them, and the ways masculinity and femininity are constructed, are central aspects of how ethnic identities are conceived and experienced. These identities reciprocally structure and condition what are defined as appropriate gender roles and behaviours. These, in turn, often serve as important ethnic boundary markers. With this in mind, I have tried, wherever possible and within the limitations of space available, always to be sensitive to the different experiences of men and women. I have not, however, attempted in Chapter 2, largely for reasons of space, to grapple with the complex conceptual task of unravelling theoretically the interconnections of race, ethnicity, and gender, although these issues are touched on in other parts of the book. Readers interested in pursuing this important task will find it helpful initially to consult Anthias and Yuval-Davis (1992) and Yuval-Davis and Anthias (1989).

My aim in this book has been to describe diversity without acceding to the idea that difference is a problem. Nevertheless, much of the book does focus on the inequalities that derive in part from the conceptualization of difference *as* a problem. The evidence of inequality, discrimination, and exclusion is so pervasive that it would be a dereliction of duty to the truth not to give it major prominence. I have tried, in doing so, to avoid a simplistic victimology but I am conscious that limitations of space mean that I have not always been able to pursue other themes as far as I would have wished.

Organization of the book

The book is organized around a series of substantive chapters. Through these run a number of recurrent themes: diversity, difference, inequality, and citizenship. Together these four concepts provide the threads that bind the whole argument together. In this edition data have been updated wherever possible. In addition, some sections have been expanded, there are discussions of new issues and there is an additional chapter, dealing with crime and criminal justice. The chapters are organized as follows.

Chapter 2 is an exploration of some of the key terms to be found in the literature on race and ethnicity in Britain. An attempt is made to introduce the reader to some areas of dispute and controversy, while making it clear how and why terms are used in the pages that follow.

Chapter 3 examines the origins of modern patterns of ethnic diversity in Britain. It focuses on the interplay of economic change and the heritage of empire in shaping patterns of migration to Britain—notably since the Second World War. It describes the development of immigration control legislation and reviews changing definitions of British nationality and citizenship. Chapter 4 maps the results of these developments by charting the pattern of ethnic diversity characteristic of Britain in the 1990s. Particular emphasis is placed on the demographic characteristics of the minority ethnic descendants of post-war New Commonwealth migrants.

Chapters 5, 6, 7, 8, and 9 each look in detail at a substantive area of social life in modern Britain. Focusing respectively on employment, education, housing and urban space, health, and crime and criminal justice, these chapters chart patterns of inequality, record evidence of discrimination, and review patterns of change.

Chapter 10 revisits the concept of citizenship first encountered in Chapter 3. Looking beyond formal legal status, it considers the evidence relating to the substantive rights of Britain's minority ethnic citizens. Reviewing the fields of immigration control, political representation, and access to welfare, it concludes by asking what are the implications of a renewed and revised emphasis on citizenship in the political rhetoric of the 1990s.

Finally, Chapter 11 considers some emerging trends and developments. It reviews the challenges and opportunities posed: by developments in the European Union; by trends in social mobility in Britain: and by the apparent emergence of new patterns of inequality and exclusion. It ends by identifying the choice between fearing difference or embracing diversity as the major challenge for the future.

Chapter 2

Concepts and Terms

Introduction

A **NECESSARY** starting point for any account of race and ethnicity in modern Britain is a consideration of the concepts and terms that will be encountered both in the account that follows and in the literature to which reference will be made. As in many other areas, both of social science and of popular discourse, there are competing terminologies and conceptual schemes in terms of which diversity and difference are described and explained. Moreover, different terminologies are frequently intended, or taken, to signify attachment to one or another political position. It is important, therefore, to commence by considering some competing usages and to be clear about how terms and concepts will be used in the chapters that follow. We begin with the terms that appear in the title.

Race and ethnicity are modern concepts. They have their origins in the global expansion of European societies that gathered pace from the late fifteenth century onwards. The processes of rapid social change that followed culminated in the transformation of European societies from primarily rural-agricultural to urban-industrial formations. This was also a period in which ways of thinking about, and explaining, natural and social phenomena also began to change as science, in a recognizably modern form, gradually developed.

Their growing exploration of other parts of the globe brought Europeans increasingly into contact with other human societies, ranging from small isolated groups of hunter-gatherers to large, complex states and empires. What appears to have struck explorers most forcefully, particularly those from England, were differences of physical appearance between themselves and others. The most striking of these seems to have been skin colour and it is notable that an early distinction emerged between those who had what was described as a 'black' in contrast to a 'white' skin. Winthrop Jordan has noted that this characterization was of considerable importance because the colours black and white were emotionally loaded concepts in the English language. Not only was the contrast one which denoted polar opposites but while 'white' represented good, purity, and virginity, 'black' was the colour of death, evil, and debasement (Jordan, 1974). Such usages linger on today in a variety of familiar expressions. As a result, it is frequently argued that great care needs to be taken in the use of language in a multi-ethnic society if the reproduction of the negative connotations of blackness is to be avoided.

As we have seen, the growth of European exploration coincided with the emergence of new ways of thinking associated with the rise of science. It is scarcely surprising, therefore, that this new curiosity about, and drive to understand, the natural world should soon begin to spawn new explanations of human difference. However, it was not simply differences of physical appearance that appeared to demand explanation. Radically different patterns of social organization also aroused Western curiosity. Moreover, and highly significantly, Europeans did not encounter other societies on equal terms. Increasingly superior technology, notably in the military sphere, meant that there were significant power differentials between Europeans and those whom they encountered. As a result, exploration quickly turned to conquest and gave rise to another phenomenon that required explanation—apparent European superiority. It was in this complex context that the concept of race made its appearance.

Race

The concept of race emerged, in recognizably modern form, between the end of the eighteenth and the middle of the nineteenth centuries (see the discussions in Banton, 1967; 1977; 1987; 1988; Malik, 1996; Stepan, 1982). Its emergence can be seen, in part, as an aspect of the general growth of scientific inquiry and explanation. Just as Newtonian physics had revealed order in the cosmos, so increasingly a drive was under way to map, and explain, a similar order in the natural and social worlds.

Part of this process was the gradual triumph of scientific over religious accounts. Thus, early accounts of human diversity were framed within the biblical story of the creation emphasizing the unity of human kind. By the middle of the nineteenth century, however, a fully fledged race science had emerged which characterized human diversity as a division between fixed and separate races, rooted in biological difference and a product of divergent heritages. Moreover, this conception of difference became inextricably linked to a notion of hierarchy in which all differences, both of history and future potential, were seen as a product of biological variation. In the words of Robert Knox, the claim was that 'race, or hereditary descent is everything; it stamps the man' (quoted in Banton, 1967: 29). So well established did this view become, that it survived the rise of theories of evolution which were, in principle, incompatible with the idea of fixity. The subtleties of Darwin's account of natural selection were hijacked by the crudities of a Social Darwinism that characterized human groups as being in a state of constant struggle to survive. Not surprisingly, those groups that appeared to be dominant were lauded as those that had won the battle. 'The survival of the fittest' became the cry which could justify both conquest and war, and which could legitimize as natural a social order that was the outcome of political and military struggles.

That this occurred alerts us to the fact that the emergence of late nineteenth-century race science was possible in part because it was in tune with wider social developments. Early discussions of racial difference had found a ready audience in those who wished to justify slavery. By the time Social Darwinism emerged, the age of empire had truly arrived, with the great powers of Europe dividing up Africa between them at the Congress of Berlin in 1885, and with Britain emerging as the dominant imperial power.[1]

A similar interaction between science and politics can be traced in the eventual discrediting of race science as the end of the Second World War signalled the beginning of the end. The revelation of the horrors of the Holocaust, and the enlistment of science in its perpetration, caused a wave of international revulsion. At the same time, modern genetic science was providing further support for evolutionary accounts and undermining notions of biological immutability. The result was a gradual disappearance of the concept of race from natural science (Banton and Harwood, 1975; Montague, 1964; 1974). This does not mean, however, that biological notions disappeared either from political discourse or from popular conceptualizations of human variation.[2] Moreover, even those who were convinced by the evidence that races in the biological sense did not exist found themselves having to confront the fact that large sections of the population, and indeed whole societies, continued to conduct themselves as though they did. Among those struggling with this recognition were sociologists.

Much has been written about the appropriate status of the concept of race in sociological investigation (see the extended discussion in Mason, 1994c). Despite the discrediting of the concept in biology, it has been common to argue that race remains a legitimate concept for sociological analysis because social actors treat it as real and organize their lives and exclusionary practices by reference to it (cf. van den Berghe, 1967).

In recent years this view has been vigorously challenged, not least by Robert Miles (1982; 1993), who has argued that race is an ideological construct. He argues that its use by social scientists serves only to legitimize it, giving comfort to those who would wish still to maintain that there are indeed real biological differences between groups of humans. For Miles, then, there are no races, biological or social. There are, however, social processes through which social relationships become racialized; that is, represented ideologically as entailing race.

Although this critique has been very influential (cf. Small, 1991), the term 'race' has not disappeared from sociological writing. Many have found the persistence of the concept in political and popular discourse impossible to ignore and have acknowledged its contested character by placing the term in inverted commas (Jenkins, 1986; Mason, 1990a; Ratcliffe, 1991). Others have, from a variety of different standpoints, sought to justify the retention of the concept for social scientific purposes (Anthias, 1990; 1992; Gilroy, 1987; Omi and Winant, 1986; Smith, 1986).

My own approach to these issues is to have some sympathy with both positions. Clearly there are no such things as races. Yet it is equally clear that large numbers of people behave as if there are. How might we retain a recognition of the social significance of race as a concept without appearing to legitimize the idea that 'races' represent a real division of the human species?

As we have seen, the race concept that emerged in the race science of the nineteenth and early twentieth centuries linked physical variation with personal, social, and cultural competencies. It was this that enabled science to be enlisted as a justification for differential treatment. Thus race was always more than just a way of thinking about and describing human difference. It was a social relationship characterized by an unequal distribution of power and resources. Beliefs about race, and the stereotyped images of others that they entailed, were among the symbolic resources that were mobilized by dominant groups in their efforts to protect their positions of power. Their success in doing so served to reinforce and reproduce those same ideas and images (see, for example, the discussions in: Fanon, 1967; Memmi, 1965; Rex, 1970; 1981).

Sociologically, then, race does not refer to categories of human beings (whether biologically or socially constituted). Rather race is a social relationship in which structural positions and social actions are ordered, justified, and explained by reference to systems of symbols and beliefs which emphasize the social and cultural relevance of biologically rooted characteristics. In other words, the social relationship race presumes the existence of racism.[3]

Racism

The term 'racism' is almost as contentious as race. It is used both as an analytic concept and as a popular political epithet; more often than not in an untheorized and sloppy way. For some writers, it is to be restricted to the realm of ideas or ideologies (Banton, 1970; Miles, 1989). For others, it is a concept denoting *both* attitudes, beliefs, and ideologies *and* social actions and structures (Anthias, 1990; 1992; Carmichael and Hamilton, 1968).

In addition there has been an increasing tendency in recent years to use the term to refer not merely to the propagation of ideas about biological race but more widely to apply to any expression of intergroup hostility or ethnocentrism. Indeed, in popular and political discourse, the term is frequently used to express disapproval of phenomena as diverse as displays of patriotic fervour and straightforward ignorance about other cultures. Many of these usages are indicative of a lack of intellectual rigour which, I contend, is out of place in social scientific analysis.

Institutional racism

The concept of institutional racism emerged in the United States in the 1960s in order to challenge the idea that racial inequality was merely the result of the attitudes of a few, pathologically prejudiced, white people. It aimed to draw attention to the systematic, structural character of racism that had its roots in the organization of societies like Britain and the United States. In practice, the term is used in a variety of ways, some of which stress intentionality and some of which discern the effects of institutional racism in any pattern of disadvantage which affects people who are not white. *For useful discussions see: Carmichael and Hamilton (1968); Gillborn (1990: 9–10); Mason (1982); and Williams (1985).* Recently the concept of institutional racism has been the subject of intense debate in Britain in the context of the Macpherson inquiry into events surrounding the racially motivated murder of Stephen Lawrence. The lack of clarity about whether the concept implies intentionality led, in part, to vigorous challenges, from a number of senior police officers, to the charge that the police were institutionally racist. Macpherson's definition, which was eventually grudgingly accepted by some, but not all, parties to the debate, was: 'The collective failure of a organisation to provide an appropriate and professional service to people because of their colour, culture, or ethnic origin. It can be seen or detected in processes, attitudes and behaviours which amount to discrimination through unwitting prejudice, ignorance, thoughtlessness and racist stereotyping which disadvantage minority ethnic people' (Macpherson, 1999, para. 6.34). For a further discussion of the Lawrence case and its relationship to issues of policing and criminal justice, see Chapter 9 below.

Ethnocentrism

Ethnocentrism refers to the practice of evaluating other groups, and their cultures and practices, from the perspective of one's own. In this basic sense, it is probably a feature of all human societies. Such judgements may, in principle, be positive or negative but will frequently entail misunderstanding. When judgements are negative ethnocentrism may, in practice, easily shade over into *xenophobia* (literally, fear of foreigners) or racism. *For a useful discussion in the context of education see Gillborn (1990: passim)*

Nevertheless, there are some arguments for a wider conceptualization of racism which deserve careful consideration. In particular, the question arises how best to recognize and interpret the similarities and historical continuities between the beliefs associated with the idea of race and other forms of inter-group hostility and conflict.

Indeed, some have argued that old style biological racism has increasingly been replaced by a 'new racism'.[4] Proponents of this idea draw attention to political arguments in favour of the exclusion of migrants, or the segregation of members of different population groups, that appeal to notions of cultural incompatibility and to the allegedly mutually disruptive and negative consequences of forcing such cultures to mix (Balibar, 1991: 21). These ideas can be found in, for example, the now famous utterances of Enoch Powell (Stacey, 1970), more widely in sections of the Conservative Party (Barker, 1981—but see note 4; Tomlinson, 1990: 27) and in arguments about so-called minority (or group) rights in South Africa.

Given what I have said about the interconnectedness of racism with the concept of race we might ask whether it is helpful to use the term racism to refer to these new kinds of arguments invoking cultural incompatibility. In addition, however, the concept of a 'new racism' raises the question of whether these arguments are any more than a rhetorical smoke-screen behind which lurk older beliefs about race. Moreover, we may also question how far these relatively sophisticated formulations have penetrated popular conceptualizations.

Although modern science has shown the old race science to be false, biological explanations of social and cultural difference have not disappeared, either from popular thought or more widely. Consider, for example, the claim by a consultant psychiatrist that the relative infrequency of a genetic trait facilitating the physiological processing of alcohol among members of the population of Japan helped to explain Japanese economic success because it discouraged the excessive consumption of alcohol by Japanese workers (Brewer, 1992). In another example a prominent newspaper sports commentator explained the success of Pakistani fast bowlers during a test match against England by suggesting that the distinctive characteristics of their sweat enabled them to impart a better polish to the ball (*Independent on Sunday*, 30 Aug. 1992: 26).

It is not unreasonable to suggest, in the context of these kinds of public pronouncements, that biological reasoning of various kinds, and of varying degrees of sophistication, remains widespread in popular beliefs about race and ethnicity as well as about other aspects of social differentiation such as gender and class. For this reason, I prefer to reserve the term racism for those situations in which groups of people are hierarchically distinguished from one another on the basis of some notion of stock difference and where symbolic representations are mobilized which emphasize the social and cultural relevance of biologically rooted characteristics.

The implication of this is also to argue against an extension of the term from ideas and beliefs to social structures and practices. The use of the term racism to include the patterns of systematic disadvantage experienced by members of subordinated groups creates a particular problem. This is because of the difficulty of determining when a pattern of disadvantage is to count as racism, rather than being seen as an outcome of other, perhaps class-based, processes. A common answer, 'when it arises from racist beliefs or practices', amounts to little more than the unhelpful circular argument that racism causes racism.

For the reasons I have tried to set out, then, I prefer to restrict the term racism to a more limited range of beliefs and utterances that stress the social significance of biologically rooted differences between human populations. This usage is deliberately and consciously much more restricted than that commonly employed both in academic and popular discourse. Indeed, the variety of ways in which the term is customarily used means that it is of limited analytical use, not least because it is often difficult to be sure whether two contributors to a debate are using it in comparable ways. As a result, it frequently obscures more than it reveals.

In this volume, the reader will see that I have been consciously economical with my use of the term. That I have done so does not, however, mean that I am blind to the systematic disadvantage, discrimination, and sometimes brutal violence which is part of the everyday experience of many of Britain's citizens who are not white. Indeed, my purpose is to elucidate, and help the reader to comprehend, precisely those patterns.

Ethnicity

We saw above that the term 'race' is often used in a way that purports to identify differences between human population groups. As we noted, however, this usage has been discredited scientifically. As a result, I argued that the only legitimate sociological usage is one that identifies race as a particular kind of social relationship constructed in, and through, racist reasoning.

An alternative way of thinking about human diversity is one that invokes the concept of ethnicity. Although there is no single, universally accepted, definition of ethnicity, not least because of the range of theoretical traditions from which the issue can be approached (cf. Jenkins, 1986; 1997; Smith, 1986; Wallman, 1986; Yinger, 1986), it is probably true to say that, if pressed for a definition, most academic commentators and policy makers would stress some sort of cultural distinctiveness as the mark of an ethnic grouping. Thus M. G. Smith has defined an ethnic unit as 'a population whose members believe that in some sense they share common descent and a common cultural heritage or tradition, and who are so regarded by others' (1986: 192). Ethnicity, then, is a more appealing and legitimate concept for social scientists both because it is intrinsically social and because it is rooted at least partly in the self-definitions of members.

Nevertheless there are, among academic commentators, differences of view and emphasis regarding the degree of negotiability of ethnicity (see the discussion in Yinger, 1986). In particular, different perspectives abound on the question of the relative significance of long-standing culture and heritage. For some there is a primordial element to ethnicity which explains the fervour of commitments to cultural identities (see the discussions in Geertz, 1963; Mason, 1986; van den Berghe, 1981; Yinger, 1986). For others, ethnicity is little more than an instrumental and situational flag of convenience (again see the discussion in Yinger, 1986: 26–31).

One way of approaching these questions is to consider the question of how ethnic boundaries are drawn. The concern here is with the way social actors define themselves and their relationships to others. An influential tradition which has attempted to capture and address the capacity of people's ethnic identities to vary in time and place is associated with the work of Fredrik Barth (1969). It is most prolifically represented in Britain in the work of Sandra Wallman (1979b; 1986). The central argument of this school is that ethnicity is more a matter of the processes by which boundaries are created and maintained between ethnic groups than it is of the internal content of the ethnic categories. Whether and how social boundaries are erected is an empirical question and not one that can be simply read off from the existence of cultural difference. Consequently, Wallman argues:

two sets of people with common cultural origins placed in similar minority positions [will not] necessarily use the same elements of their traditional culture to mark themselves off from non-member 'others'. What they do use will depend on the resources they have, on what they hope to achieve (whether consciously or not) and on the range of options available to them at the time. (1979b: 5–6)

Ethnicity is then situational. The implication is that people have different ethnic identities in different situations. Their salience is affected by such factors as the distribution of desired resources and the objectives of the people concerned. Thus it is possible to be simultaneously English, British, and European, stressing these identities more or less strongly in different aspects of daily life. Similarly, the same person might identify as Gujerati, Indian, Hindu, East African Asian, or British depending on situation, immediate objectives, and the responses and behaviour of others. It is important to note, however, that people's choices are not always unconstrained. There is considerable evidence that people's identifications are made in the context of their recognition of the ways that others categorize them. Thus, for example, a number of persons of Asian descent who responded to the *Fourth PSI Survey of Ethnic Minorities* indicated that they were inclined to think of themselves as 'black' in situations where they were in contact with white people. Among the reasons given was the belief that this was how they were defined by whites—in other words, they felt their choices were constrained (Modood, 1997c: 295–6). In this context both subtle messages about what constitutes Britishness and brutal acts of violence exercise exclusionary pressures that limit choice. (For a fuller discussion of the strengths and weaknesses of the 'ethnicity as boundary' approach, see Jenkins, 1997.)

Ethnicity in Britain

Wallman has noted of the term ethnicity that 'in Britain it signifies allegiance to the country of origin and implies a degree of choice and a possibility for change' (1986: 229). This observation highlights two aspects of British conceptualizations of ethnicity which are extremely important for our discussion. First, we may note that the emphasis on choice and change could easily lead to a naïve view that the 'absorption' or 'assimilation' of newcomers or migrants is only a matter of time. A related implication is that responsibility for continued patterns of disadvantage is to be laid at the door of those who stubbornly refuse to change—to adopt 'our ways'.

The second aspect concerns the tendency for the term 'ethnic' to refer only to those who are thought of as different from some assumed indigenous norm. The term 'ethnic' is frequently used as a synonym for those thought of as culturally different. In this connection it is interesting to note that the sole category in the ethnic classification system utilized by one of the police forces studied by Robin Oakley was: 'Ethnic' (1988: 39). Talk of an ethnic 'look' in the world of fashion is only one, relatively trivial, example of the way white British people are apt to see ethnicity as an attribute only of others—something that distinguishes 'them' from 'us'. We might, perhaps, add that the apparent denial of their own ethnicity (which is, perhaps, more properly seen as an English, rather than a British, phenomenon) also seems to be associated with a distinctively individualistic world view. Thus English people are apt to conceptualize themselves as individuals, while outsiders are seen as members of groups. The greater the degree of cultural difference between themselves and others, the more likely they are to see 'groupishness' as a characteristic of the behaviour and motivations of those others (Dhooge, 1981). In these circumstances the attribution of ethnicity to others may become part of a process of denial of legitimacy to claims on resources by those concerned (Mason, 1990b: 52–6).

It is also important to note that many of these everyday understandings may be highly contradictory. Thus, notwithstanding the emphasis on choice and the demand to change, popular and political discourse often uses the term 'ethnicity' in ways that suggest an interchangeability with distinctions based primarily upon physical markers such as skin colour and, not infrequently and erroneously, as a surrogate for biological race (Saggar, 1993: 35).

Naming diversity and difference: Alternative terminologies

Having reviewed the concepts of race and ethnicity, it is appropriate now to consider some alternative ways of characterizing the patterns of social diversity with which this volume is concerned.

Minority

The concept of minority[5] is widely used in academic circles—notably in the United States. It represents: another attempt to find a satisfactory alternative to race; an attempt to recognize the diversity of the bases upon which oppression could take place; and a means of identifying the common features of phenomena such as anti-Semitism, white racism, ethnocentrism, and nationalism. Despite its advantages in this last respect, there is a danger that it may miss the significance of the equally important *differences* to be found among various forms of intergroup conflict.

More importantly the question arises 'what is to define a minority?' In this respect, references in Britain to ethnic minorities appear to present relatively little difficulty since the groups referred to are numerically small relative to the total population. On the face of it, black people in the United States constitute a minority in a similarly unequivocal sense. Yet, as many have noted (see, for example, Simpson and Yinger, 1965: 16), their distribution has always been such that in large areas they have often been in the majority. The same is also true for people of Hispanic origin.

A solution to this problem is to deny the literal character of the term and to define it instead in terms of power; minorities being those groups in subordinate positions irrespective of their relative size. There are, however, difficulties with this option. Whatever the intentions of analysts, the literal connotations of the term may persist. There is a danger, particularly within formally democratic political systems, that the term 'minority' may embody the implication that the designated group is numerically, and hence politically and morally, less significant than the 'majority'.[6] Moreover, this terminology is confusing and, to some, offensive since it involves, for example, using the term minority to refer to women—a majority of the population in Britain—and to black people in South Africa—an overwhelming numerical majority.

Ethnic minority

In Britain the term 'minority' is rarely used on its own but is usually qualified with the word 'ethnic'. This usage reflects the characteristic features of British notions of ethnicity and entails a distinctive conception of difference. The term 'ethnic minority' is widely understood in Britain to denote a category of people whose recent origins lie in the countries of the New Commonwealth and Pakistan; in other words, in former British colonies in the Indian subcontinent, the Caribbean, Africa, and, sometimes, the so-called Far East. Two points about this usage are significant. The first is that, despite the implicit reference to cultural difference entailed in the term 'ethnic', not every group having a distinctive culture and constituting a minority in the British population is normally included. Thus, the large communities of people of Cypriot, Italian, Polish, and Ukranian origin (to name only a few) to be found in many British cities are rarely thought of as constituting ethnic minorities. The second point, which follows from the first is that the criterion which, in fact, distinguishes those to whom the term normally refers is skin colour. The essential characteristic for membership of an ethnic minority in this usage is having a skin that is not 'white'. This conflation of the concept of ethnic minority with skin colour has a number of consequences, one of which is to designate as 'ethnic minorities' members of those long-established black communities in places such as Liverpool and Cardiff who are culturally indistinguishable from their white neighbours. The people concerned frequently experience this as offensive and marginalizing. In addition, by failing to be explicit about the basis of definition, it creates considerable potential for confusion. In particular it gives rise to opportunities for policy makers and others implicitly, or explicitly, to deny the real basis of much social deprivation and exclusion, skin colour, and to focus instead upon 'ethnic' difference. It is not a large step from here to define difference itself as the problem and to blame those who are 'different' for all or some of their problems.

The concept of ethnic minority seems to have gained currency in both policy and academic circles as a reaction to the perceived inadequacies of other terminology. It appeared to recognize the inadequacies of the assimilationist assumptions embodied in references to 'immigrants' while accepting the permanence of the communities so designated. It avoided the biologically determinist associations of the concept of race and, by focusing on culture, permitted a recognition of the diversity of the groups referred to. References to 'the ethnic minority community' could easily become references to 'ethnic minority communities'.

Nevertheless, the term as commonly used embodies a number of contradictions. Thus, in order to qualify for designation as an ethnic minority, a category of people must exhibit a degree of 'difference' that is regarded as significant. An unstable combination of skin colour and distinctive culture is ultimately the criterion that marks off 'ethnic minorities' from the 'majority' population in Britain. Despite the emphasis on difference, however, 'ethnic minorities' are frequently seen to have more in common with one another than with the 'majority'. The term thus contributes to a de-emphasis on *diversity among* the groups so designated while exaggerating *differences from* the rest of the population. Even when it is argued that the basis of inclusive designation is a common experience of racism, this procedure frequently fails to take cognisance of the diverse ways in which racism may be experienced by different communities (Ballard, 1992; Field, 1987; Modood, 1988; 1990a; 1992; Modood *et al.*, 1997) or, within them, by men and women (Anthias and Yuval-Davis, 1992; Yuval-Davis and Anthias, 1989).[7]

Black, white, and non-white

The attempt to capture the commonalities in experiences of racial and ethnic exclusion has led some to argue that a single term, which accurately identifies the basis of oppression, is to be preferred. Since skin colour is a key marker of status in modern Britain, it is argued, the term 'black' is the appropriate one to use to refer to all those who are victims of the exclusionary practices of white racism (see the discussion in Modood, 1988; compare Mason, 1990a). This usage, it should be noted, frequently entails not merely a descriptive label but also a self-conscious political statement. The claim is not merely that those designated by the label 'black' share certain experiences but that they *ought* to embrace a common identity as a basis for effective mobilization and resistance.

For a number of years, this usage commanded a good deal of support in social scientific circles. However, while it was promoted with passion by some, it is doubtful whether it was ever wholeheartedly welcomed by many of those to whom it was intended to refer. In recent years, it has been increasingly questioned, not least by those who are keen to stress the diversity of cultural identities characteristic of modern Britain and the range of different ways in which racism may be experienced (Ballard, 1992; Modood, 1988; 1990*a*; 1992; Modood *et al.*, 1997).

I have argued elsewhere (Mason, 1990*a*) that these distinct political perspectives are probably irreconcilable. From a social scientific point of view, however, I suggest that the key requirement is for terminology that is sufficiently precise to enable us to analyse the patterns of social relationships that are our focus. The implication of this is that different analyses may require different terminologies. Moreover, we are most likely to develop a sensitive understanding of the needs and demands of all members of the population of Britain if we adopt language that enables us to capture its richness and diversity. Nevertheless, there will be occasions when a generic term is needed to describe general processes of exclusion which bear upon a variety of different groups of citizens. As we have seen, the term 'black' has been increasingly challenged. In these limited circumstances, it may sometimes be appropriate to refer to 'people who are not white' as a precise way of identifying the character of the exclusionary practices to which they are subject.[8]

Finally, we should perhaps note that while the term 'black' has been subject to increasing scrutiny, the same has been less true of the term 'white'.[9] Again, since it captures a key feature of the ethnic exclusivism that characterizes much of the life of modern Britain, it is less often seen as a problematic term and serves a useful shorthand function when these patterns are being explored. It is important to note, however, that the term is scarcely precise or unambiguous. It is used interchangeably with other terms, such as 'European' or 'British', in ways that reveal much about the norms against which those alleged to be different are judged. As a result, it is a term that is long overdue for some careful scrutiny for which there is, unfortunately, not space here. Nevertheless, the reader should beware taking this term, like all the others discussed here, too much for granted.[10]

Conclusion

Given the limitations of all terminologies in common currency there is a difficulty about how best to proceed. This is even more the case because of the political baggage that any system carries with it. In what follows, I proceed in the following way. I try so far as is possible to use terms that emphasize diversity as a positive and varied feature of the demographic landscape of modern Britain. I try to avoid terms that imply that difference is negative. Thus, when referring collectively to those descended from New Commonwealth migrants I usually refer to minority ethnic groups, in order to emphasize plurality. General references to ethnic diversity include white people. In quoting directly from, and in reporting the detailed results of, other people's research, I generally use the terms found in the original sources. When reporting the 1991 Census I use its categories. Where generic terms are required by my discussion, I use South Asian to refer to people who can trace their ancestry to the Indian subcontinent and African-Caribbean to refer to those whose origins lie ultimately in Africa and the Caribbean. In a small number of places, when seeking to refer to those who are subject to exclusionary practices organized in terms of skin colour, I refer to people who are not white.

Further reading

Racism After 'Race Relations' by Robert Miles (1993) is an excellent discussion, by one of the most influential contributors to the various debates, of some of the key questions surrounding conceptual and terminological issues in the field.

Racialized Boundaries by Floya Anthias and Nira Yuval-Davis (1992) is, like Miles's volume, a book which seeks to introduce the reader to some complex and difficult debates. It is particularly useful as an attempt to grapple with the way in which race, ethnicity, and gender interpenetrate.

An accessible discussion of a range of these and related issues, such as the intersection of ethnicity and gender with class, is to be found in *Fractured Identities* by Harriet Bradley (1996).

Chapter 3

Migration and Ethnic Diversity in Britain

Industrialization, colonialism, and migration

I<small>N</small> Chapter 2 it was argued that the expansion of European societies led to increasing contacts between European and non-European peoples. These contacts gave rise to two key developments: the emergence of new ways of conceptualizing and explaining human difference; and increasing international migration. The first great migrations of modern times were those associated with racial slavery and with colonial conquest and settlement in areas as diverse as the Americas, the Indian sub-continent, and Africa. As we saw, the changing relationships between Europeans and the peoples whom they enslaved and conquered were also central to emerging beliefs both about difference and about the characteristics of subordinate and dominant groups.

However, the expansion of European societies was also tied to a process of internal change and development. Hand in hand with European expansion went the gradual emergence of industrial capitalism. Nowhere was this more obvious than in Britain where industrialization is generally agreed first to have taken place. This development was to give rise, in turn, to new, and ultimately momentous, patterns of migration.

It is, perhaps, better to refer not to industrialization but to a wider process which Kumar has called 'The Great Transformation' (1978). This concept refers to the transformation of European societies from rural, agricultural to predominantly urban-industrial formations. In Britain this process had deep historical roots but is generally recognized to have dated from around the last quarter of the eighteenth century and to have developed rapidly through the first half of the nineteenth century.

In Britain, as elsewhere, these changes were associated with new and distinctive patterns of migration. Initially, these were associated with internal migrations as people left the land to move to the growing urban areas to work in the emerging industrial centres. This movement was characterized by the classic features of migrations—the combination of push and pull factors. On the one hand, a combination of the enclosure movement and the increasing capitalization of agriculture generated a surplus of rural labour. On the other, the growing consolidation of industrial production led to declining opportunities for independent household enterprise and to alternative opportunities within the factory system.

In addition to this internal migration the Great Transformation was also to lead to new patterns of immigration to Britain from outside its borders. In one sense, of course, there was nothing new about immigration into Britain. The British population was the result of successive migrations from the earliest recorded history and resulting from impulses as diverse as conquest and religious refugeedom (Kiernan, 1978). Moreover, British expansion and the growth of colonial exploitation and settlement helped to establish the economic foundations of the Great Transformation. One consequence of these developments, originating in exploration and culminating in the slave trade, was a growing black population in Britain from the sixteenth century onwards[1] (Fryer, 1984). Particularly in port cities such as Bristol, Liverpool, and London, the slave trade made a significant contribution to the establishment of permanent black settlements, as did the subsequent employment of black seamen. The long-settled descendants of these communities are most clearly represented today in the black British populations of Liverpool and Cardiff.

However, the Great Transformation altered the scale and character of this international migration. As the nineteenth century wore on, Britain's industrialization increasingly led to the immigration of people from 'less developed' (or peripheral) economies to fill specific niches or labour shortages. The most important initial source for such migration was Britain's geographically closest, and oldest, colonial dependency: Ireland.

A combination of poverty, famine, and population growth in Ireland (themselves related directly to the consequences of British colonization—see Miles, 1982; O'Connor, 1972) and labour shortages in the British economy led to the development of a pattern of migration which persists up to the present day. In particular Irish migrants filled two gaps: (a) the need for seasonal labour in an increasingly capitalized agricultural sector; and (b) specific shortages in industry and infrastructural development, such as the construction of roads and canals. By 1841, it is estimated that there were more than 400,000 Irish people living in England, Scotland, and Wales. By 1851 the Census showed that there were over 727,000 Irish immigrants in Britain representing 2.9 per cent of the population of England and Wales and 7.2 per cent of the population of Scotland (Rees, 1982: 75).

Migrants from Ireland, both temporary and permanent, have remained important sources of labour for the British economy down to the present day. Indeed the significance of this labour helps to explain the distinctive arrangements that governed Irish migration even before the introduction of provision for the free movement of labour within what is now called the European Union. Thus, even after independence had been finally sealed in 1921, and notwithstanding the fact that it had been the result of bloody conflict, citizens of the Irish Republic (Eire) continued to have freedom of entry, settlement, and the right to vote in elections. This last is a privilege not accorded even now to citizens of any other EU state who may vote in local and European, but not general, elections.

These connections between Britain and Ireland are also manifest in the continued membership of Northern Ireland in the United Kingdom. This survival reflects the colonial policies of previous British governments; notably the attempt to pacify Ireland through a policy of settlement. The importance of Belfast to the British Empire as a ship-building centre should also not be overlooked. The heritage of this colonial period manifests itself not only in the violence which has characterized Northern Ireland since 1969 but also in the persistence of anti-Irish stereotyping as an explanation for conflict (Information on Ireland, 1984; Curtis, 1971).

One result of this long history of migration and settlement is that people of Irish descent now constitute a significant proportion of the population of modern Britain. Some estimates suggest that as many as 10 per cent of the population can trace their ancestry back to Ireland (Rees, 1982: 76; cf. O'Connor, 1972: 173). There is considerable evidence to suggest that, despite their invisibility in much official data,[2] the Irish in Britain experience considerable disadvantage, discrimination and exclusion (Hickman and Walter, 1997).

Terms such as 'Great Transformation' and 'industrialization' are sometimes used in ways that imply that the processes involved represent once for all changes or events. To view any social developments as involving simple shifts from one steady state to another always does violence to the complexity of social change. However, it would be particularly inappropriate in the context of the Great Transformation since one of its key features has been a quantum jump in the pace of social, technological, and industrial change. Industrialization, then, has been a continuing process characterized by more or less distinct stages that have been passed through at different rates and sequences in different places. These different phases in industrial and economic development have, in turn, generated new patterns of labour demand (and supply) and have led to new patterns of international migration.

We noted above that Britain's population is one forged from successive historical migrations. In this respect it is not unique, although the geographical isolation conferred by island status probably helped to make those migrations

Northern Ireland

The province of Northern Ireland, formally part of the United Kingdom, consists of six of the nine counties of the historic Irish province of Ulster. It was constituted as a largely self-governing statelet in 1921. Its separate status represented a compromise in which independence was gained by the largely Catholic rest of Ireland while the North, with its Protestant and Unionist majority, remained part of the UK. The early history of the province was one of systematic discrimination against the large Catholic minority. In the 1960s, this led to the emergence of a Civil Rights Movement seeking democratic reforms. This was seen, by many Unionists, as a Republican plot aimed at forcing Northern Ireland into reunification with the Republic. Violence ensued as, sequentially, Civil Rights marchers were attacked, communities on both sides became involved in inter-communal violence, the Provisional IRA was formed, and British troops were deployed, initially to counter the partiality of the Unionist authorities. The province, since 1969, has been in a state of virtual civil war in which a cease-fire had just been declared as the first edition of this book was being completed in 1994. Some five years later, the final conclusion of the so-called 'Peace Process' is still awaited, its outcome by no means certain. The result has been one of the longest running ethnic conflicts in recent European history and it has had direct effects on British state policy in a range of areas from immigration control to policing. *For useful discussions see: Barritt and Carter (1972); Darby (1983); Edwards (1970); Farrel (1976); O'Leary (1993); and Paor (1971). For a discussion of the position of minority ethnic groups in Northern Ireland see: Hainsworth (1998).*

more palpable. The early phases of industrialization gave new impetus to inward migration as we have seen. Each successive phase of industrial change and development has been, in its turn, associated with new patterns of internal and international migration.

Thus in the period between the First and Second World Wars immigration to Britain declined sharply, being confined largely to those fleeing persecution, including many Jewish people, and a continuation of the well-established pattern of Irish migration. The deep recession experienced by Britain in common with much of the rest of the world meant that demand for labour was weak and the economic attractions of migration consequentially limited (Rees, 1982: 79).

By contrast, the economic circumstances of post-Second World War Britain were markedly different. They were to be of particular significance in giving rise to the ethnic profile of modern Britain since this period was to witness the inward migration of significant numbers of people from countries of the former British empire—the so-called New Commonwealth.[3] Indeed, in popular parlance, and in much political discourse, the term 'immigration' is now associated almost exclusively with the arrival in Britain of people whose origins lay in these countries. What were the economic forces that gave rise to this pattern of post-war migration from Britain's former colonies in Africa, the Caribbean, and the Indian subcontinent?

In the years following the end of the Second World War, Britain suffered from a severe labour shortage; especially in unskilled jobs and in service industries such as transport. This shortage had two aspects. On the one hand there was the need to engage in post-war reconstruction. Not only had British cities suffered war damage but, more importantly, industry had been run down by the war effort. There was a need both to redirect production to civilian output and also to rebuild and refurbish worn out plant. On the other hand there were more significant forces at work than this drive to reconstruct. Like the rest of the 'developed' world, the British economy was experiencing major long-term changes in the nature and organization of industrial capitalism. Industry itself was becoming increasingly large scale and capital intensive. There was a growing demand for skilled workers in emergent sectors like the motor industry. In addition new employment opportunities were opening up in the rapidly growing service industries and in a burgeoning public sector associated with the developing welfare state. Increasingly British workers had access to avenues of upward mobility which were unprecedented in recent times. As a result there was a movement into new occupations, leaving a residue of unskilled and routine semi-skilled jobs at the lower levels of the labour market. These were often dirty, poorly paid, and involved unsocial hours like night shift working. In the industrial sector they were often to be found in declining industries where cheap labour was a substitute for capital investment or an alternative to collapse (see Duffield, 1985: 85; Fevre, 1984). Given the pattern of labour shortage, these vacancies could only be filled by substantial immigration.

These features of the economic situation of Britain in the decades after the war were not unique to it. Indeed all the countries of Western Europe experienced similar pressures, albeit on slightly different time-scales depending on their demographic profile. Though precise labour needs, and the balance between capital investment and reliance on cheap labour, varied from country to country, it is no accident that large-scale immigration was a feature of all the advanced Western European economies in the 1950s, 1960s, and 1970s (Castles, 1984; Castles and Miller, 1993). Each country drew on different sources of migrant labour depending on its history and needs. In the case of Britain, a long imperial history and a still extant empire (albeit one which was in the process of transformation into the Commonwealth as more and more former colonies achieved independence) provided a ready-made source of recruitment.

A number of factors facilitated Britain's capacity to draw on this source of labour supply. One was the passing of the 1948 British Nationality Act, which gave citizens of Commonwealth countries special immigration status. Another was the 1952 passing in the United States of the McCarran–Walter Immigration

Act, which ended the system under which 'British West Indians' could enter the USA under the quota available for British citizens (Layton-Henry, 1992: 31). This partially closed a traditional destination for Caribbean emigrants. As we shall see, questions of legal status and the administration of immigration control have been key issues in the history of Britain's development as an, increasingly self-consciously, multi-ethnic society.

Migration and citizenship: Settlement, restriction, nationality, and exclusion[4]

Irish labour migration was not the only source of immigration to Britain in the nineteenth and early twentieth centuries. In addition as the nineteenth century drew to a close, increasing numbers of political refugees and economically distressed peoples from various parts of continental Europe were beginning to settle in Britain, and particularly in London. These groups included Gypsies (Holmes, 1988: 62–6), Romanians, Russians, and Italians (Foot, 1965: 88). Perhaps most significantly, a significant number were Jewish people who were often fleeing anti-Semitic pogroms in Eastern Europe (Holmes, 1988: 56–73). Many were *en route* to the United States and, although they frequently paused only briefly before journeying onwards, not a few remained and settled permanently. Between 1880 and 1920 it is estimated that the Jewish population of Britain increased fivefold from 60,000 to 300,000 (Rees, 1982: 77) Moreover, they represented a new kind of migrant in that they typically spoke no English and had not entered specifically to fill a need for labour. They settled primarily in the East End of London, where many of their descendants remain to this day. These groups were to be the focus for a campaign for immigration control inside and outside Parliament which, if not always openly anti-Semitic, was clearly focused on the Jews in particular. It resulted in the passing, in 1905, of the Aliens Act aimed at regulating the inflow of foreigners—specifically those judged 'undesirable' and 'destitute'; that is, poor. In practice, as Rees notes (1982: 78), the Act was limited in scope and not enforced with particular vigour. Its main significance lay in the fact that it represented a breach of the long-standing principle (based, as Rees points out, both on economic self-interest and humanitarian concern) that entry to Britain should be open.

The imminence of the First World War led to the passing of much more restrictive immigration control legislation aimed at 'aliens'. It gave the Home Secretary powers to exclude or deport those thought undesirable and introduced a requirement for registration with the police. British subjects, and hence the populations of British colonies, were exempt. Although introduced primarily as a wartime security measure, the Act was extended by the Aliens Restriction Act of 1919. Like its 1905 predecessor, this Act was most clearly aimed at those with limited financial resources and placed an obligation on anyone admitted without substantial means of support to obtain a work permit (Holmes, 1988: 84–114; Rees, 1982: 79).

It was noted above that the numbers of migrants to Britain, other than from Ireland, declined significantly during the inter-war period and was limited primarily to political refugees. The Second World War and its aftermath saw renewed immigration. During the war substantial numbers of Polish people, the majority of them military personnel who made a substantial contribution to the allied war effort, came to Britain. They were assisted to settle after the war by a large-scale government programme designed to promote their speedy integration into British society (Rees, 1982: 80–1). Less comprehensively assisted were large numbers of European Voluntary Workers, from such places as the Ukraine, Latvia, Lithuania, and Yugoslavia, who entered Britain in the years immediately following the war to work in areas of labour shortage. They were admitted on twelve-month work permits, were not allowed to transfer jobs, and, after 1947, were not allowed to bring in their dependants, although there was subsequently a gradual easing of restrictions (Rees, 1982: 81–3).

Just as, as British subjects, citizens of Britain's colonies had been exempt from the provisions of the 1905 Aliens Act, so in the post-Second World War period, citizens of Commonwealth countries were granted special immigration status. The British Nationality Act of 1948 conferred on them the right freely to enter, work, and settle with their families.[5] In the context of continuing labour shortages, they were specifically encouraged to do so, both by government and employers. Thus London Transport, for example, established recruiting offices in Barbados (Brooks, 1975: 256–70). As a result, through the 1950s and 1960s increasing numbers of Commonwealth migrants began to arrive, first from the Caribbean and subsequently from India, Pakistan, parts of Africa, and the Far East.

From the outset, the pattern of immigration and settlement of Commonwealth citizens closely matched the pattern of demand in the labour market. Thus migrants settled in large numbers in Greater London, where many entered service industries such as transport, in the West Midlands, where they were employed in the metal manufacturing industries, and in the North West, where they went into textile occupations. These patterns of settlement were enhanced by the tendency of later migrants to join those already settled, and for the latter to play a key role in facilitating entry to the labour market (see, for example, Brooks and Singh, 1979; Duffield, 1985; and Saifullah Khan, 1979) and in the provision of accommodation (see Ratcliffe, 1981; Rex and Moore, 1967).

From an early stage, two features dominated the situation of the new arrivals. The first is that generally immigrants found themselves occupying the least desirable jobs and housing. The second is that, despite the economic advantages to Britain of being able to call on supplies of migrant labour, a variety of social strains also emerged. The result was an increasing tide of white hostility, which manifested itself in the now infamous Notting Hill riots of 1958, when white people went on the rampage. In addition an agitation for immigration control began to develop which was to bear its first fruit in 1962. A key strain point concerned housing. Since the end of the war, successive governments had failed to satisfy demand for housing. The arrival of large numbers of migrants, particularly in inner city areas with the most acute housing problems, inevitably exacerbated already serious shortages and supplied ready-made scapegoats on whom already extant problems could be blamed (see Rex and Moore, 1967; Smith, 1989).

Gradually a campaign began to gain momentum for immigration control. White residents' associations began to spring up and their demands for action were echoed in Parliament and in the Conservative Party in particular. The agitation bore fruit in 1962 when the first of three principal pieces of legislation aimed at controlling immigration was introduced by the then Conservative government.

The **Commonwealth Immigrants Act of 1962** established controls on the entry of Commonwealth citizens for the first time. It introduced a system under which any such migrant required a voucher before being given leave to enter. Vouchers were divided into three types and were issued to different categories of would-be migrants. *Category A* vouchers were issued to those with a specific job to go to. *Category B* vouchers were available to those with specific, recognized skills or qualifications which were in short supply. *Category C* vouchers, in deliberately limited numbers, were issued on a 'first come, first served' basis to those who did not meet the criteria for the other categories.

Despite the fact that it had opposed the 1962 Act when in opposition, the Labour Party in power responded to continuing agitation about what was typically called 'coloured immigration', not only by abolishing the *Category C* voucher in 1965 but by introducing the second significant extension of controls on migration from the Commonwealth.

The 1962 Act had controlled the entry of citizens of Commonwealth countries. There was in addition, however, a major group of UK passport holders resident abroad who, as full UK citizens, were not covered by the Act. This was the group that was to become known as 'East African Asians'. Although their origins lay in the Indian subcontinent, their forebears had settled in Britain's East African colonies during the heyday of empire. When the African countries in which they lived had been granted independence, they had been given the choice either of assuming citizenship of the newly independent state or of acquiring full British citizenship. Those who had chosen the latter course had full right of entry and abode in common with any other British citizen.

The **Commonwealth Immigrants Act of 1968** was a response to the so-called Kenyan Asian crisis of 1967/8. During this period the Kenyan government began to implement Africanization policies which threatened the livelihoods of the country's many thousands of ethnically Asian residents. The prospect that these British citizens might seek to exercise their right, which had been deliberately conferred by issuing British passports, to come to Britain created a further wave of anti-immigration agitation to which the Government responded by passing the 1968 Act.

The Act created, for the first time, a distinction between those UK passport holders who had a right of entry and abode in Britain and those who did not. In order to qualify for this right, a passport holder had to have been born, adopted, or naturalized in the UK or to have one parent or grandparent who had been born, adopted, or naturalized in the UK. This principle was to become known as *patriality*. Its practical effect was to retain a right of entry for many citizens of 'old' Commonwealth countries such as Australia and Canada (and, indeed, South Africa although it had left the Commonwealth) while removing this right from many UK citizens resident in the New Commonwealth. Although distinctions of skin colour did not figure in the wording of the Act it is clear that the intention was indeed to differentiate between those whose skin colour was thought of as 'white' and those whose skin was not.

The effect of the Act was to create a group of people who, notwithstanding their formal citizenship, were effectively stateless. In practice, British governments adopted a quota system under which a gradual entry of African Asian citizens was effected. This gradualist approach broke down, however, in 1972 when emergency measures were taken to admit and settle, in the space of two months, some 28,000 UK passport holders who had been affected by measures introduced by the Ugandan government (Rees, 1982: 88).[6]

The **1971 Immigration Act** restricted still further the opportunities for migrants from the New Commonwealth to enter Britain. Effectively it meant that all those who did not qualify for right of abode under the 1968 Act now required a work permit whether they were aliens or Commonwealth citizens. Such permits were issued for twelve months and had then to be renewed. They were issued for employment with a specific employer and changes of job required permission from the Department of Employment, which was not automatic. Those working on such permits could be deported for breaching the conditions of the permit or if they were otherwise deemed to be undesirable. For many permit holders, this last provision was often experienced as a practical limitation on their ability to challenge poor working conditions or to involve themselves in any kind of political or trade union activity. After four years they could apply to have the time limit and conditions lifted. At the time of writing, the general provisions of the Act remain in force as the principal measure governing immigration.[7] The majority of work permits are now issued to professional people from non-Commonwealth countries, such as the USA.

The 1971 Act effectively put an end to all new primary immigration from the New Commonwealth. Henceforth, and with the exceptions of the admission of Ugandan Asians in 1972, family reunification became the principal source of continuing settlement. The Act, then, created a system of migratory labour closer to the model which had operated in much of the rest of Europe in the post-war period (see Castles, 1984).

The **1981 Nationality Act** had the effect of bringing back into line national-ity and immigration legislation which had become seriously out of alignment as a result of successive immigration control measures. Under the Act those qualifying for right of abode under the 1968 and 1971 Immigration Acts—so-called *patrials*—became British Citizens. Two other categories of citizenship were created: British Dependent Territories Citizenship and British Overseas Citizenship. Neither of these two last carried right of entry or settlement. The exceptional granting of such a right to a limited number of citizens of Hong Kong,[8] should they wish to exercise it, is illustrative of the decisive change in the status of Commonwealth citizens brought about by the Act.

Under the provisions of the 1981 Act, then, only British Citizens (together with citizens of other states of the European Union) are free of immigration control. Moreover, children born in the UK to non-British citizens do not acquire British citizenship unless they can satisfy the requirements of *patriality*. In principle it is not inconceivable that such children could become stateless, having formal citizenship rights in no state (for a discussion of citizenship, see Chapter 10).

Conclusion

What the patterns described in this chapter reveal is that, since the onset of the industrial revolution (or Great Transformation), the major determinant of the patterning of migration flows in Britain has been the demand for labour. This is particularly striking in the case of post-war migration. Until the advent of immigration control in 1962, migration flows roughly matched the pattern of demand in the economy (Sivanandan, 1982: 101–5). Indeed it is an oft-noted paradox that the threat of immigration control actually stimulated an upsurge in immigration as people sought to 'beat the ban'. The system operating up to

1962, then, was one of classical economic liberalism—*laissez-faire*. From this date onwards, ever-increasing government control and regulation character-ized official policy. Some have argued that this change reflected a declining demand for labour in the British economy (Sivanandan, 1982: 135–6) and there is no doubt that demand did begin to decline through the 1960s and into the 1970s. This factor alone cannot, however, explain the growth of immigration control. Not only did the major slowing down of the economy post-date the introduction of controls but in *net* terms emigration continued to exceed immigration.

Of much greater significance was the political agitation surrounding immi-gration from the New Commonwealth. This was spurred partly by the continu-ing housing crisis but also reflected a more deep-rooted hostility among British people to outsiders who were not white. This, in turn, had its roots in long-term developments, including Britain's colonial history (Rex, 1970). It is no accident that the clearly consistent theme in immigration and citizenship legislation since 1962 has been a distinction between those who were thought of as 'white' and those who were not. Each successive measure sought to close the door to dark-skinned potential migrants, while keeping it open to 'whites' from the countries of the Old Commonwealth and South Africa. The underlying theme of this aspect of official policy, then, is that difference is a problem. The greater the difference, the greater the problem. As we shall see in subsequent chapters, the assumptions to which this view gave rise have been a recurrent feature of social policy in several key areas of life in modern Britain.

Further reading

John Bull's Island by Colin Holmes (1988) is a historian's account of migration to Britain over a hundred-year period from 1871 to 1971, providing an essential historical perspective on the issues that are discussed in this chapter.

The Politics of Immigration by Zig Layton-Henry (1992) provides a highly accessible account of the political debates and struggles surrounding post-war migration to Britain and some of their consequences for Britain's minority ethnic citizens.

Chapter 4

Ethnic Diversity in Modern Britain

Introduction

W^E saw in Chapter 2 that ethnicity is—like derivatives such as 'ethnic minority'—a relational concept with highly contextual significance. Moreover, Chapter 3 made it clear that, in historical terms, the population of modern Britain is a product of successive migrations stretching back to primordial times. When we speak of and try to describe the ethnic diversity of modern Britain, then, we must inevitably make decisions about which groups to focus upon, which to give less attention to, and which groups to ignore altogether. Such decisions are structured by academic judgements about which ethnic identities and relationships appear to be the most significant in shaping life in modern Britain. They are also influenced, however, by contemporary social concerns and political forces. Moreover, the degree of detail that is possible depends upon the data available. These in turn reflect decisions made by those responsible for the Census and other survey sources, and are themselves the product of political decisions and struggles.

For reasons set out in earlier chapters, the main focus of this volume is on those patterns of ethnic diversity which post-date the Great Transformation and, in particular, on those which are a product of post-war migration to Britain from the countries of the New Commonwealth. This does not mean that other aspects of Britain's ethnic diversity are unimportant. However, in a short text such as this, there are limits to what is possible in terms of coverage. In reading what follows, therefore, the reader should constantly bear in mind that Britain's ethnic diversity is ever-changing and that there are other ethnic and national divisions that are not discussed here.

Data sources and ethnic categories

Like the conceptions of ethnicity which they reflect, the sources of data about Britain's ethnic diversity are in continual flux in response to changes in policy concerns, political priorities (both within government and outside), and patterns of political struggle, including the demands of minority ethnic communities themselves. The same is true of the categories in terms of which members of different groups are categorized.

Early discussions of Britain's growing ethnic diversity were framed within debates about immigration. The so-called 'numbers game' (Saggar, 1992: 42) was one in which competing estimates of the rate of immigration, and the potential eventual size of the minority ethnic population, were traded by the proponents and opponents of tighter immigration controls. Whatever position was taken, however, two underlying assumptions were constantly reproduced by the very fact that this debate took place at all. One was that the migrants from the New Commonwealth were a potential problem—at least if they arrived in sufficient numbers. The second, and related, assumption was that the solution was a process of assimilation—or integration—in which the migrants' 'strangeness' (Banton, 1959; Patterson, 1963) would gradually be eliminated. Both sides in the numbers game appeared to accept that this would be facilitated, the smaller the numbers requiring to be absorbed. This perspective was well articulated in the justification put forward by the then Labour government in 1968 for tighter immigration controls. The simultaneous introduction of new controls and a new Race Relations Act could be presented as part of a package designed to promote 'good race relations' (Solomos, 1988: 65).

A consequence of this immigration-led focus of government policy was that, until recently, most official estimates of the size of the minority ethnic population were based on data about the place of birth of those born outside the UK. This made some statistical sense in the early days of immigration (though it certainly was not foolproof—not all those born in, for example, India were of Indian ethnic origin (see Owen, 1993d). However, it became increasingly unsatisfactory as an ever-larger proportion of the New Commonwealth descended population came to be born in Britain. The initial solution was to count those living in households where the 'head of household' had been born in the New Commonwealth. Yet again, this could only ever be a temporary solution as the children of initial migrants increasingly came to establish their own households. Nevertheless, until data from the 1991 Census became available, estimates of this kind based on the Censuses of 1971 and 1981 were the main sources for both official and academic purposes.

The 1991 Census asked respondents for the first time to classify themselves in ethnic terms. The decision to ask an ethnic question followed a fierce debate and a lengthy process of testing potential questions (House of Commons, 1982–3; Marsh, 1993). The following schema was the one finally adopted:

White
Black—Caribbean
Black—African
Black—Other (please describe)
Indian
Pakistani
Bangladeshi
Chinese
Any other ethnic group (please describe)

These categories have also been adopted by the Commission for Racial Equality as those that it recommends for ethnic monitoring purposes.

In addition to figures derived from the Census, other sources of data include the results of a variety of surveys. The most important, and widely used, of these are the periodic surveys conducted by the Policy Studies Institute (formerly Political and Economic Planning) (Brown, 1984; Modood et al., 1997; Smith, 1976) and the results of the annual Labour Force Survey conducted by the Office of Population Censuses and Surveys. Both of these have utilized self-classification measures of ethnic group affiliation. However, they diverge not only from one another but also from the schema adopted for the 1991 Census. The result is that comparisons between these different data sources are fraught with difficulty, particularly where they involve attempts to measure change over time.

Having noted these limitations, however, it is probably also true to say that the data currently available represent an advance, in terms both of accuracy and of sensitivity to people's own identities, over those of earlier periods.[1] In the rest of this chapter and in those that follow, much of the discussion will rely upon the most recent data available from the 1991 Census, analyses of the Labour Force Survey and the work of the Policy Studies Institute. The categories used in reporting figures derived from different studies will be those used in the original sources.

Minority ethnic groups in Britain

Data from the 1991 Census[2] indicate that there are in excess of 3 million people of minority ethnic origin resident in Great Britain, representing 5.5 per cent of the population. Ethnic minorities comprise 5.9 per cent of the population of England and Wales, and 6.2 per cent of the population of England (Owen, 1992: 1–2).

Residential distribution

As we would expect, given the character of initial migration described in Chapter 3, this population is highly unevenly spread geographically. The figures above indicate that the minority ethnic population is largely concentrated in England. Within this, it is overwhelmingly resident in the most urbanized and densely populated areas. Thus, 44.8 per cent of the minority ethnic population lives in London (which contains 10.3 per cent of the white population) and 14 per cent in the West Midlands (by comparison with 9 per cent of the white population). Other areas of high minority ethnic residence are West Yorkshire, Greater Manchester, and parts of the East Midlands (Owen, 1992: 2–3).

Within this overall pattern, the distribution of individual ethnic groups varies widely. People identifying themselves in the various 'black' categories are most heavily concentrated in London and the West Midlands, this being

Table 4.1 Ethnic group composition of the population in 1991 (%)

Ethnic group	Great Britain	England & Wales	England	Wales	Scotland
White	94.5	94.1	93.8	98.5	98.7
Ethnic minorities	5.5	5.9	6.2	1.5	1.3
Black	1.6	1.8	1.9	0.3	0.1
Black-Caribbean	0.9	1.0	1.1	0.1	0.0
Black-African	0.4	0.4	0.4	0.1	0.1
Black-Other	0.3	0.4	0.4	0.1	0.1
South Asian	2.7	2.9	3.0	0.6	0.6
Indian	1.5	1.7	1.8	0.2	0.2
Pakistani	0.9	0.9	1.0	0.2	0.4
Bangladeshi	0.3	0.3	0.3	0.1	0.0
Chinese and others	1.2	1.2	1.3	0.6	0.5
Chinese	0.3	0.3	0.3	0.2	0.2
Other-Asian	0.4	0.4	0.4	0.1	0.1
Other-Other	0.5	0.6	0.6	0.3	0.2
Total population (000s)	54,888.8	49,890.3	47,055.2	2,835.1	4,998.6

Source: Owen (1992: 2)

Table 4.2 Ethnic minorities in Great Britain by region, 1991

Regions and metropolitan countries	Total Population (000s)	White (000s)	(%)	% of GB	Ethnic minorities (000s)	(%)	% of GB
South-East	17,208.3	15,512.9	90.1	29.9	1,695.4	9.9	56.2
Greater London	6,679.7	5,333.6	79.8	10.3	1,346.1	20.2	44.6
East Anglia	2,027.0	1,983.6	97.9	3.8	43.4	2.1	1.4
South-West	4,609.4	4,546.8	98.6	8.8	62.6	1.4	2.1
West Midlands	5,150.2	4,725.8	91.8	9.1	424.4	8.2	14.1
West Midlands MC	2,551.7	2,178.1	85.4	4.2	373.5	14.6	12.4
East Midlands	3,953.4	3,765.4	95.2	7.3	188.0	4.8	6.2
Yorks & Humberside	4,836.5	4,622.5	95.6	8.9	214.0	4.4	7.1
South Yorkshire	1,262.6	1,226.5	97.1	2.4	36.2	2.9	1.2
West Yorkshire	2,013.7	1,849.6	91.8	3.6	164.1	8.2	5.4
North-West	6,243.7	5,999.1	96.1	11.6	244.6	3.9	8.1
Greater Manchester	2,499.4	2,351.2	94.1	4.5	148.2	5.9	4.9
Merseyside	1,403.6	1,377.7	98.2	2.7	25.9	1.8	0.9
North	3,026.7	2,988.2	98.7	5.8	38.5	1.3	1.3
Tyne & Wear	1,095.2	1,075.3	98.2	2.1	19.9	1.8	0.7
Wales	2,835.1	2,793.5	98.5	5.4	41.6	1.5	1.4
Scotland	4,998.6	4,935.9	98.7	9.5	62.6	1.3	2.1
Great Britain	54,888.8	51,873.8	94.5	100.0	3,015.1	5.5	100.0

Source: Owen (1992:3)

particularly noticeable in the case of those classified as 'Black-Caribbean'. People of Indian origin are strongly represented in London, the West Midlands, and the East Midlands. People of Pakistani descent are somewhat more evenly distributed between the main areas of ethnic minority residence. They are less strongly represented in London but have large populations in West Yorkshire, Greater Manchester, and the West Midlands. They are also the largest minority ethnic group in Scotland. Those of Bangladeshi descent are most numerous in London and to a lesser extent in the West Midlands and Greater Manchester. People falling into the 'Chinese' and 'Other Asian' categories are more evenly distributed nationally, though again with their largest numbers in London. The group known for Census purposes as 'Other-Other' is recorded as the largest single minority ethnic group in Merseyside and Wales, 'reflecting the high incidence of persons of mixed origin in areas of long settlement such as Liverpool and Cardiff' (Owen, 1992: 3).

The minority ethnic population is, thus, geographically concentrated in the most highly urbanized areas. Within these broad areas, people of minority ethnic origin are present in largest numbers in the most urbanized parts, with representation at much lower levels in the suburban and rural areas surrounding cities (Owen, 1992: 6–7). The degree of concentration of the minority ethnic population is dramatized still further if we note that the twenty-nine local authority districts in which ethnic minorities represent more than 15 per cent of the population account for 55 per cent of the total ethnic minority population of Britain (Owen, 1992: 8—see Table 4.3).

The Census data for 1991, then, appear to reveal a long-established pattern, with members of minority ethnic groups particularly concentrated in London and the South-East, and in areas of traditional manufacturing. These data have some significance both in relation to initial patterns of migration and settlement (see Chapter 3) and in relation to the consequences of economic change in the 1980s (see below Chapter 5).

The pattern of change

Given the problems of comparing different sources of data, precise measures of the patterning or scale of change are fraught with difficulties. Some general tendencies can, however, be observed. Thus overall, the minority ethnic population does seem to have been increasing at a faster rate than the population as a whole. This should not be surprising, since this population is, on average, younger than the population as a whole and thus contains a higher proportion of people of child-bearing age. This pattern holds both nationally and regionally (Owen, 1992: 9).

Perhaps more significantly, there has been a tendency over a significant period for the minority ethnic population to become more spatially concentrated. As long ago as 1984, the third PSI survey was noting that an increasing proportion of the minority ethnic population was resident in areas of highest minority ethnic settlement (Brown, 1984: 59). Owen's comparison of 1991 Census data with available information from the 1971 and 1981 Censuses also reveals increasing concentration. This analysis, moreover, shows that a major reason for this change has been a tendency, in recent years, for population generally to shift from large cities to smaller towns and rural areas. This movement has not characterized minority ethnic groups, however, with the result that they have become a larger proportion of the residents of those major urban areas experiencing a decline in population, while their numbers have grown most slowly in the areas of fastest population growth (Owen, 1992: 9–10). Once again, these patterns have wider ramifications in the light of changes in the economy over the same period (see Chapter 5 below).

Table 4.3 Districts with largest ethnic minority percentages, 1991

District	Ethnic minorities			Largest ethnic minority	% of total population
	(%)	(000s)	% of GB		
Brent	44.8	108.9	3.61	Indian	17.2
Newham	42.3	89.8	2.98	Indian	13.0
Tower Hamlets	35.6	57.3	1.90	Bangladeshi	22.9
Hackney	33.6	60.8	2.02	Black-Caribbean	11.2
Ealing	32.3	88.9	2.95	Indian	16.1
Lambeth	30.3	74.1	2.46	Black-Caribbean	12.6
Haringey	29.0	58.7	1.95	Black-Caribbean	9.3
Leicester	28.5	77.0	2.55	Indian	22.3
Slough	27.7	28.0	0.93	Indian	12.5
Harrow	26.2	52.4	1.74	Indian	16.1
Waltham Forest	25.6	54.2	1.80	Black-Caribbean	6.8
Southwark	24.4	53.4	1.77	Black-Caribbean	8.3
Hounslow	24.4	49.9	1.66	Indian	14.3
Lewisham	22.0	50.7	1.68	Black-Caribbean	10.1
Birmingham	21.5	206.8	6.86	Pakistani	6.9
Westminster, City of	21.4	37.4	1.24	Other-Other	4.3
Redbridge	21.4	48.4	1.61	Indian	10.2
Wandsworth	20.0	50.6	1.68	Black-Caribbean	6.1
Luton	19.8	34.0	1.13	Pakistani	6.2
Islington	18.9	31.1	1.03	Black-Caribbean	5.1
Wolverhampton	18.6	45.0	1.49	Indian	11.4
Barnet	18.4	54.0	1.79	Indian	7.3
Camden	17.8	30.4	1.01	Bangladeshi	3.5
Croydon	17.6	55.1	1.83	Black-Caribbean	4.9
Hammersmith and Fulham	17.5	26.0	0.86	Black-Caribbean	5.9
Merton	16.3	27.4	0.91	Indian	3.4
Bradford	15.6	71.3	2.37	Pakistani	9.9
Kensington and Chelsea	15.6	21.6	0.72	Other-Other	3.6
Blackburn	15.4	21.0	0.70	Indian	7.7
Total		1,664.2	55.23		

Source: Owen (1992: 7)

Further evidence on ethnic diversity from country of birth data

As we have seen, data about groups classified as ethnic minorities for the purposes of the Census and other surveys do not fully capture the ethnic diversity of modern Britain. For this reason, the information collected in the Census about place of birth, though now superseded as a source of data about Britain's main minority ethnic communities, remains useful in alerting us to the presence of other significant population groups.

The 1991 Census shows that there were almost 4 million people in Britain who had been born elsewhere. Fewer than half of these had been born in the countries of the New Commonwealth.[3] People of European origin account for the majority of the remainder of those born outside Britain, with Ireland (including both Eire and Northern Ireland) representing the largest group at 1.5 per cent of the population. People from Germany constitute the largest group among those originating in other European Union countries apart from Eire. Among those from other parts of the world, groups from Cyprus and Poland stand out. The former is, of course, a member of the Commonwealth, while many of those of Polish origin would have settled in Britain after the war under the provisions of the Polish Resettlement Scheme (see Chapter 3). As might be expected from other data presented in this Chapter the size and diversity of the non-British born population is most marked in London and the South-East, with large groupings also found in the West Midlands (Owen, 1993*d*: 4–9).

Among those who were born outside the UK there are marked differences in gender balance between groups. Thus among those born in Western Europe women significantly outnumber men. The reverse is true for those from Eastern Europe and the former USSR, the Near and Middle East and North Africa (Owen, 1993*d*: 3).

Turning to smaller national minority groupings which have been identified as having special cultural or other needs, or as having been subject to racial discrimination, those of Cypriot, Turkish, and Vietnamese origin stand out. The first two groups are overwhelmingly concentrated in London, while a majority of the third is found in Birmingham, Manchester, and Inner London (Owen, 1993*d*: 19). These three groupings illustrate with particular clarity a general point that is highlighted by the discussion in Chapter 2. This is that national origin and ethnicity do not necessarily coincide. Thus Census data on Cypriots do not distinguish those of Turkish and Greek descent. The category Turkish includes Kurdish refugees from the Turkish government. Finally, those from Vietnam include a substantial proportion of Chinese ethnic origin many of whom have joined long-established Chinese communities (Owen, 1993*d*: 9–11). Owen's analysis shows, once again, that the gender balance varies between these different communities and, within them, from one place of settlement to another (Owen, 1993*d*: 11).

There is not space here to pursue further the analysis of these and other groupings. However, these data should be sufficient to indicate that the pattern of ethnic diversity in Britain is more complex and varied than is sometimes realized.[4] As was indicated in Chapter 3, this rich tapestry of cultural and social variety is no new phenomenon. Rather it can be seen as an enduring, and constantly repeated and revitalized, feature of the history both of Britain as a whole and of England in particular.

Minority ethnic groups: Gender and age structures

As is commonly (though not invariably—see Phizacklea, 1983) the case, many of the early migrants to Britain from the New Commonwealth were single men. The proportions of women in these groups increased gradually as a result of family reunification—a process partly accelerated by the threat of immigration control in the early 1960s. With the passing of the **1971 Immigration Act**, the bulk of immigration from these areas was restricted to family reunification. In addition of course, an ever-increasing proportion (46.8 per cent by 1991 according to Census data (Owen, 1993a: 12) had been born in Britain. A result of these features is that minority ethnic groups in Britain tended in the early days of migration to have heavily male population structures. The gender balance has, however, been subject to increasing equalization. Nevertheless, differences between groups remain, some of them reflecting initial migration patterns and some reflecting the relative recency of the main migrations from particular locations. Thus among 'whites', 'Black-Caribbeans', and 'Black-Others' women are in the majority, while among the main South Asian groups, men predominate (Owen, 1993a: 12).

When we turn to age structures, we find further contrasts with the pattern for the population as a whole. Generally, minority ethnic populations are younger than the white population with only Black-Caribbeans having a large population of retirement age. Among South Asian groups, Indians tend to have the oldest age structure, while Bangladeshis and Pakistanis have the youngest. The groups classified as 'Black-Other' and 'Other-Other' have particularly young populations. It is not clear to what extent this is an artefact of the classification system and people's preferred identities. In the case of 'Black-Other' it may be that it is among younger age groups that people are most likely to classify themselves as 'Black-British' or simply 'Black'. The category 'Other-Other' includes those of 'mixed' origin. Evidence from the Labour Force Survey suggests that this is a rapidly growing group reflecting the increasing numbers of children born to parents from different origins (Jones, 1993: 16, 20). Indeed some evidence suggests that about one-third of African-Caribbean adults under

30 are married to, or cohabiting with, a white partner (Tizzard and Phoenix, 1993: 1). These factors may also partly explain the apparent decline in the size of the 'Black-Caribbean' group (Owen, 1993a: 9)

Conclusion

This chapter has attempted to provide a broad overview of the ethnic diversity characteristic of modern Britain. While concentrating principally upon those of Britain's citizens who are descended from post-war migrants from the New Commonwealth, an attempt has been made to indicate that the pattern of ethnic diversity extends beyond these groups in ways which should lead us to question simplistic notions of British homogeneity.

Moreover, it should be clear that any attempt to generalize about 'ethnic minorities' is fraught with difficulty. Britain's citizens of minority ethnic origin have diverse histories, cultures, and experiences, both before and since migration. Recognizing the significance of those differences, as well as the common experiences of discrimination and exclusion explored elsewhere in this volume, is an important precondition for understanding the richness and complexity which is Britain at the beginning of the twenty-first century. It is the task of the remaining chapters in this volume to explore that complexity in a range of substantive contexts.

Further reading

The 1991 Census represents the most up-to-date source of information about patterns of ethnic diversity in Britain. Accessible discussions can be found in the *1991 Census Statistical Papers* by David Owen of the National Ethnic Minority Data Archive (see Owen, 1992, 1993a, b, c, d, 1994).

The Office for National Statistics has published a series of four volumes, entitled *Ethnicity in the 1991 Census*. Volume 3, edited by Ceri Peach (1996), provides useful profiles of a number of minority ethnic groups as well as exploring issues of categorization and identity. Volume 4, edited by David Coleman and John Salt (1996), explores the demographic characteristics of the minority ethnic populations and includes useful discussions of some of the technical and political difficulties surrounding the question inviting respondents to identify their ethnic group (Coleman and Salt, 1996).

Ethnic Minorities in Britain: Diversity and Disadvantage by Tariq Modood *et al.* (1997) is the most up to date source of data, derived from the Fourth National Survey of Ethnic Minorities, on various aspects of Britain's ethnic diversity.

Chapter 5

Employment

Introduction

C HAPTER 3 charted the recent history of migration to Britain and reviewed the development of immigration control and nationality legislation. We saw that a distinction between British citizens and others had been gradually established which placed a high implicit priority on differences of skin colour. Nevertheless, by the time the 1981 Nationality Act was on the statute book, there was already in Britain a substantial body of settled migrants entitled to full citizenship, together with a large 'second generation' of British born nationals of New Commonwealth descent, who did not fit the 'white' image of the patrial. It is the paradox of the 1981 Act, then, that it drew a clear distinction between citizens and non-citizens, insiders and outsiders, which was based on descent and was, implicitly at least, racialized. Yet at the same time it confirmed the *formal* citizenship rights of a substantial body of British citizens who were not 'white'.

However, *formal* civil and political rights are only one dimension of citizenship. More fundamental questions concern whether rights can be substantively exercised. Among the potential barriers to such exercise are the extent to which those charged with the implementation of rights make them equally available to all those who are formally entitled to them. A further question is the degree to which people have access to the resources that permit them to seize and operationalize those rights.[1]

In the chapters that follow we consider these issues from the standpoint of a variety of aspects of life in modern Britain. Since access to economic resources is often a key to people's ability to control other aspects of their lives, we commence by looking at employment.

Initial settlement and employment

In Chapter 3 it was argued that post-war migrants to Britain from the New Commonwealth came largely to fill vacancies in specific areas of labour shortage—notably in the least desirable jobs at the bottom of the labour market. We have also seen, in Chapter 4, that Britain's citizens of New Commonwealth descent have tended to continue to live in these broad areas of initial settlement and, indeed, that there has been relatively little geographical expansion. These features of the new migrants' position have had important implications for subsequent developments. In particular, they have direct effects on the range of employment opportunities which it is possible to access (see the discussion in Owen and Green, 1992).

Successive pieces of research conducted from the 1960s through into the 1980s (Brown, 1984; Smith, 1976) revealed a pattern of continuing disadvantage, with people from minority ethnic groups clustered in particular industries and occupations, and over-represented in semi-skilled and unskilled jobs. In addition, there has been a persistent pattern of exclusion altogether from the labour market, with members of minority ethnic groups experiencing consistently higher rates of unemployment than their white counterparts. In the sections which follow we explore the evidence provided by the 1991 Census, and by the work of the Policy Studies Institute (PSI) (Jones, 1993: Modood *et al.*, 1997), to provide a picture of the current situation. As we shall see it is one that reveals both continuity and change from earlier periods. Some of the explanations for each of these features will be examined.

Labour market participation

The first question to ask in any assessment of the labour market position of members of different groups is 'what proportion of those of working age are actually employed or seeking employment?' (or, to use another commonly used phrase, economically active). Working age is normally defined as 16–64 for men and 16–59 for women (this reflects differences in the statutory retirement age for men and women).

Tables 5.1 and 5.2 reveal a number of important variations in the patterns of economic activity among members of different groups. A factor of considerable importance concerns the age structures of the white and minority ethnic populations respectively (see Chapter 4). Thus, the major part of the minority ethnic population over 16 is of working age. As a result, while a majority of white

Table 5.1 Population and economic activity by ethnic group in Great Britain, 1991 (thousands)

Ethnic group	Over 16	Aged 16–59/64	Economically active	In Employment	Unemployed/on scheme	Economically inactive
White	41,846.4	31,701.9	25,475.1	22,910.3	2,564.8	16,371.3
Ethnic Minorities	2,018.7	1,887.6	1,301.7	1,030.2	271.5	717.0
Black	628.8	582.1	445.8	338.4	107.4	183.1
Black-Caribbean	390.6	350.8	285.4	224.9	60.5	105.1
Black-African	150.1	146.0	96.9	66.7	30.3	53.2
Black-Other	88.2	85.2	63.4	46.9	16.6	24.8
South Asian	951.2	892.0	576.0	458.1	117.9	375.2
Indian	592.0	547.1	395.1	336.2	58.9	196.9
Pakistani	273.3	261.6	139.3	94.8	44.5	134.0
Bangladeshi	85.9	83.3	41.6	27.2	14.5	44.3
Chinese and others	438.7	413.6	280.0	233.7	46.2	158.7
Chinese	120.3	113.2	73.9	65.7	8.2	46.4
Other-Asian	149.3	142.9	95.9	80.4	15.5	53.4
Other-Other	169.1	157.4	110.2	87.7	22.5	58.9
Entire population	43,865.1	33,589.5	26,776.8	23,940.5	2,836.3	17,088.3

Source: Owen (1993b: 1)

Table 5.2 Labour market participation by ethnic group and gender, Great Britain, 1991[2]

Ethnic group	Males Economically active (000s)	(%)	inactive (%)	Females Economically active (000s)	(%)	inactive (%)
White	14,577.7	88.2	26.8	10,897.4	71.4	50.3
Ethnic Minorities	761.9	80.2	23.9	539.8	57.6	47.0
Black	233.7	82.6	22.5	212.1	70.9	35.2
Black-Caribbean	147.4	87.5	19.9	138.0	75.7	33.1
Black-African	52.0	70.8	31.0	44.9	61.9	39.9
Black-Other	34.3	84.1	18.1	29.1	65.5	37.1
South Asian	367.6	80.1	23.9	208.4	48.1	55.5
Indian	231.5	82.8	21.9	163.6	61.1	44.6
Pakistani	103.4	76.0	26.7	35.9	28.6	72.9
Bangladeshi	32.8	74.7	27.6	8.9	22.4	78.2
Chinese and others	160.6	77.2	25.8	119.4	58.0	46.3
Chinese	41.2	72.9	29.9	32.7	57.6	46.9
Other-Asian	52.8	78.5	23.8	43.2	57.0	46.1
Other-Other	66.6	79.2	24.6	43.5	59.4	46.1
Entire population	15,339.6	88.2	26.7	11,437.2	70.6	50.1

Source: Owen (1993*b*: 2)

people who are economically inactive are retired, the reasons for economic inactivity among persons of minority ethnic descent must be sought elsewhere (Owen, 1993*b*: 1–2). Jones's analysis of Labour Force Survey data suggests that the explanation lies in the relatively larger proportions of minority ethnic than white young people remaining in full time education after the statutory school leaving age (1993: 63–4).

Once again, however, it is necessary to be cautious about generalizing too readily about 'ethnic minorities'. Thus Owen's analysis of 1991 Census data (1993*b*) reveals marked differences between groups. For example, while the proportion of 16–24 year olds of Black-Caribbean origin who are students is roughly comparable to that of white people, young people of Chinese and Indian origin display high rates of participation in post-16 education. The proportions of students among people of Bangladeshi and Pakistani descent are lower than other South Asian and Asian groups but, as Owen notes (1993*b*: 8), these groups also have relatively low rates of economic activity. Other explanations must be sought for inactivity among these groups.

This last point alerts us to other important features revealed by the 1991 Census. Thus, among all groups, economic activity rates are higher for men—90 per cent of men being active as against 70 per cent of women. Moreover, while economic activity rates are higher among white people than among people from minority ethnic backgrounds, the difference is much more marked among women. Again, however, we should note that there are significant differences between minority ethnic groups. Full details of the quite complex patterns to be uncovered are provided in Table 5.2. In general, however, we can note that those classified as 'Black', and particularly 'Black-Caribbean', have activity rates closest to white people, while among South Asians there are marked variations, notably among women (Owen, 1993*b*: 2). Jones suggests that the differences among women are 'due to differences in culture concerning the role of women in home-making and child-rearing' (1993: 63–4). In this connection we may note that Mirza has suggested that the patterns of labour market participation characteristic of African-Caribbean women reflect the specific cultural construction of femininity in communities where gender roles are more equal, and male and female roles characterized by a relative autonomy (Mirza, 1992: 164).

The data about rates of participation, of course, tell us nothing about whether people have actually been successful in gaining jobs or about the kinds of work they do. In the next two sections we consider unemployment, and occupation and job levels. Before turning to these issues, however, it is necessary to consider the balance between full- and part-time working among those in work. This is important not only because of the marked gender differentials revealed but also because of the rapid growth of part-time employment in recent years.

The data reveal that part-time employment is dominated by women, who account for nearly 90 per cent of such employees. However, a significantly higher proportion of white women in paid employment work part-time than is the case among ethnic minorities. The differences in the rate of part-time working among women from different minority ethnic groups are quite small. Moreover, the feminization of part-time working is less marked among ethnic minorities than among white people. Indeed the data reveal particularly high levels of part-time working among men of Bangladeshi, Pakistani, and Black-African origin. As Owen points out, the relatively high proportion of men among part-time workers in the Bangladeshi and Pakistani groups may, in part, be a consequence of low rates of labour market participation among women from these groups. It may, however, also reflect the over-representation of men from minority ethnic groups in insecure and poorly paid jobs in what is sometimes called the secondary labour market—a sector where the growth in part-time, as well as casualized, employment has been significant (Owen, 1993*b*: 3–4).

Table 5.3 Part-time employment rates by ethnic group, Great Britain, 1991

Ethnic group	Part time employees	% of GB total	Males (000s)	% employed	Females (000s)	% employed	% female
White	4,188.5	97.2	444.9	3.5	3,743.6	37.1	89.4
Ethnic Minorities	122.9	2.9	27.0	4.6	95.9	21.7	78.0
Black	45.9	1.1	9.4	5.6	36.5	21.4	79.6
Black-Caribbean	28.6	0.7	4.4	4.1	24.2	20.8	84.6
Black-African	11.3	0.3	3.6	10.4	7.7	24.1	68.0
Black-Other	6.0	0.1	1.4	5.6	4.7	20.7	77.6
South Asian	46.3	1.1	11.1	3.8	35.3	21.0	76.1
Indian	34.8	0.8	6.2	3.1	28.7	20.5	82.3
Pakistani	9.1	0.2	3.7	5.2	5.4	22.8	59.0
Bangladeshi	2.4	0.1	1.2	5.3	1.3	24.6	51.8
Chinese and others	30.6	0.7	6.6	5.0	24.0	23.6	78.5
Chinese	8.3	0.2	1.7	4.6	6.6	22.6	80.0
Other-Asian	10.4	0.2	2.0	4.5	8.4	23.0	80.9
Other-Other	11.9	0.3	2.9	5.7	9.0	25.0	75.4
Entire population	4,311.4	100.0	471.9	3.5	3,839.5	36.5	89.1

Source: Owen (1993*b*: 3)

Labour market exclusion: Unemployment

Perhaps the most fundamental question in any assessment of labour market position is whether or not one has access to employment at all. In this connection, we may note that successive studies (Brown, 1984; Jones, 1993; Smith, 1976; Smith 1981) have revealed that persons of minority ethnic origin are at a consistently higher risk of unemployment than are white people. Indeed, as Jones notes (1993: 112) there is evidence that unemployment among people from minority ethnic groups is 'hyper-cyclical'; that is, in times of recession, the minority ethnic unemployment rate rises faster than that of white people, while in times of recovery, it falls more rapidly. This pattern is confirmed by Labour Force data for the 1980s which show that in the first half of the decade, with the economy suffering from the recession of the early 1980s, unemployment among ethnic minority people was roughly double the rate among white people. As the economy recovered from the mid-1980s onwards, the minority ethnic unemployment rate declined to a level about two-thirds higher than that among white people (Jones, 1993: 112–23).

Table 5.4 Unemployment rates by ethnic group, Great Britain, 1991

Ethnic group	Unemployed (000s)	On scheme (000s)	Unemployment rates		
			Persons (%)	Males (%)	Females (%)
White	2,246.1	318.6	8.8	10.7	6.3
Ethnic Minorities	238.4	33.1	18.3	20.3	15.6
Black	94.0	13.3	21.1	25.2	16.6
Black-Caribbean	53.8	6.7	18.9	23.8	13.5
Black-African	26.1	4.1	27.0	28.9	24.7
Black-Other	14.1	2.5	22.2	25.5	18.3
South Asian	105.0	12.9	18.2	19.2	16.5
Indian	51.7	7.2	13.1	13.4	12.7
Pakistani	40.1	4.4	28.8	28.5	29.6
Bangladeshi	13.2	1.3	31.7	30.9	34.5
Chinese and others	39.4	6.8	14.1	15.5	12.1
Chinese	7.0	1.2	9.5	10.5	8.3
Other-Asian	12.8	2.7	13.4	14.2	12.3
Other-Other	19.5	3.0	17.7	19.7	14.8
Entire population	2,484.5	351.7	9.3	11.2	6.8

Source: Owen (1993*b*: 7)

The data in Table 5.4 report the situation as it was at the time of the 1991 Census with the economy once more having entered recession. They show the unemployment rate among people of minority ethnic descent once more running at twice the white rate among men and around two and a half times the white rate among women. They also reveal substantial differences between groups within this broad category. Thus, for example, the female unemployment rate for Bangladeshis was nearly 35 per cent, five times higher than the overall female rate of 6.8 per cent. Even among those of Indian origin, a group that, as we shall see, is often identified as experiencing progress, the unemployment rate was about 25 per cent higher than the white rate among men and twice as high among women (Owen, 1993*b*: 6).

A notable feature of unemployment is that it particularly affects young people. Unemployment rates for 16 to 24-year-olds are consistently higher than those for the economically active as a whole (Jones, 1993: 113; Owen, 1993*b*: 8). This is of considerable importance in assessing overall levels of disadvantage, given the relatively younger age structure of minority ethnic groups. Moreover, the data also show that among young people similar ethnically structured differentials can be identified as among the economically active as a whole. They suggest that only among men of African Asian origin (Jones, 1993: 113) and among Chinese men (Owen, 1993*b*: 7) are unemployment rates as low as those for white people (compare Modood, 1997*b*: 88–93). Moreover, the true position among young people may also be masked by the expansion, in the 1980s, in the number of government training schemes aimed at school leavers on which, data suggest, people drawn from the various Black groups were over-represented (Owen, 1993*b*: 7).

Unemployment rates also vary between different areas of the country. A number of urban locations in the North of England and the Midlands with high levels of unemployment are also areas of substantial minority ethnic residence. As a result the local patterns of variation between white people and those from minority ethnic groups, and between members of different such groups, diverge from the overall national pattern. The precise character of these varia-tions is too complex to be dealt with in the space available here (but see Jones, 1993; Owen, 1993*b*). However, we can note that levels of minority ethnic unemployment tend to be consistently higher than the white rate, that differ-ences are larger outside Greater London, and that, outside this area, even groups such as African Asians are likely to experience higher unemployment than white people (Jones, 1993: 113–14; Modood, 1997*b*: 88–93).

Occupation and job levels

A long series of studies has shown that in general terms members of minority ethnic groups have been employed in less skilled jobs, at lower job levels and concentrated in particular industrial sectors (e.g. Brown, 1984; Smith, 1974). More recent data such as Jones's (1993) re-analysis of the Labour Force Survey for 1988, 1989 and 1990, and the fourth PSI survey (Modood, 1997*b*), suggest that the position is becoming more complex as the experience of members of different groups has begun to diverge.

The data presented in Table 5.5 suggest that male members of some minority ethnic groups are beginning to experience employment patterns that increas-ingly approximate those of white men. This is true of African Asian, Chinese and, to a slightly lesser extent, Indian men where the proportions approximate or exceed the proportions of white workers in each of the top two categories. However, these figures conceal important variations since, although African Asian and Chinese men are more likely to be professional workers than white men, they are considerably less likely to be represented among senior man-agers in large enterprises. Among those of Afro-Caribbean, Bangladeshi and Pakistani descent, there is much less evidence of progress in the top category (although there is some convergence in the 'intermediate and junior non-

Table 5.5 Job levels of men (base: male employees and self-employed)

column percentages

Socio-economic group	White	Caribbean	Indian	African Asian	Pakistani	Bangladeshi	Chinese
Prof./managers/employers	30	14	25	30	19	18	46
Employers and managers (large establishments)	11	5	5	3	3	0	6
Employers and managers (small establishments)	11	4	11	14	12	16	23
Professional workers	8	6	9	14	4	2	17
Intermediate and junior non-manual	18	19	20	24	13	19	17
Skilled manual & foreman	36	39	31	30	46	7	14
Semi-skilled manual	11	22	16	12	18	53	12
Unskilled manual	3	6	5	2	3	3	5
Armed forces or N/A	2	0	3	2	2	0	5
Non-manual	48	33	45	54	32	37	63
Manual	50	67	52	44	67	63	31
Weighted count	789	365	349	296	182	61	127
Unweighted count	713	258	356	264	258	112	71

Source: Modood (1997b: 100)

Table 5.6 Job levels of women (base: female employees and self-employed)

column percentages

Socio-economic group	White	Caribbean	Indian	African Asian	Pakistani	Chinese
Professional, managerial and employers	16	5	11	12	12	30
Intermediate non-manual	21	28	14	14	29	23
Junior non-manual	33	36	33	49	23	23
Skilled manual & foreman	7	4	11	7	9	13
Semi-skilled manual	18	20	27	16	22	9
Unskilled manual	4	6	4	1	4	2
Armed forces/inadequately described/not stated	0	1	1	1	0	0
Non-manual	*70*	*69*	*58*	*75*	*64*	*76*
Manual	*29*	*30*	*42*	*24*	*35*	*24*
Weighted count	*734*	*452*	*275*	*196*	*60*	*120*
Unweighted count	*696*	*336*	*260*	*164*	*164*	*63*

Source: Modood, T., 'Employment', in Modood (1997*b*: 104)

manual category). Bangladeshi men in particular, 53 per cent of whom are in semi-skilled manual occupations, remain concentrated in the lower echelons of the labour market. In addition, we should note that some groups display marked bi-polarity. Thus both Indian and Chinese men are found in large numbers in both the highest and the lowest job categories. Jones argues: 'This may suggest that men from these two groups enter a relatively narrow range of occupations, either at the top or bottom end of the job market' (1993: 70).

Table 5.6 presents comparable data for women. It shows that women of all groups are less likely than men to be in the top category and, for all groups, the largest concentrations are to be found in the 'intermediate' and 'junior' non-manual categories, followed by 'semi-skilled manual'. This finding matches that of the 1982 Policy Studies Institute survey (Brown, 1984) and Jones's (1993) re-analysis of Labour Force Survey data. Both of these studies offered a similar explanation. This is that women are already disadvantaged in the labour market relative to men and that, as a result, there is limited scope for an additional disadvantage arising from ethnicity (1993: 71). Despite detailed variations between groups, therefore, there is some evidence that ' . . . gender divisions in the labour market may be stronger and more deeply rooted than differences due to race and ethnicity' (Modood, 1997b: 104).

So far as distribution between employment sectors is concerned, the data from the Labour Force Survey reflect both continuity with, and some changes in, the previously established pattern of concentration of the ethnic minority population in particular employment sectors. This concentration to some degree reflects patterns of settlement and demand for labour at the time of initial settlement (see Chapters 3 and 4). However, major economy-wide changes in the 1980s associated with the decline in manufacturing employment and the growth of the service sector have led to significant changes for members of all groups. The Labour Force Survey data for 1988, 1989, and 1990 suggest that the largest proportion of all groups, including white employees, are now to be found in distribution, hotels, catering, and repairs. Within this broad pattern people of South Asian origin are rather more likely than white people to be employed in retail distribution, while those of Chinese and Bangladeshi origin are markedly more likely than white people to work in hotels and catering. Pakistani and Bangladeshi men are particularly likely to be found in the textile and footwear sectors. Among Afro-Caribbeans there is a relatively high concentration of employees in transport and communication. Afro-Caribbean men are well represented in construction and women in the hospital and health care sectors. There is a marked concentration of women of all groups in the service sector, reflecting the general pattern of segregation of women in employment (Jones, 1993: 66–8; cf. Rees, 1992).

Some of the discussion above has indicated that caution has to be exercised in comparing groups given the data that are available. Apparently similar proportions of groups in the same occupational category may conceal important differences in status, in the kinds of enterprise worked in or in the working conditions enjoyed by members of different groups. One aspect of such differences may concern earnings and hours of work.

Brown's (1984) study found that minority ethnic employees had significantly lower earnings than their white counterparts. A number of more recent studies (Leicester City Council, 1990; McCormick, 1986; Pirani et al., 1992) have suggested that the pattern revealed by earlier studies continued into the late 1980s and 90s. This finding is further confirmed by the results of the fourth PSI survey (Modood, 1997b). These reveal, however, marked differences between groups, with African Asians and Chinese men approximating white rates. Caribbean rates are slightly lower while Indian, Pakistani, and Bangladeshi earnings (in descending order) all fall significantly behind. Among women, there is much less variation with all groups except Bangladeshis outperforming whites. We must, however, note that these figures are affected by low rates of labour market participation among some groups and by patterns of full- and part-time employment. For a full discussion see Modood (1997b: 112–17).

We should note that earnings may be significantly affected by hours worked. In this connection it is important to note that Brown's 1982 study (1984) indicated that members of minority ethnic groups were much more likely than white people to work shifts and that, when this was taken into account, ethnic differentials in earnings were larger than they at first appeared. Jones's analysis of LFS data for the late 1980s reveals that this difference in the likelihood that members of different groups would work shifts had been maintained to some degree, Pakistani male workers being significantly more likely than others to be working shifts. Among women, those of Afro-Caribbean origin were the most likely to be engaged in shift work. However, what is interesting is that this tendency to work shifts declined with age suggesting, according to Jones, that younger people 'are not following the older generations into the kinds of jobs which involve shiftwork' (1993: 75). Whether this reflects choice, employer preference, or the changing structure of employment opportunities is less clear. Given the findings of earlier research, it also the raises the question of the likely effect on earnings.

The fourth PSI survey (Modood *et al.*, 1997) attempted for the first time to produce an analysis of the *household* incomes of minority ethnic groups. This is important because the household is commonly used as the unit of analysis in analyses of living standards and economic well-being. We saw above that minority ethnic groups differed from one another and, with the exception of African-Asians and Chinese, from whites in *individual* earnings. It is a plausible assumption that individual earnings differences would be likely to feed through into household differences but the manner in which this takes place is not clear. Among relevant factors influencing outcomes will be relative household size, the number of wage earners, the number of dependants and the availability of sources of income other than earnings. The analysis undertaken for the PSI reveals that the outcomes are complex and influenced by a range of factors. It also shows that, while some of the patterns revealed by analyses of employment continue to hold, there are other patterns that differ (Berthoud, 1997: 150–84. See also Berthoud, 1998).

The analysis is too complex to summarize in the space available here. However there are some key findings which we should note. The first is the extent of poverty (defined as incomes below half the national average) among Pakistani and Bangladeshi households. As the author of this section of the report, Richard Berthoud, puts it:

Name any group whose poverty causes national concern—pensioners, disabled people, one-parent families, the unemployed—Pakistanis and Bangladeshis are poorer. (Berthoud, 1997: 180)

The data also show that only Chinese households have incomes close to those of whites. Caribbean, Indian, and African Asian households were all more likely than whites to experience poverty and less likely to have large family incomes. These results lead to an important qualification to the evidence on upward occupational mobility we reviewed above. This is that, when household incomes are taken into account African Asians as well as Indians fare less well than those of Chinese descent while Caribbeans are much better placed than Pakistanis and Bangladeshis (Berthoud, 1997: 180). These data thus provide further reasons to be cautious in assessing the significance of occupational mobility and the relative labour market placement of groups.

Another issue of extreme importance is the question of homeworking. We saw above that economic activity rates, particularly for women, vary significantly from group to group. Data on patterns of employment appear to suggest the women from some ethnic groups have very low levels of economic activity. We should not too readily assume, however, that all of those omitted from the employment figures abstain from paid (as distinct from unpaid domestic) work. There is considerable evidence to suggest that official figures seriously underestimate the volume of homeworking in the economy (Allen and Wolkowitz, 1987, especially chapter 2; Felstead and Jewson, 1996; 1999). In its most exploitative forms, it frequently preys upon women who, for child care or other domestic reasons, are unable to engage in paid employment outside the home (Bisset and Huws, n.d.; Allen and Wolkowitz, 1987). There is also evidence that women in some minority ethnic groups are particularly likely, for cultural or other reasons, to be engaged in homeworking (Allen and Wolkowitz, 1987). To the extent that this is so it alerts us to a largely hidden aspect of disadvantage. Key features of homeworking—particularly in textile and light assembly industries—often include very low rates of pay, and long and demanding hours of work (Bisset and Huws, n.d). Thus it may well be that, among those officially recorded as economically inactive, there are large numbers of women who are subject to particularly exploitative conditions of work.[3]

Self-employment and enterprise

Both the 1991 Census and the fourth PSI survey (Modood, 1997*b*) provide evidence that self-employment is generally more common among minority ethnic groups than among the white population. This generalization, however, once again conceals some significant differences among minority ethnic groups. Thus among those classifying themselves into one of the 'Black' groups, self-employment is markedly less common than among the white population. By contrast, among those classified as 'Asian' it is considerably more common. Once again, however, there are variations among Asian groups, Bangladeshis having a smaller propensity to be self-employed than other South Asians (Modood, 1997b: 122–9; Owen, 1993b: 4–6). The pattern is similar for both male and female populations, although among African Asian women levels of self-employment are similar to white women, and in all groups a larger propor- tion of men are self-employed. Labour Force Survey data also indicate that self- employment is generally concentrated into a smaller range of activities than employment in general. For all groups distribution, hotels, repairs, and cater- ing make up the largest areas of self-employment, with retail distribution being particularly prominent among the African Asian, Indian, and Pakistani popula- tions (Jones, 1993: 65–6).

Data such as these, of course, appear to confirm a number of popular stereo- types: of unbusinesslike African Caribbeans and of the thriving 'Asian' corner shop. It is important to note, therefore, that a number of studies have drawn attention to the difficulties faced by entrepreneurs from minority ethnic groups (Ward and Jenkins, 1984). Thus, there is evidence that such businesses are often undercapitalized, recent research suggesting that African-Caribbean businesses have particular difficulties in accessing bank finance (Barrett, 1999). Other work has shown that minority ethnic businesses frequently operate on the margins of profitability and are dependent on a narrow, if relatively pro- tected (Robinson, 1989: 263), ethnic market. Moreover, there is little evidence that even the more successful examples of minority ethnic business have any necessary economic pay-off for the wider community (Sills et al., 1983/4).

These limitations must be borne in mind in considering the argument that self-employment is a way for members of minority groups to avoid the effects of discrimination in the labour market. Monder Ram (1992) has argued that the constraints imposed by racism are, indeed, often key elements in pushing minority groups into self-employment. This does not mean, however, that the effects of racism are easy to transcend. Ram's research shows that many ethnic minority entrepreneurs in practice find it difficult to escape the limits of an ethnically defined market. As a result they frequently have to use white inter- mediaries or agents, and sometimes have deliberately to appoint white people to managerial posts, in order to develop appropriate contacts and establish credibility with customers.

In addition, Ram's analysis draws attention to the critical role played by the family as a resource in negotiating racism. This asset is not, however, without cost. Thus family obligations may inhibit decisions which might otherwise be seen as economically rational. More critically, Ram suggests, such arrange- ments have specific implications for women. In particular, women are rarely defined as 'managers'. This role is assumed by men, who constitute the external face of the firm. However, women play critical roles in the internal management of the enterprise, balancing conflicting demands and deploying human and financial resources. Typically, however, not only are these contributions not acknowledged but women are also usually simultaneously responsible for the domestic sphere.

Explanations of disadvantage I: Language, skill, and job search

A variety of explanations have been offered for the disadvantage suffered by members of minority ethnic groups in the labour market. Some of the most commonly expressed locate the problem in the character of minority group job seekers. Such explanations draw heavily upon assimilationist assumptions that are widely encountered in explanations of migratory labour.

A claim commonly encountered among employers is that minority ethnic workers experience 'communication difficulties' (Jewson et al., 1990). In other words, high rates of unemployment and low job levels can be accounted for by inadequate English language skills. There is, indeed, some evidence that those who have poorer English experience more difficulties in the labour market (Brown, 1984: 128–49). A study of Coventry revealed that language remained a barrier for a sizeable minority of Asian women in Coventry, giving rise to difficulties in communicating not only with white people but also with those speaking other Asian languages (Gray et al., 1993). The fourth PSI survey suggests that both age and length of residence correlate with fluency in English although it also reveals other sources of variation between members of different groups and between men and women (Modood, 1997a: 60–63). However, even if language skills play some part in employment placement, they cannot easily account for the disadvantage experienced by that increasingly large part of the minority ethnic population that was born and educated in the United Kingdom.

Another commonly encountered explanation is that minority ethnic workers suffer from a skill or qualification deficit when compared with their white counterparts. This argument is often linked to educational 'under-achievement' (see the discussion in Chapter 6). Once again, however, there are difficulties with this account. While low levels of qualification are likely to confer disadvantages in the labour market, a number of studies have shown that, when qualifications are controlled for, minority ethnic workers are more likely to be unemployed or in lower job levels than their white counterparts (Brown, 1984; Jones, 1993; Smith, 1976). Again, however, the patterns are complex and reveal significant variations, both between groups and between different types of work (Modood, 1997*b*: 91–106). In addition, we should add that there is also considerable evidence that discrimination may block ethnic minority young people at earlier training and career choice stages (Cross *et al.*, 1990; Lee and Wrench, 1981).

Finally, there is evidence that job search methods may affect people's success in getting jobs (Dex, 1978/9). It appears that those groups that rely on personal and community knowledge and networks may find successful job placement easier. A negative consequence of this method, however, is that it is likely to reinforce patterns of ethnic segregation in the labour market by ensuring that people are employed largely where they already have friends and relatives (Commission for Racial Equality, 1982; Saifullah Khan, 1979). This process may have particularly serious effects for minority ethnic women. By contrast, those who rely on formal mechanisms, such as careers advice, may have more difficulty. It is important to note in this context, moreover, that there is evidence that, intentionally or unintentionally, discriminatory practices characterize some aspects of the work of the careers service (Cross *et al.*, 1990).

Explanations of disadvantage II: Discrimination

While the kinds of explanations outlined above may account for some of the disadvantage suffered by minority ethnic groups there is considerable evidence to suggest that when matters such as language competence, skill levels and qualifications are controlled for there remains a residue which is not explained by such factors. As a result, it is difficult to avoid the conclusion that discrimination on the part of employers plays a significant part in the labour market placement of minority ethnic groups.

In this context, it is interesting to note that the fourth PSI survey found that a large majority of all respondents believed that discrimination was widespread. Indeed white respondents were the most likely to hold such a view (Modood, 1997*b*: 129–35). This belief is consistent with the findings of an overwhelming body of research evidence which has demonstrated that direct, and apparently intentional, discrimination remains a feature of employment selection decisions (Daniel 1968, Hubbock and Carter, 1980; National Association of Citizens Advice Bureaux, 1984; Brown and Gay, 1985). A common method has been to submit job applications from candidates matched in every way except ethnic origin. Using methods such as this Brown and Gay revealed continuing systematic discrimination, despite the many years of race relations legislation. Thus, although a substantial number of employers appeared to treat all candidates equally, an equally large number appeared to discriminate. In some cases, Asian applicants were treated more favourably than those of African-Caribbean origin, in others the reverse was true. Overall, however, the researchers found that while 90 per cent of white applicants were successful, only 63 per cent of Asian and African-Caribbean applicants received positive responses. In other words, white applicants were more than 30 per cent more likely to be treated favourably than those of minority ethnic origin (Brown and Gay, 1985: 13–17). The results showed no statistically significant differences in the rate of discrimination between men and women or between older and younger applicants (Brown and Gay, 1985: 19). Moreover, when compared with the results of earlier studies dating back to the early 1970s, the researchers found no evidence of a diminution in the level of racial discrimination (Brown and Gay, 1985: 25–9). The authors conclude that a major reason for the persistence of discrimination, despite two race relations acts, is that employers are very unlikely to be caught in the act of discrimination (Brown and Gay, 1985: 33).

Table 5.7 A summary of the results of Brown and Gay's test applications: men and women, older and younger applicants

column percentages

	All job types	Male applicants	Female applicants	Applicants aged 28–30	Applicants aged 18–20
(a) All three responses positive	46	47	44	47	39
(b) Asian applicant rejected	10	12	8	10	10
(c) West Indian applicant rejected	10	10	10	9	16
(d) White applicant rejected	4	4	4	5	2
(e) Asian and West Indian applicants rejected	25	22	28	24	29
(f) Asian and White applicants rejected	2	2	2	3	—
(g) West Indian and White applicants rejected	3	3	3	3	4
Base: Total vacancies	335	167	168	286	149

Source: Brown and Gay (1985: 20)

In a more recent example, research into the fate of speculative employment inquiries made to some of Britain's major companies has direct implications for the explanations examined in the previous section (Noon, 1993). Matched letters of inquiry were sent to personnel managers at the top one hundred UK companies identified from *The Times* 1,000 index. The letters were signed by fictitious applicants called Evans and Patel. They were presented as MBA students who were about to qualify and who already had relevant experience. The research compared both the frequencies of responses sent to the two applicants and their quality in terms of the assistance and encouragement offered. It found that, overall, companies were more helpful and encouraging to white candidates. Those with equal opportunities statements in their annual reports were generally more likely to treat both candidates the same. However, 48 per cent of such companies did not treat both candidates equally and where they did not do so they favoured the white candidate in proportions greater than those companies without statements. As a result, the author of the research argued that his results suggested that discrimination was taking place even in companies ostensibly sensitive to equal opportunities.

The studies reported above reveal the existence of continuing, apparently direct and deliberate, discrimination. An equally serious problem is posed, however, by what is sometimes called indirect discrimination. This is where selection criteria are applied equally to everyone but where they are such that they disproportionately affect members of particular groups. A good example is where dress requirements are imposed which cannot be complied with by members of some groups, for religious or other reasons, and where the requirements concerned are not necessary for the completion of the occupational task. Indirect discrimination may be deliberate but it may also frequently be unintentional and unrecognized. Many of the ordinary, routine, taken for granted aspects of the recruitment process and the labour market may give rise to indirect discrimination. This process is described by Richard Jenkins (1986), who argues that many selection decisions are based not on whether candidates have the right qualifications for the job but on whether they are thought to be likely to 'fit in' to the workplace without causing any trouble. Such judgements are applied equally to everyone regardless of ethnicity. They become discriminatory when they are consciously or unconsciously informed by stereotypes which managers hold of minority ethnic groups. Jenkins's research revealed, as have other studies (Jewson *et al.*, 1990), that negative stereotypes were widespread among managers responsible for recruitment decisions.

A more recent survey of Asian women in Coventry also revealed that employers frequently held negative stereotypes. Perhaps more significantly, the researchers also found that even ostensibly positive stereotypes could be dis-advantageous. Thus it seemed that changes in the nature of work were leading managers increasingly to seek employees who were flexible, able to exercise initiative, and ready to carry responsibility for checking their own work and acquiring new skills. While employers were frequently ready to characterize Asian women workers as loyal, hardworking, and uncomplaining they also argued that these 'positive' qualities were no longer what was required by the demands of the modern workplace and labour market (Gray *et al.*, 1993). These examples reveal dramatically how it is all too easy for the routines of everyday working life to operate to the disadvantage of minority ethnic groups even when there is no intention to discriminate. They also make it easy to hide intentional discrimination as the unplanned and accidental outcome of the market-place.

Patterns of change: Convergence or polarization?

The last example discussed above draws our attention to the complexity of the ways in which the rapid economic change of the 1980s and early 1990s has affected existing patterns of advantage and disadvantage in the labour market.

The studies discussed above (Jones, 1993; Modood, 1997*b*) suggest that members of some groups are experiencing significant upward mobility with evidence of a high degree of convergence between white people and at least some minority ethnic groups (see also Iganski and Payne, 1996; 1999). However, it is necessary to bear in mind, in evaluating the evidence presented that the occupational achievements of those in work must be set in the context of continuing disproportionate levels of exclusion altogether from the labour market. Moreover, as we have seen, within the broad categories utilized for analyses of this sort members of different groups may occupy significantly different positions in occupational hierarchies. In addition, to the extent that members of some groups have also made strides in self-employment, some of the upward mobility experienced by other members of the same groups may well represent a degree of internal segregation of the labour market on ethnic lines.

Other changes in the character of the labour market may have more complex effects. Thus we noted in Chapter 4 that the minority ethnic population was increasingly concentrated in urban locations, many of which have not experienced the same levels of economic progress as newer areas of population growth where ethnic minorities are under-represented. The effects of economic changes which have led to the decline of a number of traditional industries and the emergence of new employment patterns in the growing service sector have particular implications for members of minority ethnic groups (Robinson, 1989: 250–1). In the study of Coventry discussed above, for example, researchers found that many Asian women had traditionally been concentrated in low wage sectors such as retailing, other services, textiles, and electrical engineering. The recession of the early 1990s, and other more long-term changes in the nature of work, had thus had serious consequences for opportunities for those without skills. Moreover, the researchers also found that changes in the organization of specific occupations were having negative effects. In nursing, for example, innovations in training were cutting off the route from health auxiliary to nurse that many Asian nurses in the study had formerly used to enter the profession.[4] In banking an increasing division, between those in customer service roles in branches and those working in processing centres, was creating a two-tier employment structure. The former group required good language and communication skills but also had access to superior advancement opportunities. The latter had less need of these attributes but also limited promotion chances. The authors of the report commented on the fact that few Asian women appeared to be employed in the customer service side of the bank studied (Gray et al., 1993).

Conclusion

The evidence presented in this chapter reflects themes repeated throughout the volume. Thus I have emphasized the diversity of experience of members of different ethnic groups, and of men and women. At the same time I have reported the evidence of continuing and systematic discrimination. We have seen that there is evidence of some upward mobility within employment for members of some groups but have also noted continued exclusion and labour market segregation.

We return to the theme of change, and prospects for the future, in the final chapter. For the moment we need to recall the extent to which experience in the field of employment is in some ways the key to overall life chances. The needs of the labour market were central to the patterning of New Commonwealth immigration and the emerging regime of control. As we shall see, the labour market situation of those migrants and their descendants has had knock-on effects in fields such as health and housing. In turn it has been a major determinant of access to full substantive citizenship.

Further reading

Ethnicity in the 1991 Census, Vol. 4: Employment, Education and Housing among the Ethnic Minority Populations of Britain, edited by Valerie Karn, provides more detailed analysis of some of the issues discussed in this chapter

Ethnic Minorities in Britain: Diversity and Disadvantage by Tariq Modood *et al.* (1997) contains up to date data on employment. It is particularly useful in exploring, in more depth, some of the complex and diverse patterns touched upon in this chapter.

Racism and Recruitment by Richard Jenkins (1986) remains one of the best and most sophisticated discussions of the way in which disadvantage and discrimination operate on a day-to-day basis in the work situation.

Chapter 6

Education

Introduction

THE previous chapter touched upon a number of issues which raise questions about the relationship between labour markets and the education system. Of particular significance was the evidence that lower rates of labour market participation among young people of minority ethnic origin are connected to their greater propensity, when compared with the white population, to remain in full-time education after the minimum school leaving age. Nevertheless, it is by no means clear that the employment and other opportunities they enjoy by virtue of doing so are commensurate with the investment in personal development which these patterns suggest. Indeed, much of the literature in the field of education has been concerned to investigate, and debate, the alleged educational 'underachievement' of members of some groups. In this chapter we look at the evidence concerning patterns of qualification; consider the arguments surrounding relative levels of educational performance; and review some of the policy proposals and initiatives developed to address the problems discerned.

Educational participation and qualifications

As we saw in Chapter 5, there is abundant evidence that members of minority ethnic groups are more likely to remain in full-time education after the age of 16 than are their white counterparts—a finding which holds both for young men and young women (Modood *et al.*, 1997). Moreover, the evidence suggests that this is a pattern of relatively long standing, dating back at least to the beginning of the 1980s (Brown, 1984; Department of Education and Science, 1985; Drew *et al.*, 1992; Jones, 1993). In addition, it appears that, in general, minority ethnic groups are over-represented in higher education relative to their presence in the population as a whole, although this gross observation conceals some important variations (Jones, 1993: 32; Modood, 1997a; Modood and Ackland, 1998; Modood and Shiner, 1994).

There are a number of potential explanations for this pattern of post-16 educational participation. One possibility is that young people of minority ethnic origin are more motivated to do well educationally than are their white peers. A second is that levels of parental support and encouragement are higher. A third is that, among at least some groups, young people find themselves having to compensate for the degree to which the school system has failed them at an earlier stage. A final possibility—which receives some support from the fact that levels of participation in tertiary education have been increasing for all young people—is that remaining in education is an alternative to unemployment. Given the high rates of unemployment experienced by young people of minority ethnic origin which we explored in Chapter 5, it would not be surprising if at least some of the higher rate of post-16 educational participation could be accounted for in this way. It is likely that all of these explanations account for some aspects of post-16 minority ethnic participation. However, Modood (1998) has argued that it is important not to under-estimate the strength of what he calls 'ethnic minorities' drive for qualifications'. He attributes this to a strong motivation for economic betterment in which education is seen to play a key part. In this connection, the downward occupational mobility experienced by many initial migrants may have played a part in strengthening this motivation. In addition, he suggests that qualifications are seen as a means to circumvent persistent labour market discrimination.

This drive for qualifications, as well as continuing disparities and diversity can be illustrated by comparing findings of successive pieces of research into qualifications obtained by different groups. Jones's analysis (1993) of Labour Force Survey data for 1988–90 showed that, measured by highest qualification obtained by those no longer in full-time education, white men were generally more qualified than members of other ethnic groups, the most significant exceptions being those of African, African Asian, and 'mixed' origins. Men of Indian and Chinese origins, while less well qualified than whites overall, were more likely to have degrees. Among women, those of Afro-Caribbean, African, and 'mixed' origins were the best qualified. Among both men and women, those of Bangladeshi and Pakistani origin were the least well qualified (Jones, 1993: 35–6).

The results of the fourth PSI survey conducted in 1994 (Modood, 1997a; 1998) reveal both changes and continuities.[1] Among respondents aged 16–24, those of Chinese, African Asian, and Indian origin were the best qualified followed by whites, Caribbeans, and Pakistanis, with Bangladeshis at the bottom of the qualifications league. Caribbean women were better qualified than white

Higher education

Much less attention has been paid to Higher Education than to schools. Indeed this may be a reflection, in part, of the 'under-achievement' debate. Early evidence suggested that patterns established early in pupils' educational careers were repeated later in rates of participation in higher education, in subject choice and in admission to the then Polytechnics rather than Universities. Suspicions that entry to higher education might be less than completely open and fair were fuelled when it was revealed that the St George's Hospital Medical School had been using a computer programme to select candidates for admission which deliberately discriminated against women and people from minority ethnic backgrounds (CRE, 1988b). Despite this, there was little indication that institutions of higher education were willing to confront the issues or to admit that there might be a problem. Indeed, only slowly did they begin to make efforts to catch up with the best practice to be found elsewhere (Jewson et al., 1991; Williams et al., 1989).

Since 1990, however, the bodies responsible for processing admissions to institutions of higher education have been collecting and publishing systematic ethnic monitoring data. The first sets of data showed that only those classified as 'Bangladeshi' and 'Black-Other' were less well represented than whites in admissions to the then polytechnics. In universities, however, 'Black-Caribbeans' and 'Pakistanis' were also under-represented (Modood and Shiner, 1994; PCFC, 1989-90; UCCA, 1989-90).[2] Data for subsequent admissions cohorts confirm the overall picture that minority ethnic groups as a whole are over-represented relative to their presence in the population as a whole, but that within this there is significant diversity of experience (Modood and Shiner, 1994). The data for 1994-5 confirm the over-representation of most minority ethnic groups. However, it should be noted that the 'Black' groups were over-represented (strongly so) only among those aged 21 or older. (This may reflect the greater tendency of members of these groups to study part-time or to gain their entry qualifications later than members of other groups.) In addition, Caribbean and Pakistani candidates were less likely than other groups to gain admission to the (generally more prestigious) pre-1992 universities (Modood, 1998: 35-7).

Given the large numbers of minority ethnic students now present in the higher education system, it is noteworthy that the ethnic profile of those who teach them is much less balanced. Recent research (Carter et al., 1999) has shown that only about 6-6.5 per cent of academic staff are not white and, of these, fewer than half are British nationals. Among staff who are not white, Chinese, 'Asian Other', and Indians represent the largest groups while Bangladeshis, Pakistanis, Black-Caribbeans, and 'Black-Others' are significantly under-represented. Even allowing for their younger age profile and shorter lengths of service, minority ethnic staff are less likely to be professors. They are, by contrast, more likely to be in research-only posts, many of them on short-term contracts. Minority ethnic women are particularly disadvantaged. Against this background, we should note that a third of institutions did not have a racial equality policy and where these existed they were frequently limited in scope. More than ten years after the St George's Hospital Medical School investigation, therefore, it seems that racial equality issues continue to have a low priority in much of the higher education sector.

women, while Pakistani and Bangladeshi women were significantly less well-qualified than women of all other groups (although Pakistani women were well represented at degree level).

When the focus turns to those aged between 16 and 24, Jones's analysis revealed a different pattern among both men and women who were no longer in full-time education. Here LFS data suggested that those of African Asian, and Indian origin were better qualified than white people. While Afro-Caribbean men were less well qualified than white men (levels of qualification for women in these groups were comparable with one another) the gap was relatively smaller than in the population of working age as a whole[3] (Jones, 1993: 36). The PSI survey found that, among 16–24 year olds (including those still in education) Pakistanis and Bangladeshis contained the largest proportion of respondents without any qualifications, although the gap was smaller than among their elders. Caribbean men in this age group were not significantly better off than their elders while Indians, African Asians, and Chinese respondents were comparably qualified with whites, although they were significantly better placed at degree level. Caribbean women were half as likely as Caribbean men to be without qualifications. All minority ethnic women, except Caribbeans (where the gap was quite small), were better represented at degree level than whites. Overall, Pakistani and Bangladeshi women were the least well qualified.

Taken together with the evidence concerning the greater propensity of young people of minority ethnic origin to remain in full-time education post-16, the patterns identified above confirm Modood's observations about the progress made by minority ethnic groups relative to whites. Minority ethnic young women, in particular, have made great strides in educational attainment over a relatively short time span. Having said this, it is important not to overlook the evidence of continuing disadvantage. First, as we have noted, both men and women of Pakistani and Bangladeshi origin appear to be less well qualified overall than those of other minority ethnic origins and this pattern holds even when the analysis is confined to the younger age groups. Secondly, an apparent narrowing of the gap between those of African-Caribbean origin and white people to some extent masks continuing differences. In particular, the higher level qualifications of people of African-Caribbean origin are more likely than those of any other group to be vocational, rather than 'purely' academic (Jones, 1993: 42–3; Modood, 1997a).

Finally, as we noted above, there is some evidence that people of minority ethnic origin find themselves having to narrow the qualification gap between themselves and white people in the period after normal schooling (Jones, 1993: 370; Modood, 1997a: 76, 78). This raises a number of questions about patterns of achievement in the school system and about the degree to which that system meets the needs of all its pupils.

The debate about 'underachievement'

The school system, and the performance of pupils within it, has been a focus for much of the literature in the field of race, ethnicity, and education. Given the evidence just adduced about qualification levels, it is appropriate now to turn to a discussion of some of this material. As we shall see, there are serious difficulties with some of the evidence that points to variations in achievement in the school system by members of different groups. It is important to review it briefly, however, because of the assumptions it reveals both about the nature of education and the characteristics of minority ethnic groups. It is also significant because it directs our attention to issues that lie beyond the oversimplifications of the 'underachievement ' thesis.

As Troyna and Carrington (1990) point out, there has since the earliest studies undertaken been abundant evidence of 'underachievement' by pupils of African Caribbean and South Asian origin, when compared with their white peers. Most of this evidence consists of computations of the average levels of attainment by members of various groups in formal examinations—notably at 16-plus. Some of this evidence, as measured by the LFS and Youth Cohort Study (see note 3) was referred to above. Despite the convergence in overall qualification levels noted in that discussion, there is still evidence of continuing 'underachievement' in the school system prior to age 16. This has been particularly noticeable in the case of African-Caribbean pupils—especially boys (see also Drew, 1995; Gillborn, 1990: 107–10). There are, however, a number of problems with these data as measures of the underachievement of members of minority ethnic groups.

The first point to make is that, at first sight, the concept of underachievement appears to refer to the difference between the results that might have been expected and those that were actually achieved. In fact, however, the data measure differences in the average scores, in public examinations at age 16, of pupils classified by their presumed ethnicity. We may leave aside for a moment the question of whether this is the best or only measure of educational achievement—particularly bearing in mind the evidence adduced above of post-16 educational success. More significantly for the moment, as Troyna and Carrington (1990: 46–55) observe, this way of measuring achievement privileges ethnicity as an explanatory variable while at the same time taking the definition of what constitutes an ethnic group somewhat for granted. Thus much of the early data used an undifferentiated category of 'Asian'. There has, in recent years, been an increasing recognition of important differences in educational (and employment) success between groups with different South Asian origins—notably between those of Indian and Bangladeshi origin (see above and Chapter 5. See also Gillborn, 1990: 110). Yet it is rarely questioned whether the category 'Afro-Caribbean' corresponds with the identities or life experiences of those whom it aggregates (Troyna and Carrington, 1990: 47).

This is important because it connects with another significant set of criticisms of the 'underachievement' data. As Troyna has noted (1984) there is a well-established relationship between social class and educational outcomes. Given the divergent socio-economic profiles of different ethnic groups (see above Chapter 5) it would not be surprising to find that groups with relatively large proportions in manual (working-class) occupations had different patterns of educational outcome from groups with a larger proportion of people in non-manual, and managerial and professional, occupations (see the extended discussion of these issues in Gillborn 1990: 123–31). In addition, there is ample evidence that gender significantly structures the educational experiences and outcomes of members of all ethnic groups (Deem, 1978; 1980; Mirza, 1992; Sharpe, 1976). As Mirza has noted, the characteristic invisibility of gender in the literature about 'underachievement' has resulted in the relatively high performance, and aspirations, of African-Caribbean young women frequently being overlooked (1992: 1–31) or, when recognized, regarded as perplexing and counter-intuitive (Mirza, 1998).

Put another way, we can follow Troyna (1984; see also Troyna and Carrington, 1990: 46–9) in questioning whether, when comparisons of achievement between different ethnic groups are made, like is being compared with like. In reality, the experiences of all pupils are structured by a pattern of life experience and opportunity in which class, gender, and ethnicity closely interact (Drew, 1995: 70–87; Gillborn, 1990: 123–6; Tizzard and Phoenix, 1993). Moreover, as the studies of underachievement themselves demonstrate, the externally imposed definitions of, and expectations attached to, these categories represent critical aspects of that experience (Mirza, 1998). A perspective which takes the implications of differential experiences seriously must, as a first step, give up the search for single-cause explanations of 'underachievement'. Indeed, the concept of underachievement must itself be interrogated and explained. In this connection, it is important to note the conclusion of David Drew's review of the evidence and of his own research:

The data presented here confirm many of the findings of previous researchers. In particular, they reveal differences associated with ethnic background. But the analyses we have undertaken also reveal very considerable within-group differences; by merely focusing on average differences between groups, the considerable overlaps between them have tended to be obscured. At the same time, the traditional concentration on the 'high hurdle' of five or more O level (or equivalent) passes has accentuated this general perception, especially for Afro-Caribbean young people, by focusing on one comparative extreme of the statistical distribution. Approaches that provide better descriptions of the variability that exists, both between and within groups, seem important. (1995: 86)

From assimilation to multiculturalism

It could be argued that the persistence of the underachievement debate has its origins in two factors. One is the assumption, built into education policy at least since the 1944 Education Act, that the education system represents a ladder, the successful scaling of which will permit pupils to enter the competition for employment and social rewards on equal terms. In other words, that the system is meritocratic. The second assumption, born in the early days of migration from the New Commonwealth to Britain, is that the 'newcomers' were initially disadvantaged by unfamiliarity with the British education system. Commentators attributed 'underachievement' to the presumed rurality and 'backwardness' of countries of origin and to lack of facility with the English language. Theories of cultural deficit were often invoked which suggested that a variety of cultural practices or patterns of family organization held minority ethnic pupils back in the education system. These assumptions formed the basis for much government initiative in the 1960s and 70s, not only in education but also in urban policy more widely (Gillborn, 1990, especially chapters 6 and 7; Tomlinson, 1984, especially chapter 2; Troyna, 1992; Troyna and Carrington, 1990; Troyna and Williams, 1986).

The initial response to these presumed characteristics of 'immigrant' pupils was to pursue policies of assimilation which focused on getting them to adapt in ways which would enable them to fit into an education system which was seen as a model of meritocracy and opportunity. Specific policies included the provision of special language support and policies of dispersal pursued by some local authorities (Gillborn, 1990, especially chapters 6 and 7; Grosvenor, 1997; Tomlinson, 1984, especially chapter 2). Such policies, of course, defined children of minority ethnic origin as a problem. Moreover, they were formulated as much out of concern for the effects of a growing 'immigrant' school population on the opportunities of white pupils as in response to the needs of minority ethnic groups themselves. They thus pandered to the racial prejudices of white parents (Gillborn, 1990: 142–6).

Attempts to implement the assimilationist model were ultimately to prove a failure. Beyond the flawed assumptions on which it was built, a number of factors can be identified which led to its demise. As Gillborn puts it, 'The cultural variety, social cohesion and active resistance of ethnic minority groups ensured the failure of the "flattening process" [embodied in the assimilationist ideal—DM]' (1990: 147). In addition parents, who had high expectations of the education system, became increasingly dissatisfied with its failure to deliver on the promise of meritocratic achievement for all (Tomlinson, 1984; Troyna and Carrington, 1990). One result was a gradual shift of emphasis in educational policy towards the concept of multiculturalism.

There is a large literature surrounding the concept of multicultural education which it would be impossible to summarize in the space of a short chapter (for useful reviews of many of the key issues, see Gillborn, 1990; Troyna, 1992; Troyna and Carrington, 1990; Troyna and Williams, 1986). One of the main problems is the lack of an agreed definition. In addition there has been a proliferation of policies that have very different foci. In broad terms, multiculturalism entails an explicit recognition and valuing of cultural diversity. Instead of being seen as a problem, cultural difference is conceptualized as something that is of value and to which the school should respond. In practice, rather than permeating the whole curriculum as its most enthusiastic supporters recommend (Gillborn, 1990: 150), there is evidence that multicultural policies are frequently partial and ill-thought out (Troyna and Williams, 1986).

There are a number of criticisms that are commonly levelled at multicultural policies in practice. The first is that they may take the form of marginalized aspects of the curriculum, confined to special lessons or particular times of the year corresponding to minority ethnic festivals. One common justification for such policies is that they are designed to raise the self-esteem of ethnic minority pupils. However, this perpetuates the idea that the problem of 'under-achievement' is centred on the characteristics of pupils rather than on the educational provision made available to them. The result, some have argued, is a conceptualization of minority cultures as exotic ephemera. Policies embodying this view have been criticized as substituting a concern for the 3 Ss (saris, samosas and steel bands) for the real education of minority pupils (Stone, 1981; Troyna and Williams, 1986: 24–5). Indeed, some have argued that there is, in the end, little to distinguish the underlying assumptions of multiculturalism from earlier assimilationist perspectives and that they amount to little more than attempts at social control (Carby, 1982: 194–5). It is of considerable significance in this context that multicultural initiatives have often been seen as having relevance only for schools with significant minority ethnic populations. Often there is a view that it is not necessary for white pupils living in other parts of the country to be exposed to other cultures (Gaine, 1995). Sally Tomlinson reports the view of a Conservative Education Minister expressed in a speech to HMI in 1986:

I believe that in areas where there are few or no members of ethnic minority groups, there is a genuine and not dishonourable fear that British values and traditions—the very stuff of school education—are likely to be put at risk if too much allowance is made for the cultural backgrounds and attitudes of ethnic minorities. (1990: 27)

'School effects', school racism, and anti-racist policies

Despite these criticisms of multiculturalism in practice, it is possible to argue that the rise of a multicultural perspective represented an advance over the old assimilationist models in at least one respect. This is that it, in principle, problematized the curriculum, if only in limited ways, and recognized that there was an onus on the school to respond to at least the cultural needs of minority ethnic pupils. This represented a change of considerable importance because of the mass of evidence that the character of schooling itself is a key variable in giving rise to the differential outcomes which have been taken as evidence of 'underachievement'.[4] One aspect of this is the mounting evidence of what is sometimes called a 'school effect' in determining educational outcomes (Drew, 1995; Mirza, 1992: 32–52; Smith and Tomlinson, 1989).[5] The work of Smith and Tomlinson in particular has shown how, against a background of patterns of differential attainment, individual schools have been able to achieve markedly different patterns of results and, most importantly, to achieve startling levels of progress among pupils whose backgrounds and prior levels of attainment would normally have given rise to more gloomy predictions of outcomes (Smith and Tomlinson, 1989). It is important to understand that Smith and Tomlinson's arguments are complex and relate to levels of progress rather than in simple terms to absolute attainments. They have been erroneously taken in some quarters to suggest that minority ethnic students are not subject to any systematic disadvantage in the school system and that differences of attainment are a product either of differential effort or variations in effectiveness between schools (see Gillborn, 1990: 130–9 for a discussion of these issues).

In fact, Smith and Tomlinson's results do not bear such an interpretation.

While they provide further evidence of the inadequacy of the original 'under-achievement' thesis, they do not undermine the considerable evidence that many schools and teachers have been at best ill-informed and insensitive, frequently ethnocentric (Gillborn, 1990: 10) and, at worst, explicitly racist in their treatment of pupils of minority ethnic origin (Mirza, 1992: 56–60).

We encountered above the criticism of the 'underachievement' thesis that it depended upon problematic comparisons between groups defined by their presumed ethnicity. These comparisons, we saw, took no account of social class differences. This was but one respect in which, as Troyna (1984) argued, they did not compare like with like. There is in addition, however, a large body of evidence which points to systematically different treatment of members of different groups within the school system. Such differential treatment is not simply a consequence of the prejudices of individual racist teachers. It can also be a product of the systematic labelling of members of particular groups. Thus there is abundant evidence of stereotyping, for example, of African-Caribbean boys as disruptive and of Asian girls as submissive. Such labelling also characterizes the talents and skills seen to reside in particular groups, those of Afro-Caribbean origin often being seen as talented in the sporting field but not as potential intellectual successes (see, for example, Mac an Ghaill, 1992 and 1988; Gillborn, 1990: 113–14; Troyna and Carrington, 1990: 50–5; Wright, 1992 and 1987). Such labelling has serious consequences for all members of the group concerned, often leading to discouragement. For some, however, it can be particularly devastating. This was the case for those black pupils who, as Bernard Coard's now famous paper (1971) showed, were disproportionately likely to be classified as 'educationally subnormal'. This, Coard argued, resulted not only from low teacher expectations, but from a system that was rigged against black children, not least because of culturally biased testing procedures. Similarly there is evidence of systematic overrepresentation of black children among those excluded from schools (Bourne *et al.*, 1994).

It is important to stress that the disadvantaging of pupils in the school system does not depend solely, or perhaps even mainly, on *intentional* discrimination. As Sally Tomlinson has put it:

Evidence does seem to be accumulating that normal school processes, not designed to be racist and often operated by liberal and well-intentioned teachers, can have the effect of disadvantaging pupils from particular ethnic groups, in addition to those from lower socio-economic groups and some girls. (1987: 105–6)

This observation was made in the context of a study of the process by which option choices were made by students in their third year of secondary education. Such choices were typically structured by staff assessments of ability (not all of them based on formal testing) motivation, and behaviour. They had the effect of determining at what level students would be entered for 16+ public examinations and in what subjects. It is not difficult to see how this system offers all sorts of scope for the operation of the kinds of labelling processes discussed above.

Perhaps even more significantly for the issues discussed in this chapter, it is crucial to stress the degree to which such choices may be part of a cumulatively disadvantaging process. Thus the pattern of option choices determines the range of subjects which students may henceforth study, not only to 16 but at A level and beyond. In addition, it places an upper limit on the level of attainment that is possible for any student. This is extremely significant for the issue of 'underachievement' discussed above (see the discussion in Drew, 1995).

Option choices do not represent the only way in which 'normal' school processes may disadvantage pupils from minority ethnic backgrounds. A number of students in Mac an Ghaill's study (1988; 1992) also clearly perceived what they saw as an ethnocentric curriculum to be one which held them back—not least by reinforcing feelings of being outsiders and 'different'. Manifestations of ethnocentrism may range from history curricula which focus exclusively on British history to the exclusion from school of pupils who, for religious or other cultural reasons, are unable to participate in the full range of school activities— such as mixed swimming lessons. As Gillborn notes, such curricula features illustrate the degree to which assimilationist and integrationist values continue to find expression in school policies and the views of teachers (1990: 161). Such problems are likely to be perpetuated as long as neither teachers nor school governing bodies are representative of the communities they serve (Deem et al., 1992; Osler, 1997).

If the disadvantaging effects of the operation of normal school processes cannot always be described as intentionally racist, the same cannot be said to be true for another area of serious concern—racial violence and harassment. The title of a report by the Commission for Racial Equality, Learning in Terror (1988b), aptly sums up the issue. The most dramatic and newsworthy incident of such harassment in a school context was probably the stabbing to death of Ahmed Iqbal Ullah by a 13-year-old white fellow pupil in a Manchester school in 1986 (see Macdonald et al., 1989). Yet, as the CRE's report makes clear, this example represents only the tip of a large iceberg. Moreover, in addition to racial harassment within schools, many young people from minority ethnic groups have daily to run the gauntlet of persistent racist attacks on their way to and from school (Commission for Racial Equality, 1987. For discussions of racial harassment more generally see Virdee, 1997; and Chapter 9 below).

It is not difficult to imagine the debilitating effects of such persistent fear for one's safety. Nor would it be surprising if, in such circumstances, minority ethnic pupils were to become demoralized and discouraged in ways that led

The Swann Report

The Swann Committee report, *Education for All*, was published in 1985 (Department of Education and Science, 1985). It was the culmination of an inquiry that had begun in 1979. During a somewhat troubled history, it had had its terms of reference reformulated to be more restrictive and, critics allege, to reflect the new priorities of a Conservative government. In addition, its first chairman, Anthony Rampton, was replaced. In this context it is perhaps not surprising that the report has been the subject of much controversy (see Chivers, 1987). In particular, it has been criticized for being anodyne, for overemphasis on 'underachievement', and for failing to confront the problem of racism. This last accusation was greatly assisted by the tone of the Chairman's guide to the report, which failed to use the word racism even once. Close inspection of the report's more than 800 pages, however, reveals substantial sections where racism is discussed. Moreover, issues of curriculum design explicitly raise the need to tackle racism. The report's recommended principles for evaluating the curriculum give a flavour of points on which others might build (p. 329):

- *The variety of social, cultural, and ethnic groups and a perspective of the world should be evident in visuals, stories, conversation, and information.*
- *People from social, cultural, and ethnic groups should be presented as individuals with every human attribute.*
- *Cultures should be empathetically described in their own terms and not judged against some notion of 'ethnocentric' or 'Euro-centric' culture.*
- *The curriculum should include accurate information on racial and cultural differences and similarities.*
- *All children should be encouraged to see the cultural diversity of our society in a positive light.*
- *The issue of racism, at both institutional and individual level, should be considered openly and efforts made to counter it.*

them to under-perform. What is perhaps remarkable, then, is the resilience of individuals and communities subjected to these and other forms of racism and discouragement. The evidence in fact suggests that, even among those groups alleged to be most prone to underachievement, levels of commitment and motivation are as high or higher than among white pupils. Moreover, rates of post-16 educational participation reinforce this point.

This does not mean that the daily experience of overt hostility, violence, and condescension has no effect. If minority ethnic students achieve as much as they do in the face of disadvantage and discrimination what, we may ask, would be possible in its absence? This question brings us back to the 'school effect'. It suggests that those schools which are likely to be most effective in generating high levels of performance and attainment among all their pupils are those which provide high quality academic education for all. This entails not ignoring racism and racial disadvantage, as some interpretations of Smith and Tomlinson's work have suggested (see Gillborn, 1990: 136), but seeking to counter it in their organization and curriculum.

This process of actually seeking to counter disadvantage and discrimination is seen by many to entail going beyond the celebration and valuing of diversity implied by multicultural policies—even those which are most fully integrated into the whole curriculum. Instead it entails developing what have become known as anti-racist policies. (For a useful discussion see Gillborn, 1995.)

The concept of anti-racism is both controversial and difficult to define simply and precisely. As in the case of multiculturalism, in practice it embraces a wide variety of policies with different aims and underlying theoretical and political philosophies. Broadly, however, it may be said to entail taking racism seriously. In other words, it seeks to confront and counter all manifestations of racism, whether they take the form of individual prejudices or structural disadvantage rooted in the organization and practices of the school or the wider society. Such policies are frequently criticized for being unnecessarily confrontational. Those who consider themselves free of prejudice often claim to be insulted by the implication that they need to engage in anti-racist practice. As a result there is an ongoing debate within education about the relative advantages and characteristics of anti-racist and multicultural policies. Moreover, anti-racism has also provided a focus for attack from those who would wish, for political or other reasons, to dispute the pervasiveness of racism in education. Recently May (1999) has suggested that the debate between these two perspectives has been unnecessarily polarized in Britain. In other countries, he suggests, multiculturalism has itself embraced a more critical anti-racist perspective and has been more sensitive to the complexity of cultural variation and identity than has often been the case in the UK. (There is, unfortunately, insufficient space here to explore these debates in detail. For useful discussions, see Carter and Williams, 1987; Gillborn, 1990, especially chapter 6; May, 1999; Troyna, 1992; Troyna and Carrington, 1990.)

Educational reform

To whatever extent, and in whatever form, schools and individual teachers embrace, or have embraced, anti-racism (or multiculturalism), they have in recent years found themselves having to pursue such policies in the context of wide-ranging, rapid and on-going changes in the education system. Resulting from central government legislation, these changes are associated with a series of legislative changes stemming from the Education Reform Act of 1988.[6]

Among the most significant developments from the point of view of this discussion has been the elaboration of a compulsory national curriculum for state schools which has sought to define both the content of the curriculum and the proportion of time devoted to each major subject. One consequence has been that the time available for the inclusion in the school's programme of matters defined as peripheral to the core academic curriculum has been severely curtailed with obvious implications for some aspects of multicultural and anti-racist policy. (This is not to say that there is no scope for committed teachers to incorporate such matters into the mainstream curriculum.) Moreover, the attempt by government rigidly to circumscribe the content of the curriculum in key areas has taken a form which many teachers and minority ethnic communities have seen as at best insensitive and at worst deliberately marginalizing. Relevant issues here include: demands for the prioritization of British history; attempts to insist on the use of 'standard' English; and the prioritization of Christianity in religious education and celebration (Gillborn, 1990: 166–71; Troyna and Carrington, 1990: 76–111). Indeed, some have suggested that the new requirements might be better designated as a national*ist* curriculum (Gillborn, 1990: 206).

Other significant aspects of the Education Reform Act from the point of view of this discussion include the development of arrangements, known as local management of schools, under which school governing bodies are given relative independence from local authorities and acquire direct responsibility for finance and curricula matters. One consequence is to free schools from the obligation to pursue local authority initiated equal opportunities, multicultural, or anti-racist policies. Given the pressures created by the national curriculum, it is not difficult to imagine what might be the consequences for practice in these areas.

On the other hand, it might be argued that one of the government's intentions in reforming the management of schools was to bring them closer to the communities they served by involving parents and other local independent persons more closely in their management. In principle, this would seem to offer at least the possibility that the long-held concerns of ethnic minority parents about the quality of education offered to their children could be addressed. Indeed, in places where communities have organized effectively there is some evidence that such an outcome is possible. However, as Deem *et al.* have shown, there is also evidence that governing bodies under the new arrangements are far from representative. Moreover, the uneven distribution of capital, both financial and cultural, between schools having different ethnic and class profiles appears to remain the strongest determinant of the quality of education and the effectiveness of parental influence (Deem *et al.*, 1992; 1995). It is by no means clear that the quality of consultation with minority ethnic communities has improved over that reported by Gibson (1987) on the basis of research conducted before the Act.

Opting out and opting in

We have on several occasions in this chapter noted the widespread and long-standing dissatisfaction of parents in minority ethnic communities with the education system. One response to those concerns has been the establishment of variously named supplementary, voluntary, or Saturday schools. As Tomlinson (1984, chapter 5) notes, the motivations underlying the establishment of such projects may range from a desire to preserve cultural traditions to a wish to respond to the perceived inadequacies of state education. (For further discussions of voluntary schools, see Chevannes and Reeves, 1987; Reay and Mirza, 1997)

In principle, it seems that a further provision of the government's educational reforms might be relevant to these developments. This is the process of allowing schools to opt out of local authority control and seek 'grant maintained status', being funded directly by central government. In practice, however, the government has until very recently been unsympathetic—notably to requests by Muslim groups for the right to state funding equivalent to that available to Church of England and Catholic schools. In a change of approach, however, the government introduced in 1993 a measure under which other religious groups could seek to set up their own grant maintained schools.[7] More recently the rules governing the treatment of applications to set up new schools where surplus places already exist were relaxed. This process was defined as 'opting in'. What is interesting is that the initial response of Muslim groups—who remain in the forefront of those seeking state funding for schools responsive to the demands of minority cultures—seems to have been a negative one. Their argument was that grant maintained status embodies the principle of inequality and privilege. What they sought instead was voluntary aided status within the mainstream state system (*Times Education Supplement*, Friday, 1 July 1994).[8] While this response to some degree represents a resistance to the national curriculum which would become compulsory under such conditions, it also reflects the view of many ethnic minority parents, reported by Sally Tomlinson (1984, chapters 4 and 5), that the state system offers potentially high quality education if it can be made sufficiently responsive to the needs of minority communities and their children. As Troyna and Carrington (1990) note, this theme of dissatisfaction and distrust, mixed with a determination to succeed, has been one of the most consistent findings of research in the field of race, ethnicity, and education.

Conclusion

In this chapter, we have seen that complex patterns characterize the experiences of young people of minority ethnic origin in the education system. They vary both by specific ethnic background and by gender. Nevertheless, there are some general observations that can be made. The most important is that, whatever disadvantage and discrimination is encountered in the school system, the aspirations of minority ethnic young people, like their white peers, remain high. High levels of participation in post-16 education are testimony to a determination to succeed and to overcome past failures of the system adequately to provide for their needs.

The second is that, whatever the precise pattern of achievement in the education system, it is apparent that the oversimplifications of the underachievement thesis must be challenged. Indeed, they are being challenged by young people themselves.

The third point is that, whatever the final outcome of the debate about 'school effects', it is clear that both schools and individual teachers do have a role to play in examining their approaches and assumptions, and in challenging racist beliefs and practices. In this respect, and whatever its detailed deficiencies, the policy thrust offered by *Education for All* (the Swann Report) does offer scope for the agenda to be pushed further towards genuine non-racial equality of opportunity (Rex, 1987).

Having said this, we need also to acknowledge that some have argued that educational equality of opportunity is no more than a myth of the British education system. So far from being meritocratic, it is actually designed to reproduce and legitimize unequal outcomes (see the discussion in Gillborn, 1990: 105–23). This argument reflects a long-running debate about the nature of equal opportunities which is encountered in a wide variety of spheres (see, for example, Jewson and Mason, 1992). It may in fact be that, in modern societies, equality of opportunity can never mean anything more than having an equal chance to be unequal. The question that this raises, however, is whether it would nevertheless be an advance if this chance were to cease to be structured by race and ethnicity. As the discussion in Chapter 5 made clear, while qualifications do not entirely protect people of minority ethnic origin from labour market disadvantage, their non-possession weights the scales further against them. Rates of post-16 educational participation appear to suggest that young people of minority ethnic origin recognize this only too clearly.

Further reading

'Race' Ethnicity and Education by David Gillborn (1990) is an excellent overview of the main issues and debates in this field. It contains both empirical material and an assessment of various of the competing theoretical and political positions.

'Race', Education and Work: The Statistics of Inequality by David Drew (1995) is a review of the evidence concerning the underachievement thesis.

Racism and Education edited by Gill, Mayor, and Blair (1992) and Racial Inequality in Education edited by Barry Troyna (1987) both contain useful collections of essays reviewing some of the most significant issues in the field.

Chapter 7

Housing and Urban Space

Introduction

WE saw in Chapter 3 that, as post-war migration to Britain from the countries of the New Commonwealth increased, housing quickly emerged as a
key point of social strain and as a focus for the anti-immigration hostility
mobilized by those agitating for controls. Nowhere was this clearer than in
Birmingham, where these factors contributed to the successful election of a
Conservative Member of Parliament in the Smethwick constituency in the
General Election of 1964. It was widely believed that this success, against the
national trend in what should have been a safe Labour seat, owed much to
conflicts surrounding housing and to a campaign in which, it was alleged, the
local Conservative Party deployed the slogan 'if you want a nigger for a neigh-
bour vote Labour' (Holmes, 1988: 264; Layton-Henry, 1992: 77–8; Saggar, 1992:
76–7).

In fact, housing has been a recurrent social and political problem in post-war
Britain and was a key focus of the battle between the major political parties in
General Elections up to, and including, that of 1979.[1] Not only is decent housing
of significance in its own right, providing shelter and security, it is also clearly
linked to a number of other indicators of well-being. It is, for example, difficult
to secure and hold down a job without a permanent address, while the capacity
to buy and sell, or easily to rent, property is a key influence on the mobility of
labour (Karn *et al.*, 1985). In addition, there is clear evidence of a link between
housing quality and health (see Chapter 8). Finally we should note that housing
is linked directly to wealth. Thus, particularly during the second half of the
twentieth century, there has been a steady redistribution of personal wealth in
Britain towards middle-income groups (but not the very poorest). A major reason for this change has been the fact that housing has come to constitute a
growing proportion of personal wealth. As a result the spread of home ownership has had direct implications for the distribution of wealth (Saunders, 1990:
135–6).

For all these reasons, housing patterns are key indicators of social well-being. Differences of access to housing between ethnic groups are likely, therefore, to be important *prima facie* measures of inequality. As we shall see, the history of housing for members of minority ethnic groups in Britain has, in general, been one which paralleled other aspects of their experience (see Bhat *et al.*, 1988: 103–46).

Housing and initial settlement

Chapters 3 and 4 indicated the extent to which post-war New Commonwealth migrants to Britain settled in a limited number of urban locations in London and the South-East, the Midlands, and the North. This settlement, we saw, reflected the demand for labour in the British economy. Within these broad urban locations, however, there was a further process of clustering as new-comers sought to satisfy their housing needs. Thus migrants generally settled in cheaper inner city housing which was typically located close to their work-places (Patterson, 1963; Peach, 1968; Rex and Moore, 1967). As we saw in Chapter 3, they frequently replaced earlier migrant groups in what some have described as 'twilight zones' or 'zones of transition' (Rex, 1968; Rex and Moore, 1967; Sarre *et al.*, 1989: 7).

For the most part, early migrants did not qualify for public housing. A large proportion comprised single men and there were complex residence and other qualification rules which effectively denied them access (see below). As a result, they were dependent either on private renting or upon owner-occupation. Both solutions brought with them their own problems and established patterns of disadvantage which have been long-lasting. They also gave rise to persistent contrasts between the patterns of housing tenure characteristic of different minority ethnic groups. In all cases, discrimination on the part of what have become known as 'urban gate keepers' (Karn *et al.*, 1985: 119–20; McKay, 1977: 85–91)—estate agents, private landlords, and local authority housing depart-ment officials—has been a major background variable to the solutions adopted by members of different groups (Commission for Racial Equality, 1990; Cross, 1978: 66; Daniel, 1968).

In very broad, and admittedly oversimple terms,[2] we can characterize the initial experience of the main migrant groups as one in which those of African-Caribbean origin were likely to resort to renting from those private landlords who did not exclude them altogether. Often they found themselves accom-modating their entire families in one or two rooms (Ratcliffe, 1981: 163). By contrast, migrants from India and Pakistan were more likely to solve their housing needs by buying large, cheap, run-down inner city houses.[3] One mechanism which helped to facilitate this was the pooling of resources among kin, which permitted the accumulation of sufficient funds at least to afford a deposit. We should note, moreover, that since building societies were frequently unwilling to mortgage such properties, prospective purchasers often had to resort to taking out short-term loans at high rates of interest (Cross, 1978: 65; Karn et al., 1985; Rex, 1973: 127–36). The subletting which this sometimes necessitated, together with the pooling of resources referred to above, meant that those Asian migrants who initially rented frequently did so from relatives (Ratcliffe, 1981: 164).[4] The development of areas containing large numbers of properties of this kind, which Rex and Moore describe as lodging houses (1967), was often a further source of stress as well as a pretext for discrimination and anti-immigrant agitation. Thus, accusations of overcrowding were commonly levelled against migrant communities, while local authorities sometimes used their powers of control selectively against migrant landlords and households (Rex and Moore, 1967).

These processes were to help entrench patterns of social segregation which have been long-lasting (see Chapter 4; Smith, 1989) while also establishing systematic housing disadvantage. As Karn et al. (1985) have shown more generally, the purchase of poor quality, run-down, inner city property frequently creates a range of knock-on disadvantages which are difficult to transcend. These include problems of servicing loans, high maintenance and repair costs, and geographical and social immobility caused by unsaleability. In these circumstances disadvantage in the housing system can, all too easily, become part of a vicious circle, reinforcing and entrenching labour market and other deprivations.

Although the early circumstances described above set the framework in which subsequent developments occurred, it would be wrong to suggest that no changes have taken place in patterns of tenure. Once again, however, subsequent developments have been characterized by a divergence of experience between groups. Thus people of African-Caribbean origin have had a greater tendency to move from private to publicly rented property[5] (though by no means exclusively so) while people of South Asian descent have tended to move into owner-occupation—especially of cheaper terraced housing (Robinson, 1989: 260).

By 1982, Brown's data show that 41 per cent of people of African-Caribbean descent were owner-occupiers, by comparison with 59 per cent of the white population and 76 per cent of people of South Asian origin. Some 46 per cent of African-Caribbean people, 30 per cent of whites, and 19 per cent South Asians lived in publicly rented accommodation. Relatively small numbers of all groups lived in privately rented or housing association accommodation (Brown, 1984:

Table 7.1 Tenure patterns among members of the main ethnic groupings, 1982

row percentages

	Owner-occupied	Publicly rented	Privately rented	Housing association
White	59	30	9	2
West Indian	41	46	6	8
Asian	72	19	6	2
Indian	77	16	5	2
Pakistani	80	13	5	1
Bangladeshi	30	53	11	4
African-Asian	73	19	5	2

Adapted from Brown (1984: 96)

68–127). Within the South Asian group, it is notable that the lowest rates of owner-occupation were found among people of Bangladeshi origin, who were also significantly more likely to live in publicly rented accommodation than members of any other group.

Despite high levels of owner-occupancy among South Asian groups, there was continuing evidence of a tendency for them to inhabit older, poorer quality, terraced housing than members of other groups. Regardless of tenure type, they were also more likely to have to share facilities such as bathrooms and WCs and to experience overcrowding (Brown, 1984: 68–127; Cross, 1978: 60–1).

Public housing: Incorporation and marginalization

As we saw above, early migrants were largely excluded from access to public housing by complex residence and qualification rules. The former restricted access to those who had been resident in the locality for a minimum period (five years was not uncommon—Rex and Moore, 1967: 24; see also Cross, 1978: 65–6). As a result, migrants typically had to wait a considerable number of years before becoming eligible to join housing waiting lists. For the most part qualification arrangements utilized 'points' systems which favoured families, those who were otherwise homeless or those who were being compulsorily rehoused. Points were also commonly allocated for such things as overcrowding, lack of facilities, period on the waiting list, and war service (Rex and Moore, 1967: 24). Even when they reached the waiting list, however, migrants might or might not qualify for high priority depending on such matters as the slum clearance policies of the local authority and the relative length of the queue.

Over time, of course, increasing numbers of members of Britain's minority ethnic communities came to satisfy residence and other qualifications. However, this did not mean that equitable treatment became the order of the day. In fact a pattern of differentiation emerged which was to provide prima-facie evidence of discriminatory practices by local authority housing departments in many parts of the country. The opportunities for discrimination were introduced by the discretionary elements that typically formed part of the assessment procedures used by authorities. Thus, in their study of Sparkbrook, Rex and Moore concluded that the assessments of housekeeping standards by housing visitors played a role either in excluding minority ethnic citizens from council housing altogether or in ensuring their allocation to the least desirable housing (1967: 26–7). It is important to note that housing visitors' judgements could be a product of prejudice and discriminatory intent. However, they could also reflect the operation of more unconscious ethnocentric stereotypes or culturally determined differences of view about what constitute good housekeeping practices (Commission for Racial Equality, 1984; Cross, 1978: 65–6).

Whatever the detailed cause, however, it is clear that allocation procedures did result in systematic differences between members of different groups in access to, and type of, public housing allocation. Generally, as in the private sector, minority ethnic clients were more likely to be housed in older properties with fewer amenities, frequently on less popular estates (Commission for Racial Equality, 1984; 1986; Cross, 1978: 62; Phillips, 1985; Robinson, 1989: 262; Simpson, 1981: 34; Smith, 1989: 92–8). They were also more likely to be allocated flats rather than houses (Brown, 1984: 83–4; Robinson, 1989: 262). Often they were caught up in policies of dispersal which sought to limit the numbers of minority ethnic households in any given area (Simpson, 1981: 261; Smith, 1989: 99–101).[6]

Studies of both Liverpool and Hackney by the Commission for Racial Equality have revealed evidence of systematic disadvantage of minority ethnic clients, leading in the Hackney case to the issuing of a non-discrimination notice under the 1976 Race Relations Act (CRE, 1984; 1986. See also Bowes et al.1991; Smith 1989: 81–104). In some areas research indicates that one of the consequences of these circumstances is that members of affected communities were particularly likely to be rendered homeless. Thus data for 1986 indicate that, although people of Bangladeshi origin represented 9 per cent of the population of Tower Hamlets at the time, they made up 90 per cent of the homeless and 80 per cent

Table 7.2 Housing conditions of the members of main ethnic groupings in publicly rented accommodation, 1982

row percentages

	% in flats	% in detached or semi-detached houses	% in dwellings built before 1945	% lacking exclusive use of bath, hot water, or WC
White	27	39	27	3
West Indian	54	9	34	3
Asian	54	11	35	7

Adapted from Brown (1984: 102)

of households in temporary, bed and breakfast, accommodation (Robinson, 1989: 262).

We should, in addition, take note of some evidence that ethnic inequalities in allocation outcomes may be significantly gendered. Thus Peach and Byron (1993) found that for African-Caribbean men, class factors appear to explain much of the pattern of housing tenure. However, among female heads of household, class factors explain relatively little, while gender differences appear highly significant. Thus the authors found an over-concentration of African-Caribbean female heads of household in the poorest quality local authority accommodation. These patterns, they argue, must be a result of allocation practices. This may suggest that the operation of ethnic stereotypes in the allocation process is highly gendered.

Minority ethnic housing: Evidence from the 1991 Census[7]

Table 7.3 presents data on housing tenure patterns revealed by the 1991 Census. They show about two-thirds of households now living in owner-occupied accommodation. As in previous studies, the evidence shows that people of South Asian origin had the highest rates of owner-occupation. About two-thirds of white people fell into this tenure category, while the figure for those groups classified as 'Black' was well under 50 per cent. Among all groups, the proportions in publicly rented accommodation had fallen although the overall patterns remain similar with 'Black' groups over-represented and South Asians under-represented. A notable change had been an increase in the proportions of Bangladeshis in owner-occupied accommodation and a corresponding decline in the proportion publicly renting. This group continued, however, to exhibit a contrasting pattern to all other South Asian groups. Levels of private renting were low for all groups, reflecting the general long-term decline in this sector of the housing market. Members of some minority ethnic groups were, however, more likely than the population as a whole to inhabit this type of accommodation.

It is important to note that some of the changes that have occurred in patterns of tenure reflect developments in the housing market as a whole and result, in part, from the policies pursued by government since the early 1980s. In particular, a strong boost has been given to home ownership and many council tenants were given the right to buy their homes. Financial incentives were made available to encourage a high rate of take-up. In addition, local authorities have been discouraged from building new property for rent and a general policy of reducing the proportion of housing in local authority control

Table 7.3 Housing tenure by ethnic group in Great Britain, 1991

Ethnic group	Households (000s)	Owner-occupied (%)	Households renting from		
			Local authority (%)	Housing Association (%)	Private Landlord (%)
White	21,026.6	66.6	21.4	3.0	7.0
Ethnic Minorities	870.8	59.5	21.8	5.9	10.8
Black	328.1	42.3	36.8	10.1	9.2
Black-Caribbean	216.5	48.1	35.7	9.7	5.6
Black-African	73.3	28.0	41.1	10.8	17.8
Black-Other	38.3	36.7	34.5	11.2	13.6
South Asian	357.2	77.1	11.1	2.5	7.6
Indian	225.6	81.7	7.8	2.2	6.5
Pakistani	100.9	76.7	10.4	2.2	9.6
Bangladeshi	30.7	44.5	37.0	6.1	9.6
Chinese and others	185.5	56.1	15.9	4.9	19.9
Chinese	48.6	62.2	13.1	3.5	17.0
Other-Asian	59.0	53.9	13.6	4.4	24.5
Other-Other	77.9	54.0	19.3	6.2	18.2
Entire population	21,897.3	66.4	21.4	3.1	7.1

Source: Owen (1993c: 8)

has been pursued. These changes may be of particular importance in interpreting differences between ethnic groups in their propensity to chose owner-occupation. Describing the results of research into the housing experience of minority ethnic groups in Scotland, Third and MacEwen argue that:

owner occupation can be a very different experience for minority ethnic groups than for white households. Whilst among the general population, home ownership may imply affluence and freedom of choice for some, this may not be so for households who are forced to buy. Many . . . households . . . expressed a preference for renting, but had found it difficult to do so. (1997: 66)

While we cannot generalize from the Scottish situation to Britain as a whole, these findings may nevertheless be of significance in the light of the evidence that minority ethnic owner-occupiers tend on average still to inhabit less desirable and well-appointed properties.

A significant thrust of policy has been the drive to replace local authority provision with rented property controlled by housing associations. Although, in 1991, this source of accommodation remained small in total size, it is one that was expected to grow (Owen, 1993c: 8). Moreover, it is an important source of accommodation for members of some minority ethnic groups including those classified as 'Black' and Bangladeshis (see Table 7.3).

There is some evidence that the procedures by which housing associations allocate property to prospective tenants have on occasion been overly informal and subjective (Dalton, 1991) and there have also been instances of associations having been found to be discriminating on racial grounds (MacEwen, 1991a: 253–78). Despite the formal equal opportunities guidance issued by the Housing Corporation (which has overall responsibility for the regulation of housing associations) MacEwen concludes that opportunities for discriminatory practices remain (1991a: 277–8).

An important development in recent years has been the growth in the numbers of what are often called black housing associations (MacEwen, 1991a: 278–80; Harrison, 1995). These target groups for whom there is inadequate provision in the mainstream sector. By December 1987, there were 38 such associations, mostly in London, targeting a range of special needs such as black single homeless, the elderly, and Bangladeshi widows. These self-help schemes are of considerable importance and illustrate the importance of community initiatives in addressing the failings of mainstream provision (Harrison, 1995, 82–110. Compare the discussion of health initiatives in Chapter 8). Nevertheless, as MacEwen notes (1991a: 280), the bulk of minority ethnic housing needs addressed by this sector are likely to continue to be satisfied by mainstream associations. There will continue to be a need, therefore, to ensure that their services are delivered equitably.

The Census also provides data on the distribution of physical amenities within homes. Table 7.4 sets out the results of Owen's analysis of these data. (See also the discussion in Lakey, 1997.) To some degree, the general improvement of the housing stock that has taken place in recent years has mitigated some of the worst features of physical deprivation. Nevertheless, the data do indicate continuing differences between white and minority ethnic groups. Thus a significantly higher proportion of ethnic minority than white households contain more than one person per room, with almost half of Bangladeshi households being in this position. More than twice as many ethnic minority as white households do not have self-contained accommodation. A similar differential applies to the exclusive use of a bath or WC. This is particularly significant in the case of Bangladeshi households, where those in this position contain on average twice as many people as others in the same circumstances. Finally, it should be noted that more Pakistani and Bangladeshi households are likely than other groups to lack central heating, a fact which probably reflects the age of property purchased by members of these groups and is, in turn, a measure of relative economic deprivation (see Chapter 5).

Concentration or segregation?

We have seen that both the initial settlement and current residential location of Britain's minority ethnic citizens is characterized by a high degree of concentration (see Smith, 1989: 36–45). Not only are these populations concentrated in a limited number of urban areas, but there is typically significant clustering at a much more local level. There are differences of view in the literature about whether these patterns should be characterized as segregation. For some, the systematic disadvantage experienced by many ethnic minority citizens in inner city areas is comparable to the much more obvious patterns of segregation characteristic of parts of the United States. Others argue that clusters of minority ethnic population in Britain are neither so large nor so ethnically exclusive as those found in the USA[8] and do not justify the use of the term 'segregation'.

A further set of arguments concerns the consequences of concentration or segregation. As we saw in Chapter 5, the geographical location of the minority ethnic population was in part a product of the demand for labour in the early days of migration. As the economy changed, notably in the 1980s, that same clustering led to the emergence of changed employment opportunities and new (or renewed) patterns of labour market exclusion—especially in the inner cities. From this point of view, geographical clustering is often (though not

Table 7.4 Households experiencing physical housing problems by ethnic group in Great Britain, 1991

Ethnic group	More than 1 person/ room	Not self-contained accommo-dation	Without exclusive use of bath or WC		Without central heating	
	(%)	(%)	(%)	(persons per household)	(%)	(persons per household)
White	1.8	0.9	1.2	1.50	18.9	2.16
Ethnic Minorities	13.1	2.4	2.1	2.09	17.8	3.33
Black	7.2	3.1	2.3	1.69	17.4	2.33
Black-Caribbean	4.7	2.0	1.4	1.65	17.4	2.30
Black-African	15.1	6.5	5.1	1.73	15.8	2.46
Black-Other	5.6	3.2	2.4	1.67	20.2	2.27
South Asian	20.5	1.1	1.4	3.08	19.5	4.43
Indian	12.8	1.0	1.1	2.65	12.4	3.59
Pakistani	29.7	1.2	1.7	3.31	34.2	4.95
Bangladeshi	47.1	1.3	2.0	4.17	23.6	5.19
Chinese and others	9.4	3.6	3.0	1.78	15.0	2.62
Chinese	10.6	3.5	3.2	1.95	16.0	2.82
Other-Asian	11.0	3.7	3.0	1.79	12.1	2.83
Other-Other	7.4	3.7	3.0	1.67	16.7	2.39
Entire population	2.2	1.0	1.3	1.54	18.9	2.21

Source: Owen (1993c: 9)

always) negative, creating and reinforcing both labour market and housing disadvantage (see the discussion in Green, 1997).

Others have argued that, notwithstanding these negative consequences, there are also positive advantages to be derived from ethnic clustering. These include the potential to exercise influence on the outcomes of elections and the availability of relatively protected ethnic markets for entrepreneurs (Robinson, 1989: 263–4). Smith concludes that, whether or not there are positive as well as negative features to residential segregation, it is ultimately an expression of a pattern of inequality expressed in, and reinforced by, a variety of aspects of the lives of Britain's minority ethnic citizens (Smith, 1989: 38).

Urban policy

The term 'inner city' has in the last thirty years become almost synonymous with deprivation. In the 1960s, the focus was on a housing crisis associated with overall shortage and the persistence of slum dwellings. More recently the concern has shifted to the consequences of economic restructuring and counter-urbanization which have become associated with high levels of unemployment and urban decay. In this context, governments have developed a succession of policy measures aimed at addressing the perceived problems of inner cities. There is not space here to deal adequately with the shifts and turns, nor with the detail, of these ever-changing approaches.[9] Nevertheless, it is important to identify some of the key features of policy which have relevance for our theme.

An enduring feature of urban policy in Britain has been its generally 'colour-blind' character. In other words it has typically been targeted at deprived *areas* rather than specific group needs (Edwards and Batley, 1978; Rex, 1982; Robinson, 1989: 264–5; Smith, 1989: 67–77). There has been a general reliance on non-targeted social policy. Instead of seeking directly to address minority ethnic needs, the presence of ethnic minorities has frequently been seen as part of the problem requiring attention. Indeed, for many years the presence of significant minority ethnic communities was taken as an index of deprivation (Owen, 1993c: 9). This conception of policy is part of a consistent theme in post-war government policy, which sees the presence of minority ethnic citizens as a problem. All too often, as we explore elsewhere in this volume, the policy response has been one which has ignored the ethnic diversity of modern Britain and relied on an, often unspoken, assumption that over time problems would be overcome by means of a process of assimilation. It appears to have taken the urban disorders of the 1980s to shake up these assumptions and to generate a greater willingness to conceive of policy objectives targeted at minority ethnic groups (Smith, 1989: 72–3).

Urban areas as sites of struggle

The 1980s saw a number of episodes of serious rioting in British cities (Benyon and Solomos, 1990; Solomos, 1986). Those that attracted most public attention took place in inner city locations and involved, though by no means exclusively, young members of minority ethnic communities. A variety of contrasting explanations have been put forward to account for these episodes of urban disorder. Thus, for the government, the riots were outbursts of anarchic criminality, often fomented by outside agitators. For radical members of the communities involved, they were often presented as legitimate insurrections against an oppressive and racist state (Kettle and Hodges, 1982). Perhaps most commonly, the disorders were explained as a response to high levels of economic and social deprivation characteristic of inner city life (Scarman, 1981). None of these explanations is, on its own, entirely satisfactory (Jewson, 1990). Moreover, it would be a mistake to see the events as identical. In practice they involved very different communities, contrasting social and physical environments and varying proximate triggers (Rex, 1982).

Nevertheless, it is possible to argue that the riots shared certain features, which are acknowledged in different ways by the explanations discussed above. First they challenged, and signalled the bankruptcy of, colour-blind social policies that relied on continuing assimilationist assumptions (Holdaway, 1996: 111–12; Jewson and Mason, 1994: 597). Second, they were almost always triggered to some degree by community responses to some action of the police (see Chapter 9). Thirdly, they all constituted in some measure an attempt by members of local communities to assert a degree of control over the urban space they occupied. This might be in response to what were seen as outside intrusions (such as those by the police or by members of extreme right wing groups), in protest against urban deprivation and unemployment or as a symbolic demonstration of control and resistance. It is instructive that the response of government, whatever its rhetorical commitment to the claim that the events were evidence only of criminality, was to develop more closely targeted measures aimed more explicitly than hitherto at the perceived needs of the communities concerned (Smith, 1989: 72–3).

Conclusion

Many of the themes of this chapter have had, in the context of the volume as a whole, a familiar ring. Housing, like so many other aspects of the experience of Britain's minority ethnic communities, has been characterized by systematic patterns of disadvantage and discrimination. At the same time social policy responses have manifested the all too familiar features of 'colour-blindness' and assimilationism. However, it is important also to note that, in the fields of housing and the management of urban space, the state, both national and local, has played a particularly prominent role. As a result, we can argue that these arenas provide particularly important and visible test cases of governments' commitment to equitable treatment of all Britain's citizens. We return to and develop this theme further in Chapter 10.

Further reading

1991 Census Statistical Paper No. 4 by David Owen of the National Ethnic Minority Data Archive (1993c) gives information on the housing situation of Britain's minority ethnic citizens as revealed by the 1991 Census. See also Volume Four of *Ethnicity in the 1991 Census*, edited by Valerie Karn (1997) and *Ethnic Minorities in Britain*, by Tariq Modood *et al.* (1997).

The Politics of 'Race' and Residence by Susan Smith (1989) places the housing experience of minority ethnic groups in the context of a more wide-ranging discussion of the political context of segregation in modern Britain.

Race, Community and Conflict by John Rex and Robert Moore (1967) remains a classic text, reminding us of the early significance of struggles over housing and urban space in the construction of contemporary patterns of exclusion and inequality.

Race and Racism in Britain by John Solomos (1993) contains a wealth of useful information on such matters as urban policy, policing, and urban unrest.

Chapter 8

Health

Introduction

ISSUES of health and health care are of critical importance in assessing the relative status and well-being of people within modern societies. There are clear links between people's health and economic position, not least because good health is generally a prerequisite for a successful employment history. There is growing evidence that ill-health and unemployment are positively correlated (Schwefel et al., 1987; Smith, 1987; Warr, 1987) and there is also a well-established link between ill-health and poverty (Blackburn, 1991; Payne, 1991; Trowler, 1991). Health can in addition be linked with housing status (Ineichen, 1993; Leaper, 1980; Lowry, 1991). Moreover, the evidence of public opinion surveys appears to indicate that the provision of health care services is high on the political agendas of large sections of the population and, indeed, is seen by both electors and political parties as a key index of citizenship.[1]

For all these reasons no discussion of race and ethnicity in modern Britain would be complete without a discussion of the relative health status, and access to health care, of different ethnic groups. However, to provide an introduction to the relevant issues in a brief text of this kind presents more than usual difficulties. This is because the literature is very fragmented and much of it is written from the standpoint of medical specialisms that are not always sensitive to the nuances of ethnic difference and racial oppression to which we have tried to draw attention in other chapters of this book. Not only does much of the literature operate with unacceptably gross categories when describing and seeking to account for differences between populations (Andrews and Jewson, 1993), but the relative power of the medical profession (Freidson, 1970; Larkin, 1983) has helped to ensure a high profile for research operating within a largely biomedical model of health and illness (Ahmad, 1993a). One consequence has been a level of insensitivity, if not indifference, to people's own definitions and understandings which amounts, in the estimation of some commentators, to outright racism (see for example Ahmad, 1993a; see also the discussions in

Kelleher and Hillier, 1996). A manifestation, or perhaps a result, of this state of affairs is that the data on the health status of different ethnic communities is fragmentary and uneven in quality (Smaje, 1995).

It is no exaggeration to say that the field of health is one in which the kinds of assimilationist assumptions which have characterized most of the areas discussed in this book have been slowest to begin to yield to alternative views. We saw in Chapter 6 that major influences in challenging the dominance of these perspectives in the education field were the demands and resistance of pupils, their parents and communities. By contrast, while it would be wrong to suggest that minority ethnic communities have been passive, it may be that the relative power of the medical profession makes such challenges in the health field more difficult—notably in establishing research priorities.

Two consequences flow from this state of affairs. One is that there is still a strong tendency for explanations of variations in the health status of different ethnic communities to be rooted in oversimplistic culturalist explanations which trace differences in health to variations in behaviour, which in turn are linked to cultural difference.[2] This emphasis on *difference* is not, it should be noted, one which *celebrates* diversity. Rather it emphasizes divergence from some presumed norm that can all too easily resonate with ethnocentric beliefs and racist prejudices (Ahmad, 1993a, Bowler, 1993; Kelleher and Hillier, 1996). It is no accident, perhaps, that scares about health have frequently been mobilized in anti-immigration campaigns[3] while public concern about health issues affecting members of minority ethnic groups is all too often directed towards those which confirm popular stereotypes.[4]

The second and related consequence of the pattern of medical dominance referred to above is that research is highly likely to focus disproportionately on high status areas of medical practice. It may be no accident in this context that research into the apparently high rate of coronary heart disease among people of South Asian descent has had a significantly higher public profile than research into hypertension among people of African-Caribbean origin. Illnesses which primarily affect minority ethnic groups (such as sickle cell disorders and thalassaemia) appear to come still further down the research priority pecking order (Anionwu, 1993).

In the remainder of this chapter, I review some of the evidence on the health status of members of different groups and consider the kinds of explanations mobilized to account for them. I conclude by drawing out the implications both of the patterns discerned and the way in which they have been 'explained' for the overall theme of the book.

Patterns of health inequality

We noted above that links between economic status and health are well established in the social science literature (Townsend and Davidson, 1982; see also
Davy-Smith *et al.*, 1990). The evidence we have reviewed in the fields both of
employment and housing suggests that members of minority ethnic groups
are, on average, economically less well placed than white people (though, as we
saw, this generalization is subject to considerable qualification). In particular
unemployment, which is a particularly serious problem among members of
minority ethnic groups, has been identified by the Child Poverty Action Group
as a major contributor to poverty (Oppenheim, 1993). Partly as a result, people
from minority ethnic groups are disproportionately represented among the
poor.[5]

Given these findings it would not be surprising to find that there were
significant health inequalities between people of different ethnic groups. The
evidence of the fourth PSI survey is that there are, indeed, important health
differences between the white and minority ethnic populations. These are
manifested in differences of general health and in the incidence of specific
conditions, such as coronary heart disease, which disproportionately
affects those of South Asian origin. Overall, those of Pakistani and Bangladeshi
descent reported a 50 per cent higher risk of poor health than white people,
while the figure for Caribbeans was 30 per cent higher. Interestingly, however,
the differences from whites reported by those of Indian, African-Asian, and
Chinese descent were small and were not statistically significant (Nazoo, 1997:
237). The PSI data also show that, although not explaining all the variation,
socio-economic factors make a more important contribution to such variations
than has been suggested by other studies (Nazoo, 1997).

Unfortunately, the task of accurately measuring, tracking, and assessing
alternative explanations for ethnic inequalities is made extremely difficult by
the very poor quality, coverage, and reliability of statistical data in this area
(Andrews and Jewson, 1993; Skellington, 1992: 77; Smaje, 1995). In particular,
many of the available data report differences between groups classified according to the birthplace either of the individual patient or the head of household.
These data do not, of course, include those people of minority ethnic origin
born in the UK—a fact that seriously reduces their usefulness. Nevertheless,
there are some well-established patterns which provide evidence of systematic
health inequalities and which suggest that there is a link with economic
deprivation (see, for example, Carter *et al.*, 1990).

Maternity and child health

A number of these patterns are concerned with maternity and child health.[6] Thus, for example, there is evidence that women born in the New Commonwealth are significantly more likely to die in childbirth than are those born in the UK (Bhat et al., 1988: 179, 181; Parsons et al., 1993). Another phenomenon which is widely taken as a measure of health inequality is the likelihood of a child surviving after birth.[7] Successive surveys have shown that, particularly in the first month of life, death rates among children born to mothers who were themselves born in the New Commonwealth tend to be higher than those for children of UK born mothers (Bhat et al., 1988: 179-87; Parsons et al., 1993). However, these same surveys, together with more recent evidence (Andrews and Jewson, 1993), also show that there are significant variations among different minority ethnic groups. Moreover, it appears that the rates of mortality among infants have been falling—in the case of those of Bangladeshi origin, at a remarkably rapid rate (Andrews and Jewson, 1993). We consider below the implications of these data for explanations of ethnic inequalities. For the moment we should merely note that they indicate that the situation is a complex one about which it would be unwise to make sweeping generalizations. We should also remind ourselves that these data tell us nothing about the children of mothers born in the UK—an increasing proportion of the minority ethnic population.

Rickets

A disorder of some significance in the context of this discussion is rickets. This illness, resulting largely from a deficiency of vitamin D, began to be noticed in the 1960s among children, adolescents, and pregnant women in the Asian communities of a number of British inner city areas (Donovan, 1986: 47; McNaught, 1988: 63-4). The disease, which was prevalent in British working-class communities before the Second World War, is one which, in the past, has been commonly attributed to the effects of poverty. Interestingly, however, most of the early attempts to explain and remedy the illness among Asian patients concentrated on matters that were thought to be specific to Asian lifestyles. Thus explanations for the illness put forward by researchers included: the alleged inadequacy of 'the Asian diet'; inadequate exposure to sunlight[8] caused by cultural prohibitions on the exposure of the skin (especially among women); failure of Asian women to take advantage of antenatal advice; and a preference for ghee (or clarified butter) over margarine, which was routinely fortified with vitamin D (Donovan, 1986: 47-52). The most notable feature of these explanations is the way in which they place the onus for remedying the problem on the sufferers (McNaught, 1988: 63). One study went so far as to suggest that 'the long-term answer to Asian rickets probably lies in health education and a change towards the Western diet and lifestyle' (quoted in Donovan, 1986: 49). As we shall see, such recommendations largely ignored the lessons of earlier campaigns against the disease in Britain.

Sickle cell disease and thalassaemia

There is no evidence that genetic factors are implicated in the occurrence of rickets. There are, however, some inherited illnesses that are disproportionately prevalent among minority ethnic communities. The most well-known are sickle cell disease and thalassaemia. Because they are, to all intents and purposes, diseases that only affect particular groups, they provide an important test of the responsiveness of the health services to the specific needs of these groups. We take up some of these issues in a later section. For the moment, it is important to sketch out the main features of these disorders.

The trait for sickle cell is carried by around 1 in 10 people of African-Caribbean origin and as many as 1 in 4 from West Africa. The trait has adaptive advantages in giving partial immunity to malaria. It causes problems, however, when two carriers of the trait have children together. In such circumstances, there is a 1 in 4 chance that a child will not carry the trait, a 1 in 2 chance that it will be a carrier like its parents, and a 1 in 4 chance that it will have the full-blown disease of sickle cell anaemia. Under specific circumstances, including stress, after exercise or during pregnancy, the disease causes the red blood cells to change to a half moon or sickle shape and then clot or block smaller blood vessels. In sufferers this produces a range of painful, distressing, and potentially life-threatening symptoms. (For detailed discussions of the disease see Anionwu, 1993; Donovan, 1986: 53–6.)

Thalassaemia is also a disorder of the haemoglobin. It affects a variety of groups of Mediterranean, Middle and Far Eastern, and Asian origin. In Britain the trait is carried by approximately 1 in 7 people of Cypriot descent, 1 in 12 Greeks, 1 in 20 people of South Asian descent but only 1 in 1,000 white British people (Anionwu, 1993; Donovan, 1986). As in the case of sickle cell disease, its effects manifest themselves in 1 in 4 children born to couples where both partners carry the trait. It takes a variety of forms, some causing stillbirth and others resulting in the onset of severe anaemia in early childhood. In the latter case, the treatment entails monthly blood transfusions. There are not infrequently complications associated with this treatment and, despite recent advances, relatively few patients survive into their twenties and thirties. (Again, for detailed discussions of the disease see Anionwu, 1993; Donovan, 1986: 55–6.)

Mental health and illness

An area of special and increasing concern is that of mental health and illness. This is an issue of particular difficulty and controversy with the result that it is especially problematic to attempt the kind of brief summary for which there is space in this volume.[9] Nevertheless, the topic is one of considerable importance for the issues with which this book is concerned since it demonstrates with particular clarity the way in which apparently unambiguous indices of difference or disadvantage are social constructions, with quite different meanings for the various parties involved. This characteristic is not unique to the question of *mental* health and illness but it is dramatized by it. This is because, in addition to the problems of inadequate data and problematic ethnic classification categories already referred to, the very question of what constitutes mental health and illness is widely contested (Pilgrim and Rogers, 1993; Szasz, 1971; 1972). This highlights the extent to which, when data on health and illness are collected and presented, they frequently tell us as much about the diagnostic practices of doctors as they do about the actual incidence of any disease.

Mental health and illness is assessed by reference to the presence of symptoms. As in many other kinds of illness, these symptoms frequently rely upon the patient's own reports for their identification—with obvious implications for issues of communication. More significantly, they are typically behavioural in form; the presence of mental illness being inferred from the judgement that a particular pattern of behaviour diverges from some presumed norm. Indeed, some have argued that this feature calls into question the very existence of mental illness (Szasz, 1972). Even if one does not go that far, however, it is easy to see how cultural differences could seriously complicate and distort diagnoses (cf. Donovan, 1986: 58–9).

These issues should be borne in mind in assessing the evidence concerning the incidence of mental illness in different ethnic groups. Moreover, it is also important to note that, notwithstanding the evidence that people of minority ethnic origin are disproportionately represented among those diagnosed as suffering from particular disorders, available data also suggest that members of these groups make less use of psychiatric services than do white people (Donovan, 1986: 57). Despite this, data concerning rates of admission to mental hospitals show a somewhat different pattern. These suggest that African-Caribbean born males and females have tended to have a somewhat higher rate of admission to in-patient facilities than white people. There is also some evidence which suggests that among some groups of South Asian born people, particularly those originating from India and Pakistan, both men and women may have raised rates of admission (see Bhat *et al.*, 1988).

When we turn from rates of admission to patterns of diagnoses, somewhat clearer patterns emerge, though their meaning and significance remains far from unambiguous (Bhat *et al.*, 1988; 194–200). The datum that people of African-Caribbean origin are more likely than white people to be diagnosed as schizophrenic is now well established. Different studies yield different esti-mates, but it seems clear that diagnosis of schizophrenia is around five times more likely for African-Caribbean males and three times more likely for Asian males, when compared with their white counterparts. Similar differentials can be found among women (Bhat *et al.*, 1988: 196). What is particularly interesting about these figures is that there appears to be a corresponding tendency for members of these groups to be less likely than their white peers to be diag-nosed as suffering from depressive illnesses. Bearing in mind what was said above about the reliance of diagnosis on behavioural symptoms it is perhaps not surprising that some writers have suggested that this pattern to some degree reflects the potential for cross-cultural misunderstanding and mis-representation. Bhat *et al.* quote Littlewood and Lipsedge's view that 'whatever the empirical justification, the frequent diagnosis in black patients of schizo-phrenia (bizarre, irrational, outside) and the infrequent diagnosis of depression (acceptable, understandable, inside) validates our stereotypes' (1988: 197).

There are at least two other respects in which those of minority ethnic origin who are admitted as psychiatric in-patients appear to experience differential treatment. First, there is evidence that they are more likely than white patients to be subjected to harsh and invasive forms of treatment such as intra-muscular medication and electro-convulsive therapy. In addition, African-Caribbean patients appear more likely to be placed in secure units, and to be described as 'aggressive', than uncooperative white patients (Bhat *et al.*, 1988: 199). Finally, it seems that patients of minority ethnic origin are more likely than white patients to have been hospitalized compulsorily under the Mental Health Act, a procedure often involving police intervention (Bhat *et al.*, 1988: 199–200).

Adequately explaining these differences poses serious problems. It may be that poor service delivery to minority ethnic communities results in a failure to identify problems until they become emergencies (Bhat *et al.*, 1988: 200). Equally, it is possible that ethnocentric assumptions, failures of cross-cultural diagnosis, or the operation of straightforward racist stereotypes leads to differential treatment that is not related to real differences in rates of susceptibility to illness. Moreover, writing of the epidemiological evidence on schizophrenia, Sashidharan and Francis argue that currently available data, and the thrust of much of the research, is so seriously flawed as to reveal little about differential patterns of mental illness. Rather they suggest that the concentration of many studies on single variable comparisons focusing on ethnicity—but ignoring class, marital status, geographical location, and levels of economic activity—has led psychiatry to become a powerful vehicle for articulating ideas about race rather than advancing our understanding of illness and its effects (1993: 112–13).

Explaining ethnic variations in health

Having selectively reviewed some of the evidence on variations in the health status of members of different ethnic groups, we turn now to a consideration of the ways in which these variations have been explained. In considering these questions, it is essential to bear in mind at all times the qualifications raised above about the quality of the data on which both evidence and explanations are based.

We have several times commented on the prevalence and persistence of assimilationist assumptions in attempts to account for inequalities between members of different ethnic groups. Such explanations assume that differences and inequalities will disappear as 'newcomers' adopt the customs and practices of 'the host society'. In the health field, the consequence of these kinds of assumptions is that differences in health status are highly likely to be attributed to differences of culture. The discussion of rickets in the previous section provides a good example of these kinds of explanation. Thus we saw that the occurrence of the disease among Asian residents of inner cities was frequently attributed to alleged deficiencies in the Asian diet and to a variety of other cultural practices. The onus for addressing the problem was, then, placed on Asians themselves, who were urged to change their behaviour. However, as Donovan points out, this kind of explanation largely ignores the experience of earlier campaigns against rickets: 'rickets was largely eradicated among white Britons only when margarine was fortified and milk was given free to children in schools' (1986: 49). Despite this, demands for the fortification of foods popular among the groups at risk have not met with government favour. At the same time, explanations which focused on sunlight deprivation, resulting from cultural restrictions on behaviour, largely ignored the fact that the sufferers tended to live in inner cities with potentially limited access to open space and with freedom of movement restricted by the fear of racial attacks (Donovan, 1986: 51–2). Such cultural explanations rarely consider the significance of material conditions such as housing, poverty, and discrimination for explanations of ill-health. Yet there appears to be ample evidence that rickets, as well as other diseases such as tuberculosis from which people of minority ethnic descent have been shown to suffer, is directly linked to various indices of deprivation (Bandaranyake, 1986; Donovan, 1986: 52–3).

As in the case of class differences in health (Townsend and Davidson, 1982), there is a well-established link between ill-health and economic deprivation. In the case of class too, there have been those who have argued that differences of social and cultural custom and practice between members of different groups affect their health status. It is not the intention here to deny that such links and influences exist. Rather it is to suggest that cultural explanations have been more dominant and more persistent in the field of ethnicity than in the realm of class.

Is the implication that we should substitute crude materialism for an inadequate and simplistic culturalism? It may be useful to return to the issue of death among infants to consider this question. There is well-established evidence that economic deprivation directly affects the rate at which children die in early infancy, as well as other aspects of child health (Carter *et al.*, 1990; Townsend and Davidson, 1982). Given the evidence about the relative economic status of members of different ethnic groups, we should expect economic circumstances to play a large part in explaining differences between them in respect of health and illness. Andrews and Jewson's review of evidence concerning infant death suggests that at least some of the data relating to such risks among members of minority ethnic groups confirm the materialist case. There are, however, patterns that are difficult to explain simply by reference to indices of deprivation. Thus, not only are the rates of infant death among members of the Bangladeshi population lower than other groups, but they have been declining at a faster rate. This is so despite evidence that the Bangladeshi population suffers some of the highest levels of economic deprivation (Andrews and Jewson, 1993). Andrews and Jewson suggest that this should lead us to reappraise our explanations, not by simply abandoning materialist accounts but by recognizing that health and illness is a product of a complex interplay of influences—both material and cultural.[10]

As we have seen, many cultural explanations of ethnic differences in health status define cultural variation as a problem. As a result, they fail to recognize the positive contribution that cultural difference may make. Thus, as Donovan notes, discussion of 'the Asian diet' in the context of rickets largely failed to note that this same diet comes close to that regarded as ideal by the World Health Organization (Donovan, 1986: 49). Moreover, '(a) person's cultural heritage may also provide her/him with a set of tried and tested traditional remedies which have been largely ignored by researchers and the medical profession' (Donovan, 1986: 64. See also the discussion in Kelleher and Hillier, 1996).

Finally, we should note that there is considerable evidence to suggest that many illnesses are associated in some way or another with stress. The experience of racism, discrimination and harassment are likely to be key sources of stress for many members of Britain's minority ethnic communities. It would

Alternative medicine: The Hakim

The relationship between Western scientific medicine and alternative therapies of various kinds has rarely been a harmonious one. Issues of medical power and dominance are, of course, at stake. Nevertheless, when the alternative remedies are also the products of marginalized cultures, particular issues arise. Waqar Ahmad (1992) has argued that despite the growth of interest in alternative therapies in Britain and across Europe, and the indications of some degree of rapprochement with the medical establishment, the hakim as a practitioner of 'Asian' traditional medicine continues to be treated as an outsider and a scapegoat for all manner of ills. Ahmad notes that the inconclusiveness of much research has not prevented the stereotyping and stigmatization of the hakim. While allegedly harmful preparations, or hazardous interactions between them and Western drugs, have been blamed for a variety of conditions, he contends that no real attempt has been made at systematic evaluation studies comparable to those conducted on homeopathic remedies. *See Ahmad (1992)*.

not be a surprise to find that stress generated in this way may be an element in the causation or exacerbation of a variety of illness conditions. To the extent that this is so, we should also expect the resources of such communities, including a shared culture and patterns of political organization, to be key elements in assisting their members in coping with such stress and its effects.

Addressing health inequalities: Service delivery

Not surprisingly, the measures adopted to address illness and to deliver services are closely related to the way in which the incidence of any condition is explained. They are also related to the degree of priority attached to any particular disease or group of patients. In this connection, explanations that place the blame for a condition, or responsibility for rectifying it, on the patients themselves, may result in low levels of priority being attached to it.

The failure of the National Health Service to be responsive to the specific needs of minority ethnic groups has been the subject of much comment (Bhat et al., 1988; Johnson, 1993; McNaught, 1988: 47–82; Torkington, 1991). Some authors have pointed to a failure to provide services aimed at addressing the specific needs of minority ethnic patients. The case of rickets described above represents an example of the way in which responses to a condition when it affects minority ethnic groups appear to diverge from measures thought appropriate when it occurred more widely. In the case of illnesses specific to minority groups, such as sickle cell disease and thalassaemia, a general failure to provide adequate services is taken by some writers to contrast unfavourably with the likely reaction were the sufferers white (Anionwu, 1993).

Even when services are provided, they may not be equally accessible to all groups of patients. The Black Report showed how access to services was affected by class differences related to economic resources and opportunities (Townsend and Davidson, 1982: 76–89). When we add to such inequalities those arising from cultural differences, such as religious requirements or limited facility in English, it is not difficult to see how minority ethnic communities might have problems in accessing even those services that are available.

The response of the National Health Service to such access problems has been the subject of much criticism (Johnson, 1993). It would be wrong to suggest that there have been no initiatives but these have often been highly local in character and frequently rely upon the initiative of committed individuals or groups. In many cases, it has been the mobilization and demands of minority ethnic groups themselves that have been critical in stimulating action (Anionwu, 1993; Torkington, 1991). In the system as a whole, it appears that positive action is still *ad hoc* and fragmentary.

Moreover, even positive initiatives must be seen against a background of the continuing stereotyping both of ethnic minority patients and their cultures. Bowler (1993) has shown, for example, how midwives stigmatize their Asian patients. Staff in her study expressed irritation with their patients' lack of facility in English and made little attempt themselves to remedy the potential for misunderstanding. In addition, they were prone to characterizing Asian patients' behaviour in terms of a tendency to make an 'unnecessary fuss' and frequently claimed they lacked normal maternal instincts. Further evidence is provided by studies of health professionals' perceptions of the health, and health care needs, of Asian patients. These have revealed a widespread tendency to identify the major issues as those surrounding the supposedly problematic features of patients and their cultures rather than focusing on their specific health problems and needs (Bhopal and White, 1993).

It is for this reason that many would argue that greater sensitivity to the needs of an ethnically diverse population requires that those responsible for organizing and delivering care are more representative of the populations they are required to serve. In this context it is of some significance that research has highlighted a continuing under-representation of minority ethnic groups on the Boards of Health Authorities. A 1989 survey by the King's Fund Equal Opportunities Task Force revealed an under-representation of black and Asian people among the membership of health authorities. Three years later, in 1992, a survey by the Ethnicity Research Centre of the University of Leicester (Jewson *et al.*, 1993*a*, *b*) revealed that not only had there been no improvement but ethnic minority representation had actually fallen, the decline in African-Caribbean representation being particularly sharp.

The significance of these findings lies in the fact that the functions of Health Authorities include the setting of priorities and the monitoring of service targets, sensitive to local community needs (Department of Health, 1992). It is difficult, however, to see how these functions can be effectively and credibly discharged unless members are drawn from a broad cross-section of the population served. The presence of minority ethnic members would seem to be a key element in the successful placing of ethnic differences and needs on the local health agenda.

National Health Service employment

If people of minority ethnic origin are present in very small numbers on the Health Service Boards which control key aspects of service provision, the same cannot be said of their presence in the workforce of the NHS. Indeed, systematic, planned recruitment of staff from the New Commonwealth was a key feature of the large-scale post-war migration described in Chapter 3 (McNaught, 1988: 36–9). That they are present in considerable numbers, however, does not mean that people of minority ethnic origin are represented across the full range of occupational functions or that they have access to genuine equality of opportunity. As the CRE has noted, there have been a substantial number of industrial tribunal cases in which Health Authorities have been found to have unlawfully discriminated against employees or job applicants. 'In addition, as numerous reports have shown, there are still many, often glaring disparities between white and ethnic minority employees in terms of training and career opportunities, grade and specialism' (1991: 6).

There is not space here to deal in detail with all the relevant issues.[11] However, we can point to a number of indicators of systematic inequality. Thus, until the recent introduction of a single system of training for nurses, there were two distinct levels of qualification: the State Enrolled Nurse and the State Registered Nurse. The former was of lower status and typically enjoyed fewer opportunities for promotion to more senior positions. Evidence suggests that nurses of minority ethnic origin are markedly over-represented among SENs (Ward, 1993). There is similar evidence of systematic disadvantage affecting doctors. Thus doctors of minority ethnic origin appear to be over-represented among those practising in low status specialisms, such as psychiatry and geriatrics, and under-represented in such areas as general surgery. These differentials are more marked still when we consider occupational grade, with minority ethnic doctors over-concentrated in lower grades. The proportions of minority ethnic consultants (the most senior grade) are lowest of all in high status specialisms such as general surgery (McNaught, 1988: 40; Ward, 1993).

As in employment more generally (see Chapter 5), there are a variety of potential explanations for these patterns. Once again, however, it is clear that discrimination plays a major part in the pattern of allocation to jobs, as the CRE's report shows. (See also the discussions in McNaught, 1988: 41–6 and Ward, 1993.) The difficulties entailed in addressing such discrimination were well illustrated by the case of Doctors Esmail and Everington, who sought to investigate medical hiring practices by using the well-tried method (see Chapter 5) of submitting matched applications (ostensibly submitted by white and minority ethnic candidates) for junior doctors' posts. The result of their efforts was to be arrested by the Fraud Squad for making fraudulent applications. In the event the police case was dropped and the General Medical Council found no case of unprofessional conduct against them (*Independent*, 20 April 1993). Moreover it is important to record that the doctors were strongly supported in an editorial in the *British Medical Journal*, which commented that 'the public and professional importance of the question being asked seems to justify the small element of deception' (Smith, 1993). Nevertheless, the fact that this incident occurred at all suggests that the development of appropriate sensitivity to issues of discrimination in the Health Service may yet have some way to go.

A recent initiative of some importance in this connection is the launching of a programme of action to achieve equality of opportunity for minority ethnic staff in the National Health Service. The programme's stated aim is to 'achieve the equitable representation of minority ethnic groups at all levels in the NHS (including professional staff groups), reflecting the ethnic composition of the local population'. Health Authority Boards and Trusts were enjoined to set out time-scales, for addressing under-representation, in their business plans. Goals specified by the programme include: improving staff development with an emphasis on identifying the needs of minority ethnic groups; ensuring workplaces are free of racial harassment; increasing the numbers of black and ethnic minority chairs and non-executive members of NHS Authority and Trust Boards in order to reflect the composition of the population served; improving service delivery to ethnic minority clients; ensuring that the time spent in higher specialist training by ethnic minority doctors is equivalent to that spent by white doctors; achieving equitable representation of nurses at higher grades; and increasing ethnic minority applications for, and participation in, management training and career development schemes (*Equal Opportunities Review*, January/February, 1994; March/April 1994).

Against this background we should note that recent research on medical school admissions has shown continuing ethnic differentials in success rates (McManus, 1998). Similarly, the results of studies of recruitment to the nursing and midwifery professions also suggest that progress in meeting national objectives is painfully slow (Beishon *et al.*, 1995; Iganski *et al.* 1998). A study, conducted for the English National Board for Nursing, Midwifery and Health Visiting (Iganski *et al.*, 1998) revealed evidence of significant under-representation of members of Asian minority ethnic groups among those applying for training. In addition, when the outcomes of applications were considered, all those minority ethnic groups, whose numbers were large enough to permit analysis, were less likely than white applicants to have commenced training or be holding offers to do so. Given these patterns, and the national commitments referred to above, it is surprising that case studies of nurse education centres, carried out by the research team, identified few positive action provisions which were part of a systematic strategy for improving recruitment from minority ethnic communities. They also identified a number of selection practices that were potentially problematic. The researchers concluded that the various arguments for equal opportunities and positive action measures were neither fully and widely understood nor wholeheartedly embraced and the problem was compounded by the fragmented organizational structure of the NHS.

As we saw above, this is not a matter that is relevant only to considerations of fairness and justice to current or potential employees. Under-representation of particular groups is likely to impact directly on the quality of service that can be provided to patients from those same communities (Anionwu, 1996; Baxter, 1997; Gerrish, *et al.*, 1996; Jennings, 1996).

Conclusion

In this chapter, we have reviewed the health care status, and access to health care, of Britain's minority ethnic citizens. The evidence suggests that the assimilationist assumptions that have been prominent in a number of areas of social policy have been particularly resistant to change in the health field. The result is that both explanations of health inequalities and the organization of service provision have tended to problematize minority ethnic cultures. This tends to result in the victims of ill-health being blamed for their own situation while only limited attempts are made to accommodate cultural diversity. In short here, as in so many other fields, difference is defined as a problem rather than as something that presents a challenge, and a potential source of alternative solutions.

Further reading

'Race' and Health in Contemporary Britain edited by Waqar Ahmad (1993*b*) contains a series of essays, written from a critical perspective, on a range of aspects of health and health care in modern Britain.

Health, 'Race' and Ethnicity: Making Sense of the Evidence by Chris Smaje (1995) is a useful review of the often fragmentary and incomplete evidence in this area.

The King Edward's Hospital Fund for London also publishes regular reviews, research reports, and notes of practical guidance in this area.

Chapter 9

Crime and Criminal Justice

Introduction

THE racially motivated murder of Stephen Lawrence, and the subsequent
publication of the Macpherson report (Macpherson, 1999) into the circumstances surrounding it, have raised the public profile of a range of issues concerned with crime and the criminal justice system as they impact on minority
ethnic communities. As we shall see, many of these issues are of long-standing
and represent a key respect in terms of which members of minority ethnic
communities have felt that their full citizenship has been compromised.

Minority ethnic groups in the criminal justice system

The operation of the criminal justice system has long been the focus for some of
the most serious questions about racial and ethnic equality in modern Britain.
A particular area of concern has been the over-representation of people of
African-Caribbean descent in prison. Home Office data for 1997/8 indicate that
people from this group constitute 12 per cent of the male prison population
(about six times greater than their representation in the population at large
over the age of 10) and one-quarter of women prisoners (Home Office, 1998: 5,
31).[1] This pattern is of long standing (see Hood, 1992: 193), the numbers having
been relatively constant over an extended period, although there is evidence
of a slow increase in the proportion of male prisoners who are black. These
circumstances have led some to claim that the criminal justice system is permeated by systematic, and institutionalized, racism (Gordon, 1983). While there
is certainly evidence that would tend to support such a view, the quality of
statistical data available and the small number of systematic studies make

it difficult in practice to identify exactly where in the system disadvantage occurs. Moreover, the patterns revealed by such research as is available are complex and difficult to unravel (Hood, 1992; Kirk, 1996; Mhlanga, 1997) and there seem to be systematic differences between the experience of different minority ethnic groups.

In general, however, available evidence suggests that there may be a process of cumulative disadvantage in which differences of treatment at successive stages of the criminal justice system mount up to generate significant differences between ethnic groups in their representation in the prison population. Thus, among both men and women, people of African-Caribbean origin are more likely to be arrested and charged than their white counterparts for similar offences. Home Office data for 1998, for example, show that there are significant differences between groups in their likelihood of being stopped and searched by the police under the provisions of the Police and Criminal Evidence Act, 1984 (PACE). Thus, of the approximately one million stops and searches recorded in 1997/8, 11 per cent were of black suspects, 5 per cent of Asian suspects and 1 per cent of 'other' non-white suspects. Overall, black people were five times more likely to be stopped than white people, although there were significant variations across the country. In general, only between 8 and 14 per cent of suspects were arrested following a stop and search, although black people were more likely than white people to be arrested in these circumstances (Home Office, 1998: 13–14).

Of the 1.96 million arrests made in 1997/9, 7 per cent were recorded as being of black people, 4 per cent of Asians and 1 per cent of 'other' non-white groups. Thus, black people were 5 times, and Asian people up to 3 times, more likely than white people to be arrested, although again there were regional variations (Home Office, 1998: 19–20). Once arrested, several disposals are possible. Thus an arrested person may be charged, formally cautioned, dealt with informally or released without further action. There is evidence of considerable differences between police forces in their use of the formal caution. However, overall, evidence suggests that cautioning is used less frequently for black people than it is for whites or those of Asian descent (Home Office, 1998: 5, 20). According to the Home Office:

Variations in the use of cautions may reflect ethnic differences in the following: whether it was first offence, the seriousness of the offence, the admission of guilt, whether the police officer perceives the offender as showing remorse as well as local cautioning policy and practice (1998: 20).

It is not difficult to see how the operation of some of these criteria could be subject to prejudiced interpretation or the intrusion of stereotyped judgements about the characteristics of particular groups. However, it is worth noting that evidence suggests that black suspects are less likely than whites to admit guilt—a fact which may impact not only upon the decision not to caution but also on subsequent disposals (Fitzgerald, 1993).

Once they come before the courts, there is evidence of differences between white and minority ethnic offenders, and between those of different minority ethnic origins, in whether or not they receive a custodial sentence. Here the effects of a range of variables, such as the seriousness of the offence, make it difficult to demonstrate with precision the size of any 'ethnic effect'. Nevertheless, Hood's study found that black offenders overall had between a 5 and 7.6 per cent greater probability of receiving a custodial sentence than whites, while Asian offenders had a lower probability—largely because they were generally convicted of less serious offences (1992: 198). We should note, however, that there appeared to be significant differences of outcomes between geographical areas and between individual courts.

There is also evidence which suggests that, if convicted, black people are likely to receive a harsher sentence and, where they re-offend, will tend to graduate more quickly to custodial punishment (Gordon, 1983; Hood, 1992; Jefferson et al., 1992; NACRO, 1986; Waters, 1990). Home Office data for 1997/8 indicate that 61 per cent of black adult males, and 59 per cent of Asian males were serving sentences of more than four years compared with 47 per cent of white prisoners. Among adult women sentenced prisoners, 58 per cent were serving more than four years compared with 31 per cent of whites.[2] Once again, it is difficult to identify with precision the reasons for these differences. However, Hood's study did suggest that one source of variation was that black and Asian prisoners were more likely to have been sentenced without a Social Inquiry report about their background and circumstances being available. This in turn was often due to the fact that such prisoners were more likely than whites to have pleaded 'not guilty' to charges against them (see also Shallice and Gordon, 1990) although there remained differences between groups even when this factor was controlled for. Even where Social Inquiry reports are available in respect of both black and white offenders, there is evidence that their contents may have negative implications for black defendants. This is because those who write them may, often inadvertently, include material that has the unintended effect of reinforcing stereotyped views of offenders and their families. Kirk (1996) found that processes of this kind helped to account for differential sentencing of young offenders in a juvenile court.

This example illustrates how easy it is for the normal processes of the criminal justice system to have negative consequences for black citizens, even in the absence of intentional discrimination (see also the discussion in Kalunta-Crumpton, 1999). This is not to say, of course, that there are no examples of racially prejudiced judges, magistrates or probation officers. It is, however, to argue that more subtle processes are at work which derive, in part, from the difficulties that many key national institutions have in acting with sensitivity towards the needs of minority ethnic citizens. One reason for this, as in other walks of life examined in this volume, is the under-representation of minority ethnic groups in a range of important criminal justice occupations. Most significantly, data suggest that minority ethnic officers represented only 2 per cent of serving police officers in March 1998, the highest ranking of whom was an Assistant Chief Constable (Home Office, 1998: 37). Among Prison Service staff, 3 per cent of 'non-industrial' staff were from minority ethnic groups as were 2.3 per cent of Prison Officers and Governors. There is some evidence of an increased rate of recruitment of minority ethnic staff in recent years but rates of retention remain below those for white staff (Home Office, 1998: 38). Turning to the judiciary, data suggest that in August 1988, 'there were believed to be 5 ethnic minority circuit judges, 13 Recorders and 13 Assistant Recorders' (Home Office, 1998: 37). There was an increase from 4 to 6 in the number of stipendiary magistrates over the previous year. Among lay magistrates, where ethnic monitoring data are only available with respect to appointments, there was a fall from 6.5 to 4.1 per cent in the numbers recruited from minority ethnic groups (Home Office, 1998: 37).

Among other professions and occupations associated with the criminal justice system there is some evidence of an, albeit slow, increase in the representation of minority ethnic staff. Examples include the Probation Service where 8.3 per cent of staff were of minority ethnic origin, the Crown Prosecution Service (8.4 per cent), and staff in magistrates courts (6.9 per cent) (Home Office, 1998: 37). In the Home Office as a whole, minority ethnic representation is high among administrative grades but falls progressively as one ascends the hierarchy. Such a pattern is, of course, consistent with recent improvements in recruitment but could also indicate continuing disadvantage in access to higher grades. In the legal profession as a whole, minority ethnic groups remain underrepresented at the higher levels. Thus only 17 of 974 Queen's Counsel (QCs) were of minority ethnic origin in April, 1998. This compares with 8.5 per cent of qualified barristers in independent practice and 25 per cent of students enrolling on the Bar Vocational Course in October 1997. Among solicitors, 8.2 per cent on the Roll in England and Wales were of minority ethnic descent compared with 14.9 per cent of those admitted to the profession in 1996/7 (Home Office, 1998: 37–8). Again these figures are consistent with increasing recruitment of minority ethnic personnel and, other things being equal, would lead us to expect increasing numbers at higher levels in these professions in future years. Such a pattern would also be consistent with the evidence reviewed in Chapters 5 and 6 about the aspirations of minority ethnic young people and existing patterns of upward occupational mobility.

The police

Since the police represent probably the first point of contact for most people with the criminal justice system, their behaviour and probity in dealing with members of minority ethnic communities will be a key issue in establishing the availability of full substantive equality before the law. Moreover, as we have seen, decisions taken by police officers have implications that feed through into later stages of criminal procedure. However, it has been in precisely this area that there has been some of the most serious evidence of a lack of trust between the police and such communities.[3]

The riots that occurred in a number of British cities during the 1980s brought relations between the police and the communities involved into direct and public scrutiny. As we saw in Chapter 7, these events were variously characterized as expressions of criminality, as uprisings against oppression; and as responses to deprivation (see the discussion in Jewson, 1990). In point of fact their participants were by no means exclusively members of minority ethnic groups. Moreover, in a longer historical perspective the disorders were by no means a new phenomenon. However, they were widely seen to break a long period of relatively stable public order (Holdaway, 1996: 113). Perhaps more significantly, the disorders were routinely characterized as 'race riots'. From a conservative perspective their apparent novelty could be ascribed to the transformation of Britain's inner cities by post-war migration. From more liberal and radical standpoints, they could be portrayed as the inevitable result of neglect and racial exclusion.

Whatever the variations to be found among them, and however inadequate the 'race riot' label, the riots nevertheless shared a number of features (see Chapter 7 above). In particular, a key trigger point in almost every case appears to have been relations with the police. Thus, in his official report, Lord Scarman (1981) argued that the 1981 Brixton riots had been finally precipitated by an, at best, insensitive police operation. The crucial point about these circumstances for the present discussion is not simply that relations between the police and the communities involved had deteriorated to the point of open conflict. It is that the police were to become the focus for a more general sense of disillusionment and exclusion from full participation in the life of the nation. Since the police were highly visible representatives of the state, poor relations with them could become a symbol of a wider sense of exclusion from full citizenship. These themes are clearly articulated in Scarman's account of the background to the riots and, in particular, in the significance he attributed to unemployment and urban decay (1981). (See also Holdaway 1996: 111–16; Jewson, 1990).

There is, however, a good deal of evidence to suggest that police–community relations were more than a cipher for a general feeling of exclusion. They were also a source of a continuing sense of injustice in their own right (Benyon, 1986). There have been widespread and persistent reports of police officers acting unjustly and with unnecessary violence towards minority ethnic citizens, as well as claims of racial abuse and harassment (Mason, 1994a; Virdee, 1997: 281–5).[4] Acts of alleged excessive police force were widely held to be triggers for episodes of violent confrontation between the police and communities, including the Broadwater Farm Estate riot in 1985 (Holdaway, 1996: 122). In addition, more routine police activities, such as the stop and search practices discussed above, have come under scrutiny as have the police's apparently differential propensity to arrest black youths. There may well be operational reasons that account for some of the differences in the way officers exercise their powers. There is no doubt, however, that these are reinforced by a strong occupational culture which reproduces a world view in which citizens, law-abiding and otherwise, are divided into relatively closed and fixed categories (Reiner, 1992: 115–21). There is also evidence that policing practices have been shaped by, and in turn have helped to shape, stereotyped characterizations of the criminality allegedly characteristic of minority ethnic communities (Reiner, 1992: 118–19; 156–60). These in turn produce self-fulfilling prophesies in which operational decisions about how to deploy police resources—in particular areas or on specific groups—inevitably produce results that confirm the apparent veracity of the assumptions on which they are based (Reiner, 1992: 114–15).

During the 1970s, the police began to make much more conscious efforts to communicate with and through the mass media (Reiner, 1992: 173–82). In particular, police forces regularly released statistics which appeared to justify their own priorities and practices, even though the arrangements for monitoring were less than systematic and precise (Hall et al., 1978). In the process they contributed to a widespread acceptance of many of their own stereotyped characterizations. This was reinforced as examples of crimes committed by minority ethnic citizens were widely reported by the press in ways that helped to reinforce such stereotypes.

The example of 'mugging' represents a good case in point of the interaction of police public relations activities and press reporting. From the early 1970s (Hall et al., 1978), until as recently as 1995 (Gabriel, 1998: 140), there have been repeated moral panics about the alleged lawlessness of young black men. The Metropolitan Police, in particular, regularly released data about 'mugging' which then became the focus for relatively long running media campaigns representing young black men as disproportionately responsible for this category of crime. In the most celebrated recent case, the Commissioner of the Metropolitan Police wrote to community leaders in London stating, *inter alia*, that 'very many perpetrators of muggings are very young black people' (Gabriel, 1998: 140). His letter was leaked to the press and fuelled a resurgence of press coverage of the issue which tapped into a well-spring of popular prejudice and anxiety, helping to reproduce a 'common-sense, racialized understanding of mugging' (Gabriel, 1998: 140).

Yet 'mugging' is quintessentially a social construction. It is not, itself, a crime but is a term used to denote a range of different street crimes such as theft, assault, and robbery. It thus represents an arbitrary lumping together of criminal acts more usually classified separately. Even then, there is evidence that data for London were selectively utilized in the creation of a moral panic. Thus even in London, 'muggings' represented only 4 per cent of all crime in 1994 while research in other cities has suggested that 'mugging' is in fact more likely to be committed by white people (Gabriel, 1998: 140–1). The socially constructed category 'mugging', therefore, appears in both police and media reports not only to have highlighted the alleged criminality of black youth but to have underplayed the extent and significance of the much larger class of crimes for which whites were overwhelmingly responsible.

As Gabriel has argued, ' "Mugging" fuelled the white imagination . . . because it tapped into ideas of black masculinity which had a much longer lineage' (1998: 139). In this connection we should note that Grover and Soothill (1996) found, in an analysis of newspaper reporting of rape, that cases involving minority ethnic (and particularly black) men were much more likely to be widely reported. In addition reports tended to focus on particularly violent attacks, often involving the use of knives, and cases which also involved robbery. Here, Grover and Soothill argue, 'the construction of the black, knife-armed mugger . . . is being partially maintained through the reporting of rape searches in the press' (1996: 576). This construction resonates with '(t)he popular imagery of black men as one of violence and sexual threat . . . ' (Grover and Soothill, 1996: 568).

'Mugging' represents a dramatic example of how operational policing decisions, informed by the routine categorizations central to police occupational culture, can interact with stereotypes of minority ethnic groups in ways which have implications far beyond the day to day activities of police officers. In addition, however, a number of pieces of research also revealed the persistence of more overtly racist attitudes among police officers (Gabriel, 1998: 135–8; Holdaway and Barron, 1997; Reiner, 1978; 1992: 125–8; Smith and Gray, 1983). Some of the evidence suggests that these reflect views held more widely in the population but there is no doubt that studies have shown that recruits to the police force have been shown to exhibit very hostile attitudes to minority ethnic groups. There is some evidence that such attitudes may be ameliorated to some degree by training but are then accentuated during work experience

Crime and the media

Research indicates that the mass media play a critical role in producing and reproducing negative stereotypes of minority ethnic groups, in caricaturing their beliefs and cultures, and in stimulating moral panics around issues such as crime. The press reporting of issues surrounding immigration (especially illegal immigration and asylum seekers), of urban disorders, and of crimes (particularly those which are portrayed as specific to particular groups) represent only a few of the ways in which the press contributes to the definition of difference as a problem. In addition, all too often the ethnicity of those alleged to be involved is stressed where this is irrelevant to the matters being reported. *See the discussions in: Cohen and Gardner (1982); Gabriel (1998), Gordon and Rosenberg (1989); Grover and Soothill (1996); Hall et al. (1978); Hartmann and Husband (1974); Twitchen (1990); and Van Dijk (1991).*

(Reiner, 1992: 128). In this context, Holdaway has questioned the effectiveness of training, particularly about minority ethnic cultures, in reducing the impact of negative attitudes and stereotypes on day-to-day police practice (1996: 109). Reiner has argued that such negative attitudes do not necessarily feed through directly into police behaviour on the streets (1992: 126), a view for which there is some evidence (Smith and Gray, 1983: 388). Nevertheless, it would be difficult to ignore the co-incidence of evidence about the prevalence of such prejudices, more generally stereotyped views about minority ethnic groups, and disproportional stop and search and arrest rates.

Critical to an understanding of how these various elements interrelate is their place in police occupational culture. As Simon Holdaway has shown, this places great emphasis on the team. Officers need to be able to trust one another in situations which involve confrontations with members of the public and which may entail real physical danger (Holdaway, 1996: 158–67; 1997a: 25–6). Even if much routine police work is solitary and lacking immediate danger, rank and file occupational culture nevertheless defines it as team-work. In this context, a variety of devices is used to create and sustain a sense of solidarity. These include drawing sharp distinctions between the police and civilians (Reiner, 1992: 115–16) and using humour and banter to cement and celebrate that distinction. Given what we have seen about the prevalence of stereotyped images of minority ethnic groups, and the incidence of outright racial prejudice, it is not surprising to find that much of the humour and banter used in this context has a strongly racist flavour. In perhaps the most dramatic and publicly visible example, an Independent Television programme, *World In Action*, broadcast tape recordings of the comedian Bernard Manning addressing a gathering of Greater Manchester police officers in 1995. Manning was recorded not merely uttering racially offensive remarks and jokes but deliberately targeting a black police officer in the audience (see the discussion in Gabriel, 1998: 137–8). More generally, derogatory language and terminology has been found to be widespread in day-to-day police culture while the emphasis on team solidarity means that even those officers who might personally disapprove are constrained to participate if they are to demonstrate their loyalty (Holdaway, 1996: 1; 1997a). The day-to-day operation of occupational culture, then, serves to reproduce and perpetuate negative constructions of minority ethnic citizens among police officers, whatever their individually held views.

In recent years a number of police forces have made efforts to eliminate such behaviour. However, reports of racist utterances, harassment, and discriminatory selection practices continued to surface (Mason, 1994a). A report by Her Majesty's Inspectorate of Constabulary published by the Home Office in 1993 identified continuing problems of unchallenged racist banter among police officers and a general scepticism about senior officers' commitment to equal opportunities. It is against this background that we have to understand the effects of attempts to make police ranks more representative of the population as a whole.

In 1999, only 2.0 per cent of police officers nationally were of minority ethnic descent. The proportions ranged from 0.1 per cent in parts of Wales to 4.5 per cent in Leicestershire. These figures must of course be set against the proportions of the population locally who were of minority ethnic descent. Thus in London, where 25 per cent of the population aged between 18 and 54 were of minority ethnic descent, only 3.3 per cent of police officers were drawn from these groups (Home Office, 1999: 11–13). In July 1999, in the wake of the report of the Macpherson Inquiry (Macpherson, 1999), the Home Secretary set recruitment targets for the police based on the size of the local minority ethnic population with a minimum target set at 1 per cent. Only in a small number of areas did current levels of representation come close to matching these targets (Home Office, 1999).

This initiative was the latest in a long line of attempts to improve minority ethnic representation in the police service that stretched back to the mid-1970s (Holdaway, 1996: 138–41). All of these initiatives have foundered, however, at least in part as a result of the problems generated by the patterns of behaviour described earlier in this section. As Holdaway has put it:

The attractiveness of a police career to a black or Asian person is not immediate. Highly publicised individual cases where a black person has received poor treatment at the hands of the police; question marks about the handling of riots; concern about how one will be treated by future police colleagues; and other, related issues will be weighed in the balance when a police career is considered. (1996: 142–3)

Moreover, as Holdaway's recent research shows, the treatment received by minority ethnic officers in post also affects rates of retention, as well as being likely to be related back to the communities from which they come. Thus minority ethnic officers report having to cope with a continual stream of racist remarks and banter, if not outright harassment (Holdaway, 1996: 142; 1997a; 1997b; Holdaway and Barron, 1997). In addition to these features, however, Holdaway's data show that the ability of minority ethnic personnel to fit into the organization is directly related to their capacity to participate in the occupational culture of the police and the extent to which they are allowed to do so. Their willingness to do so is, at the same time, a key to their acceptance by other officers. There is, in other words, a potentially vicious cycle of exclusion which it may be difficult to break. The problems are particularly acute where the occupational culture is centred on activities from which some personnel are excluded. Muslim officers, for example, may feel unable to participate in activities centred on the consumption of alcohol while their lack of participation may be seen by other officers as an unwillingness to commit to the team (1997a: 25–7). Once again this example reminds us how easy it is for exclusionary processes to operate even in the absence of deliberate discrimination.

Racial violence and harassment

In addition to concerns about the treatment of minority ethnic suspects by the police, it has also long been claimed that the police have routinely failed to take seriously crimes committed against minority ethnic citizens. This has been particularly the case in relation to complaints of racial harassment and violence (Benyon, 1986; Gordon, 1983; Holdaway, 1996: 25–71).

On 22 April, 1993, a black young man, Stephen Lawrence, was assaulted and murdered by a gang of white youths while waiting for a bus in London. Following the murder, there were persistent complaints, led by the victim's family, that the police response and subsequent investigation had been variously, dilatory, incompetent and characterized, at best, by insensitivity and, at worst, by racism. In particular, there was, for a significant period, a reluctance on the part of the police to accept that a racial motive was involved, although there is now widespread acceptance that there was unequivocal evidence that this was the case (Macpherson, 1999).

However, the Lawrence case represents only the most publicly known example of the extreme end of a continuum of harassment and violence which have been the daily experience of many of Britain's minority ethnic citizens. The phenomenon is not new, although it has come increasingly onto the public policy agenda since the 1980s (Virdee, 1995: 12–13). In 1986, the Home Affairs

Select Committee described racial attacks as, 'the most shameful and dispirit-ing aspect of race relations in Britain' (quoted in Holdaway, 1996: 45). Since then, a number of official reports, as well as several local studies, have high-lighted the problem and provided evidence of its persistence and scale (Holdaway, 1996; Virdee, 1995). Nevertheless, there have been continuing com-plaints that the police have failed to take racial attacks seriously (Virdee, 1997: 278–80), and have significantly under-recorded their occurrence.

The terms 'racial attack' and 'racial harassment' are shorthand for a range of offences from murder, through damage to property (ranging from arson to the daubing of racist slogans), to 'verbal and other forms of personal abuse of an isolated or persistent nature' (Holdaway, 1996: 45). Members of all groups can be victims, but 'it remains the case that the overwhelming proportion of victims of racial violence and harassment in Britain today are the "visible minorities"' (Virdee, 1995: 14).

It is impossible to know with any precision what the overall size of the prob-lem is. Different data sources have produced different results, partly as a result of differences in recording practices and partly because of different definitions. Thus early police data classified as 'racial' all incidents which were seen as 'inter-racial'. This included all events where there were perceived differences in the ethnic group membership of victim and perpetrator, whether or not a 'racial' motive was present (Virdee, 1995: 14). This had the effect of inflating the numbers of white victims in police data. More recently, the significance of 'racial motivation' in the definition of such incidents has been accepted and a standard definition was adopted by all police forces in England and Wales in 1995:

Any incident in which it appears to the reporting or investigating officer that the complaint involves an element of racial motivation; or any incident which includes an allegation of racial motivation made by the person. (Home Office, 1998: 35)

The number of racial incidents reported to, and recorded by, the police has risen steadily from 4,383, in 1988 (Virdee, 1995: 15), to 11,006 in 1993/4 and 13,878 in 1997/8 (Home Office, 1998: 35). As the Home Office acknowledges, some of this increase is probably a result of improved adherence to the above definition but it remains the case that there is still significant police under-recording. Thus, in 1996, while police data recorded 12,220 incidents, the British Crime Survey identified some 140,000 which victims perceived to be racially motivated (Home Office, 1998: 35).

Some of the most recent data relying on the reports of victims are provided by the results of the fourth PSI survey (Modood et al., 1997). On this basis, Satnam Virdee has concluded that in a twelve-month period, about 20,000 people were racially attacked, 40,000 had been subject to racially motivated damage to property and 230,000 were racially abused or insulted (Virdee, 1997: 288). The PSI data are important not only because they expose the extent of the direct misery caused by racial harassment and attacks. They also reveal the degree to which minority ethnic citizens are forced to employ avoidance strategies which cause them to modify their lifestyles in ways that constrain their opportunities in the fields of leisure, employment, and education (Virdeee, 1995: 42–7; 1997: 284–6). The survey also indicated that South Asians were more likely to have been victims than Caribbeans although both groups reported similar levels of racial abuse at the hands of the police. Approximately half of respondents who had reported incidents to the police were dissatisfied with the response, alleging either indifference or racially motivated sympathy with the perpetrator (Virdee, 1997: 288).

These data suggest that the police still have some way to go in addressing long-standing concerns both about officers' behaviour and about their sensitivity to the needs and concerns of minority ethnic citizens. This view was reinforced by the report of Sir William Macpherson into the murder of Stephen Lawrence and the subsequent police investigation. The report contained trenchant criticism of a number of aspects of police conduct during the case and concluded that a significant problem lay in the prevalence of institutional racism within the police service. The report generated heated debate, particularly on the issue of the extent to which police officers as a group could be described as intentionally racist. Yet it is clear that Macpherson did not argue that individual officers were, without exception, motivated by racism. Nor did he claim that the policies of the Metropolitan Police Service were intentionally racist. Instead, he provided the following definition:

The collective failure of an organization to provide an appropriate and professional service to people because of their colour, culture, or ethnic origin. It can be seen or detected in processes, attitudes and behaviours which amount to discrimination through unwitting prejudice, ignorance, thoughtlessness and racist stereotyping which disadvantage minority ethnic people. (Macpherson, 1999, para. 6.43)

He went further to identify the ways in which the concept of institutional racism was relevant to an understanding of police actions:

Institutional racism is in our view primarily apparent in what we have seen and heard in the following areas:
(a) in the actual investigation including the family's treatment at the hospital, the initial reaction to the victim and witness Duwayne Brooks, the family liaison, the failure of many officers to recognise Stephen's murder as a purely "racially motivated" crime, the lack of urgency and commitment in some areas of the investigation.
(b) countrywide in the disparity in "stop and search figures". Whilst we acknowledge and recognise the complexity of this issue and in particular the other factors which can be

prayed in aid to explain the disparities, such as demographic mix, school exclusions, unemployment, and recording procedures, there remains, in our judgment, a clear core conclusion of racist stereotyping;

(c) countrywide in the significant under-reporting of "racial incidents" occasioned largely by a lack of confidence in the police and their perceived unwillingness to take such incidents seriously. Again we are conscious of other factors at play, but we find irresistible the conclusion that a core cause of under-reporting is the inadequate response of the Police Service which generates a lack of confidence in victims to report incidents; and

(d) in the identified failure of police training; as evidenced by the HMIC Report, "Winning the Race" and the Police Training Council Report, and the clear evidence in Part 1 of this Inquiry which demonstrated that not a single officer questioned before us in 1998 had received any training of significance in racism awareness and race relations throughout the course of his or her career. (Macpherson, 1999: para. 6.45)

In Macpherson's discussion of institutional racism, then, we find a replay of many of the issues explored in this chapter—issues that have been a source of continuing concern over several decades with respect to minority ethnic citizens' experiences of the criminal justice system. The report suggests that progress has been slow and that there is some way to go before all Britain's citizens enjoy full equality before the law, in the widest sense of that term.

Conclusion

This chapter has reviewed some of the evidence about the experiences of Britain's minority ethnic citizens, both as victims of crime and at the hands of the criminal justice system. Much of that evidence has concerned relations with the police as highlighted by the conclusions of the Macpherson Inquiry report. This focus has been inevitable because of the key role the police play as gatekeepers to the criminal justice system for the vast majority of citizens. Against that background, it is important to echo another observation of the Macpherson report:

Racism, institutional or otherwise, is not the prerogative of the Police Service. It is clear that other agencies including for example those dealing with housing and education also suffer from the disease. If racism is to be eradicated there must be specific and coordinated action both within the agencies themselves and by society at large, particularly through the educational system, from pre-primary school upwards and onwards. (Macpherson, 1999: para. 6.54)

This is an important cautionary note. Each of the chapters of this volume has reported on some aspect of the pervasive experience of racism and exclusion that has been the lot of Britain's minority ethnic population. In the next chapter we explore further the implications of this evidence for their access to full, substantive citizenship.

Further reading

The Racialization of British Policing by Simon Holdaway (1996) is a useful discussion of developments in this area over an extended period.

Resigners? The Experience of Black and Asian Police Officers by Simon Holdaway and Anne-Marie Barron (1997) explores the situations of minority ethnic police officers and identifies barriers to their increased representation.

Ethnic Minorities in Britain: Diversity and Disadvantage by Tariq Modood *et al.* (1997) contains up to date data on racial harassment and relations on the police.

The report of the Macpherson Inquiry (1999) brings together a number of issues raised in the chapter in the context of a tragic individual case of racially motivated murder.

Chapter 10

Citizenship Revisited

Introduction

IN Chapter 3 it was argued that the 1981 Nationality Act introduced a more exclusive definition of British nationality. This had the effect of excluding from potential membership in the national community many people of New Commonwealth descent who were not able to claim patrial status. As we saw, it effectively, though not formally or explicitly, distinguished between potential citizens substantially on the basis of skin colour. On the other hand, this same Act also confirmed the formal citizenship of many others of New Commonwealth descent who were already resident, or had been born, in Britain. In this chapter we explore the extent to which that *formal* citizenship is matched by the capacity to exercise those *substantive* day to day rights which might be expected to accompany full membership in the national community.

The concept of citizenship

The term 'citizenship' is one that is used in a variety of ways. In its formal legal sense, it designates those who are entitled to membership in the nation-state and, hence, to the rights and duties associated with membership. As expressed in the provisions of the British Nationality Act, for example, it defines who has right of entry and abode in Britain. Beyond this, it confers the right to vote in elections and access to various aspects of state provision in such fields as health, education, and social security.

Looked at from this point of view, citizenship is very much an either/or matter: people are either citizens or they are not. In fact the situation is more complicated than this. As a result, citizenship has come to acquire a more complex set of meanings within the literature of social science (see, for example, Marshall, 1950; 1964; Turner, 1986; 1993). An influential discussion, and one that forms the starting-point for many subsequent accounts, is provided in the work of T. H. Marshall (1950).

For Marshall, citizenship expresses full membership in the national political community. The process by which citizenship rights were historically extended to the mass of the population in Britain was, for Marshall, one of the gradual incorporation of previously excluded classes into the body politic. Different sets of rights were extended at different periods and this represented a process of gradual accommodation to mass demands. Thus *civil rights*, in the form of equality before the law, were largely established in Britain in the seventeenth and eighteenth centuries. *Political rights*, in the form of extensions of the franchise and representative democracy, developed through the nineteenth and into the early twentieth centuries. *Social rights*, by which Marshall meant the right to a basic level of material and social well-being as represented by the welfare state, were increasingly demanded and fought for in the twentieth century, and were still incompletely established at the time he was writing. For Marshall, this process of gradual accommodation and incorporation was an alternative outcome of processes of class struggle from that posited by Marxist notions of proletarian revolution.

It follows from this account that, in a context where ever more sections of the population are able to regard themselves as full members of the national community, anyone deprived of access to all or some citizenship rights is, in effect, an outsider—defined as not really belonging, or as marginal to the mainstream of social life. This process of exclusion is likely to be most obvious, and keenly felt, when it affects collectively defined groups of people.

Exclusion from citizenship rights most obviously affects those who are formally defined as non-citizens (see the discussion of immigration and nationality law in Chapter 3). However, formal exclusion from access to all or some of the rights attaching to citizenship is not confined to legal non-citizens. Indeed, Marshall's account, by focusing on the British experience and by being framed within the debate about class, tends to present a rather unidirectional, evolutionary model of citizenship which to some degree obscures this issue. As Mann has pointed out (1987) other societies have experienced different trajectories and sequencing of the development of citizenship rights. Perhaps more importantly for our discussion, women were incorporated into the British body politic generally later and on a different pattern from that experienced by men. This is true of their later acquisition of the vote. It also manifested itself in the fact that, in relation to such matters as divorce and marital property rights, their formal equality before the law was much slower to be achieved. Indeed, a number of writers have argued that citizenship in modern Britain continues to be significantly gendered, with rights and duties asymmetrically distributed between the sexes (Walby, 1992; 1994; Yuval-Davis, 1993; Yuval-Davis and

Anthias, 1989. For a thoroughgoing examination of the concept of citizenship from a feminist perspective see Lister, 1997).

Differential placement in relation to *formal* citizenship is not the only respect in which individuals or groups may be disadvantaged. The formal possession of citizenship rights may not necessarily be matched by their substantive availability. Thus, for example, if some of those who are formally citizens are not able to claim social benefits because they are homeless, we may argue that they are deprived of substantive social citizenship rights. Similarly, Britain's citizens who are not white may, as a result of deliberate racism or because they are unconsciously defined as outsiders, be denied access in practice to some of the rights and benefits of citizenship to which they are formally entitled.[1] It is to a discussion of some of these issues that we now turn. It is important to remember, however, that many of the matters discussed in previous chapters have direct implications for citizenship conceived in this way.

Citizenship and Britain's minority ethnic communities

Immigration controls and their enforcement

Since citizenship has been linked so explicitly by government to immigration, it will be appropriate to begin our survey with a discussion of the operation of immigration controls. This is particularly apposite, moreover, since entry to the country represents the precondition for an ability to access the other rights of citizenship. As we saw in Chapter 3, although this was never expressed formally, the principal intention of the immigration controls introduced from 1962 onwards was increasingly to exclude potential migrants who were not white. In this climate, it would not be surprising to discover that having a skin colour other than white might arouse suspicions about citizenship status. The evidence of a number of studies suggests that this has, indeed, been the case. Those seeking entry have been more likely to encounter suspicion if they appear to be members of a minority ethnic group. Moreover, even those with a legitimate claim to enter have on occasion been subjected to extra scrutiny or refused entry entirely. They have included: dependants with a legal claim to join relatives; those seeking only to enter as visitors; those travelling on business and even, on occasion, full British citizens. (For a discussion of these and related issues see CRE, 1985; Gillespie, 1992; Gordon, 1985; Moore and Wallace, 1975.) Moreover, given a frequently reiterated concern that illegal immigrants

were evading the system of control, attempts to prevent illegal entry have frequently extended beyond ports of entry, into the wider community. Thus so-
called 'passport raids', involving both immigration officers and police, have
been widely reported to have occurred in a number of areas of Britain (Gordon,
1985; Moore and Wallace, 1975). Many have complained that such practices
have the effect of placing the citizenship of all members of minority ethnic
communities continually in doubt, as well as providing an occasion for harassment. Once again, the subtle message received by many of Britain's minority
ethnic citizens is that they are second class citizens. Such messages are only
reinforced by the nature of press coverage of scares about illegal migration and
allegedly bogus asylum seekers (Gabriel, 1998: 97–128).

Political representation

Although in formal terms Britain's minority ethnic populations are fully
incorporated politically—that is they have access to political citizenship rights
in Marshall's terms—it has been common to argue that their needs have not
been fully represented in the political system. One reason for this is that the
British parliamentary system is dominated by two major parties which have
not always apparently seen it as vital to their interests to cater too directly to
minority ethnic constituents. The willingness of both the Conservative and
Labour parties to play the race card during the period of large-scale New Commonwealth migration is indicative of the extent to which both have been most
responsive to the demands of white voters (Layton-Henry, 1992, chapters 4, 7,
and 8; Saggar, 1992, chapter 5).

  In the latter half of the 1990s there has been some waning of political focus
on the issue of immigration. Although there is no evidence of a reduction in
popular hostility to the continuing migration of those who are not white, the
now very low levels of such immigration, together with a considerable measure
of agreement between the two main political parties on the issue, have meant
that the issue did not figure highly in the 1997 general election campaigns
(Saggar, 1998). Instead, there has been a growing focus on the apparently
increasing numbers of asylum seekers arriving in Britain from areas of the
world experiencing natural disasters or, more commonly, fleeing war, geno-
cide, and religious and ethnic persecution. Those fleeing the conflict in Kosovo
have, in particular, been the focus for recent expressions of concern in some
parts of Britain (see, for example, *The Times*, 1 April 1999, 3; 2 April 1999, 8). The
result has been a renewed debate, similar to one taking place in other parts of
Europe, about whether asylum seekers are 'genuine' or are merely 'economic
refugees' in search of enhanced welfare and economic opportunities. The result
has been the development of increasingly restrictive rules regarding the

processing and acceptance of applications for asylum and a reduction in the availability of state provision for those awaiting a decision.

The potential of these debates to fuel generalized hostility and prejudice was well illustrated by the debates surrounding the 1996 Immigration and Asylum Act (Gabriel, 1998: 105–6). In this context it is interesting to note that, in anticipation of the Parliamentary debate on the 1999 Immigration and Asylum Bill, the leaders of the political parties represented in the House of Commons signed a statement drawn up by the Commission for Racial Equality, the Refugee Council and the United Nations High Commissioner for Refugees:

We, as leaders of the Parliamentary parties in England, Scotland and Wales, agree that all MPs, MEPs, councillors and officials of our respective parties should undertake:

- Not to publish, cause to be published, or in any way endorse any material which incites hostility or division between people of different racial, national or religious groups, or which might reasonably be expected to stir up or incite such hostility or division.
- To ensure that in any dealings with the public no words or actions are used which may stir up racial or religious hatred, or lead to prejudice on grounds of race, nationality or religion.

We call upon all others who are in any way involved in the passage or reportage of the Immigration and Asylum Bill, especially the media, to do the same.

It is interesting to speculate whether their willingness to do so was enhanced by the recognition that the race card no longer seemed to yield discernible dividends.

There may, of course, be other considerations. As long as elections were not determined by marginal constituencies in which large minority ethnic populations potentially held the balance of power, the relative neglect of issues of concern to minority ethnic voters was likely to persist. Changes seem to have begun gradually as the Labour Party's hold on power in some inner city constituencies and local authorities began increasingly to depend on its becoming more responsive to the needs of the minority ethnic voters who had traditionally supported it (Layton-Henry, 1992, chapter 5; Saggar, 1992, chapter 6). In this respect the concentration of these populations in a limited number of urban areas may have conferred a degree of influence. Indeed, Robinson (1989: 263) has argued that this was responsible for the return, in 1987, of the first minority ethnic Members of Parliament for some time. The significance of these kinds of considerations may have been enhanced in the early 1990s as political parties appeared to be running closer to one another in opinion poll standings. In the general election of 1992, six minority ethnic Members of Parliament were returned, including the first Conservative since 1900 (Layton-Henry, 1992: 120)

In the 1997 general election, nine MPs from minority ethnic backgrounds were elected. This was an increase of only three over the previous result and the members concerned represented only 1.4 per cent of the total of 659 members of the House of Commons. By contrast, a Parliament reflecting the population more accurately would contain 36 minority ethnic MPs (Weir and Beetham, 1999: 74). Weir and Beetham argue that, making up at most a quarter of the population of those constituencies in which they are most heavily represented, minority ethnic voters are unable to determine the result in Britain's single member constituencies (1999: 74). Nevertheless, there is some evidence that minority ethnic groups can exercise an important influence. Thus, Curtice and Steed note of the 1997 general election, which saw an overall 10.3 per cent swing from Conservative to Labour across Great Britain:

In Bethnal Green and Bow where Conservative support rose by nearly 5 per cent, and in Bradford West where it fell by less than 1 per cent, the Conservative candidate was a Moslem while the Labour candidate was from a different ethnic minority. Both seats contain a significant Moslem minority who were evidently attracted into the Conservative camp by the religious affiliation of the local Conservative. Never before has such ethnic voting occurred on this large scale in Britain. (1997: 308–9)

In this connection, we may note that there is evidence of Asian communities beginning to organize, with some success, within Labour Parties to get their candidates selected (Weir and Beetham, 1999: 74; see also Fielding and Geddes, 1998). Indeed, this phenomenon may not be entirely limited to the Labour Party. In the 1997 general election, the BBC's Constituency guide listed 42 minority ethnic candidates. Of these 12 were Labour, 17 Liberal Democrat, 12 Conservative and 1 SLP. Of these five were sitting MPs, while three more (two Labour and one Conservative) were selected to fight seats already held by their party (BBC, 1997: 2–6). This may suggest that, despite an apparent upward trend, progress remains slow in increasing the representation of minority ethnic groups—particularly as candidates in 'safe' seats.

Moreover, notwithstanding limited positive trends, we should note that some have argued that minority ethnic communities have derived little direct benefit from their involvement in mainstream politics at either local or national level. Saggar (1993) has argued, for example, that the transformation of race issues in British political discourse in recent years has owed as much to a continuing white liberal agenda as to the direct effects of minority ethnic participation. Similarly, Geddes (1993) suggests that the increasing number of Asian and African-Caribbean councillors in local authorities has done little to remedy overall under-representation. Moreover, even this level of success has been highly skewed, with Asian men in the majority. In addition, Geddes questions whether their presence has made any effective difference. Finally, we should note that an analysis of recent voting patterns by Saggar and Heath (1999) suggests that minority ethnic voting patterns in 1997, isolated examples such as the one noted above notwithstanding, represented a continuation of

Minority ethnic representation in the Labour Party

The feeling that, despite their loyal support over many years, black people were not properly represented in the organizations of the Labour Party was fuelled in the late 1970s and 1980s by a continued failure by the party to select minority ethnic candidates in winnable seats. The result, was a spate of resolutions to Annual Party Conferences calling for the setting up of Black Sections on the model already established for women. The argument was that this would provide an organizational forum in which black people could take responsibility for policy formulation on issues affecting them and which would give them the power base in the organization which they lacked. These efforts were resisted by the Party hierarchy for a number of reasons. Among some there was a genuine fear of separatism and ghettoization, among others there was concern about press reaction and the danger of being seen to be endorsing 'the loony left', among yet others there was almost certainly a fear that traditional power bases in the Party would be threatened. This opposition was greeted with dismay, and as a scarcely veiled manifestation of racism within the Party, by many supporters of the Black Sections movement. The sense of betrayal was heightened when almost all the black MPs elected in 1987 subsequently deserted the cause. In the end a much diluted form of black organization within the Party was approved in 1990. More recently, evidence of substantially increased minority ethnic membership in some Constituency Labour Parties has led to expressions of concern about 'entryism'—or systematic attempts to take over local parties. That these concerns are expressed has, in turn, led to claims that the Labour Party remains permeated with racism and a reluctance to take racial equality seriously. *For discussions see: Fielding and Geddes, (1998); Layton-Henry (1992: 163–9); and Saggar (1992: 132–3).*

past patterns. Rather than representing evidence of new strategic ethnic voting, their analysis suggests that, '(m)inority voters in 1997 broadly pursued a similar path to their white counterparts . . .' (1999: 122).

Social rights: access to the welfare state

There is also evidence of limits to the substantive access of minority ethnic communities to full social citizenship. We noted above, that the questioning of formal citizenship often extended beyond ports of entry into aspects of daily life. Storey (1986), for example, has shown how immigration controls impacted directly upon access to the welfare state, with the production of passports often being demanded as proof of entitlement (Gordon and Newnham, 1985; MacEwen, 1991b; 71). More generally, a report by the National Association of Citizens' Advice Bureaux (1991) produced evidence of a general lack of sensitivity in the social security system to the needs of minority ethnic clients.

Not only did the report reveal evidence of racism among staff but the provision of necessary services, like interpreters, was highly variable. In addition, the report revealed a general lack of understanding of cultural differences in patterns of family life and an assumption that conformity to some presumed norm was a legitimate precondition to the provision of support.

Nationality and nationalism in 1980s Britain

We have already noted how the legal framework for access to full formal citizenship was set by the 1981 Nationality Act. The redefinition of British citizenship that it entailed can be seen as part of a general process, in the 1980s, in which government sought a reinvigoration of British nationalism. This process was reflected in events as diverse as the Falklands war and conflicts with the European Commission. A key feature of the conceptions of Britishness deployed on these occasions was an emphasis on the antiquity of British national culture, traditions, and institutions. Not only were these portrayed as being under threat but they were also represented as a slowly evolving network of mutually supporting elements that were interfered with only at the nation's peril.

A key element in this patchwork was a renewed emphasis on a unified and unitary British national culture.[2] On the one hand this could be said to offer the possibility of belonging. Thus in the 1983 General Election campaign a Conservative Party poster, depicting a black person, carried the legend: 'Labour says he's black, we say he's British.' On the other hand this left people of minority ethnic origin with a stark choice. They could be British, with all the cultural allegiances that implied, or they could be 'ethnic'—and therefore potential outsiders who might even threaten to 'swamp' the nation with 'alien cultures'.[3] This position was succinctly expressed by the senior Conservative politician, Norman Tebbit, when he suggested that an appropriate test of people's Britishness was which national cricket team they supported (see Faulks, 1998: 163–65). This approach delegitimized policies aimed at addressing collectively defined special needs and defined as unBritish any but the most minimal manifestations of cultural difference.[4]

Citizenship in 1990s Britain

By contrast with the stridently nationalist conception of British citizenship that was openly promoted in the 1980s, by the 1990s all political parties were offering rather different and, they argued, enhanced conceptions of citizenship. Their main feature was the promise of wider, more extensive, and more active involvement of citizens, *as consumers*, in education, health, and social security, as well as the market-place. The new emphasis, then, was upon citizenship as an expression of the contract between an enabling state and individuals who were free to choose and direct their own destinies. As Faulks (1998) has noted, one consequence of this conception was that it created an implicit distinction between those who had the resources that enabled them to exercise this citizenship and those who did not. Faulks argues that, in its Conservative manifestation this distinction was explicitly expressed in the concept of *active* citizenship, with its implied partner, *passive* citizenship. The former was seen as virtuous and to be encouraged. The latter, by contrast was either a manifestation of commitment to deviant lifestyles or a result of having sunk into a state of dependency manifested in the notion of underclass (Murray, 1990). The former were to be policed and controlled, the latter discouraged through the disciplines of increasingly marketized welfare. This emergent distinction then, created a new manifestation of a key feature of citizenship; namely that it simultaneously includes and excludes. We have seen how formal citizenship rules have excluded minority ethnic groups. It is not difficult to see how this new conception could also exclude them both because their lifestyles were defined as deviant (or alien) and because to exercise active citizenship requires resources which, as we have seen, are unevenly distributed. This pitfall has been recognized in the concept of 'social exclusion' embraced after the 1997 general election by the new Labour government. The conquest of social exclusion has been given high priority by the government but there is as yet little sign that policy initiatives are having major success in reducing it. Moreover, some government critics have charged that it remains too closely wedded to the previous Conservative government's underlying assumptions about its origins.

This renewed emphasis on citizenship, then, raises important questions. 'What is the relationship between a concept of citizenship embodying the individual freedom to choose consumption patterns and lifestyles, and the notions of Britishness being promoted in the 1980s and still prominent in some sections of the political right?' Moreover, 'What arrangements are in place for ensuring that those citizenship rights which are formally available can be exercised in practice?'

We consider an important test of the first question in the next section. So far as the second is concerned, the changed view of the role of the state and of citizenship characteristic of the 1990s does seem to have manifested itself in a number of changes in the tone and content of both Conservative and Labour government initiatives and utterances. A notable development was the Employment Department's *Equal Opportunities Ten Point Plan for Employers*, which was launched by the then Secretary of State for Employment, Michael Howard, in March 1991. This document urged employers to adopt a range of detailed measures including systematic ethnic monitoring and the setting of equality targets. Many of these had been regarded as, at best, controversial during much of the 1980s and had frequently been associated with what was sometimes described as 'the loony left'. Since then Governments have associated themselves with campaigns such as *Opportunity 2000* and *Racial Equality Means Business*, private sector sponsored campaigns to improve equal opportunities for women and minority ethnic groups respectively. In addition, governments have been more proactive in seeking to promote racial equality in the public services.

The *Programme of Action to Achieve Equal Opportunity in the Civil Service for People of Ethnic Minority Origin* was launched in 1990. The Office of Public Service and Science published its third progress report on the programme in 1994. It indicated that overall representation of ethnic minorities in the Civil Service increased slightly from 5 to 5.2 per cent between April 1992 and 1993, a figure that compared with the 4.9 per cent of the economically active population which was of minority ethnic origin. Despite increases, representation remained low in management grades and at higher levels, only 2.1 per cent of civil servants at Grade 7 and above being of ethnic minority origin. Even this figure, however, represented an increase from the 1.8 per cent recorded the previous year and was the largest year on year increase since 1989. The report nevertheless recognized that there was room for further improvement and the Office of Public Service and Science announced a review of procedures and an exploration of the scope for outreach work. By 1998, the overall representation of minority ethnic groups in the Civil Service had risen to 5.7 per cent. However it was still the case that only 2.1 per cent of staff at grade 7 or above were of minority ethnic origin. In the light of these figures, a *Charter for Action to Redress the Under-Representation of Ethnic Minorities in the Senior Civil Service* was launched in February, 1999.

Given the apparently slow rate of progress, it might be argued that these developments are of no more than rhetorical significance. However, there are grounds for arguing that they represent a change of some importance when taken together with the new emphasis on citizenship. This is because the concept of citizen is one that emphasizes notions of freedom and opportunity. As a result, it can be argued that equal opportunities issues are, in principle, at the heart of inclusive modern citizenship. Given the political agenda of governments in the 1990s, the developments described do appear to represent a significant change in direction and in the level of commitment to this project. It remains to be seen, however, whether they can extend beyond rhetoric to deliver genuinely enhanced access to full citizenship. Moreover, they would need to be matched by a corresponding commitment by employers in the private sector if they were to secure long-standing change.[5]

Perhaps more significantly, the question arises of whether they can transcend the limits imposed by deeply rooted notions of Britishness which were so assiduously cultivated by government during the 1980s.

Equal opportunities policies

Equal opportunities policies, aimed at a variety of disadvantaged groups (including women, people with disabilities, and members of minority ethnic groups) have been an increasingly common feature of employment practice (and service delivery) in both public and private sectors in recent years. Such policies take a variety of forms and are pursued with varying levels of seriousness and conviction. Often the objectives of policy are unclear or the subject of dispute, a major distinction being between those which seek equality of opportunity and those which aim for equality of outcome. In addition, there is evidence that the needs of women often command a higher degree of legitimacy than those of minority ethnic groups. Nevertheless, as changes in government policy have shown, there is a growing consensus about what the key formal elements of policy should be. *See the discussions in: Braham et al. (1992); Employment Department (1991); and Mason and Jewson (1992). See also the discussion in Chapter 11 below.*

A test case? Equal opportunities and the armed forces

It is arguable that there are fewer clearer expressions of full citizenship than being granted the right and opportunity to participate in the defence of one's country. In this connection, we may note that the British armed forces have made remarkable strides in recent years in extending the range of opportunities open to women (BMSG, 1991; Dandeker and Segal, 1996). Following a ruling that it was contrary to European Union law to require women to resign from the armed forces upon becoming pregnant, rapid and far-reaching changes have taken place. Thus, for example, women are now fully integrated into the Royal Navy, including service at sea on all types of warships other than submarines. Women are being trained and have qualified to fly combat aircraft, including fighters, for the Royal Air Force, and women's exclusion from the band of the Royal Marines has been ended.

According to the Strategic Defence Review White Paper (SDR), '96% of posts in the Royal Air Force and 73% of the total posts in the Royal Navy and Royal Marines have been open to women for some time. On 1 April 1998, the Army increased the posts open to women from 47% to 70%' (MOD, 1998, Supporting essay 9, para. 39). Moreover, 'Servicewomen currently represent around 7% of the total strength of the Armed Forces. More women are joining the Forces and fewer are leaving. In the last year 14% of all new recruits were women and there was a 30% decrease in the numbers leaving' (MOD, 1998, Supporting essay 9, para. 40). A debate continues about the integration of women into the principal roles from which they remain excluded in the Army, Royal Air Force Regiment and Royal Marines; namely those requiring them to 'close with and kill the enemy'—specifically infantry and armour. It is noteworthy, however, that the SDR did not rule out future changes in this area (MOD, 1998, Supporting essay 9, paras. 39 & 40).

By contrast with this picture of rapid change, progress in increasing the recruitment and retention of members of minority ethnic groups has been slower and, until recently, had a lower public profile. In recent years, however, there has been a series of embarrassing allegations of discrimination and harassment (Mason, 1994a). Together with an investigation by the Commission for Racial Equality (CRE, 1996), these events have combined with recruitment pressures to produce a greater recognition, on the part of the armed services, that the under-representation of minority ethnic groups is a problem. Thus at January 1, 1999, minority ethnic groups comprised 1.04 per cent of the total UK regular forces and 1.44 per cent of civilian personnel within the services. Within this already low level, South Asian minority ethnic groups are particularly underrepresented among uniformed personnel (DASA, 1999).

A high profile Army recruitment initiative and a new Equal Opportunities Directive are among the most visible manifestations of public commitments to change, which were reinforced by commitments set out in the SDR (EOR, 1999; MOD, 1998, Supporting Essay 9, paras. 41 and 42):

41. **Ethnic Minorities**. We are determined that the Armed Forces should better reflect the ethnic composition of the British population. Currently some 6% of the general population are from ethnic minority backgrounds, but they make up just 1% of the Services. This must not continue. We have set a goal of attracting 2% of new recruits this year from ethnic minority communities for each Service. We want that goal to increase by 1% each year so that, eventually, the composition of our Armed Forces reflects that of the population as a whole.

In the light of the fact that progress towards racial equality in the armed forces has hitherto been painfully slow we may reasonably ask what might be the obstacles to delivering on these commitments.

A central feature of military organizations is that they are structured around hierarchies and authority. Members of military organizations are required to conform to strict codes of discipline. Moreover, conformity is also central to the social integration of military units and organizations. It is a key component of the notions of comradeship and *esprit de corps* which are characteristic of military self-image and organization. Its most visible manifestation is the uniform which de-emphasizes individuality and emphasizes similarity and sharing. These features of military organizations have, in principle, problems in coping with difference of any kind—a fact that may help to explain some of the difficulties they encounter with homosexuality.

There are, however, some distinctive features of British history and culture, with particular resonances within military culture, which make embracing *ethnic* differences particularly problematic. The contrast between the increasing participation of women in wider military roles and the continued difficulties experienced by Britain's citizens of minority ethnic descent may be instructive in this regard. This is because Britain's minority ethnic citizens continue to be routinely represented as different from their white peers—whether for reasons of biology, culture or history. Indeed, the relationship between citizenship and nationality poses particular problems because of the way in which both 'Englishness' and 'Britishness' have been represented as uniquely long-standing and primordial attachments (Colley 1992; Rich, 1994). The significance of this appeal to historical continuity is greatly heightened when we consider the fact that all armed forces tend to place a very high value on tradition and history. This is not just a product of a desire to learn the lessons of past campaigns. Rather it represents a further way in which conformity and *esprit de corps* are reproduced by emphasizing continuity with the past, and fellowship with ancestral role models. In the case of the British armed forces this emphasis on history is of particular significance for the subject-matter of this volume.

Much of the military history of Britain over the last two centuries or so is the history of colonial involvement. Many of the campaigns fought by the British armed forces were either campaigns against colonized peoples or campaigns to protect imperial territory from other colonial powers. Thus the recent forebears of many of Britain's citizens who are not white were either enemies or colonial subjects.[6] In these circumstances, it may be difficult to view their descendants as co-nationals—whatever their formal citizenship—because they lack both the common origins and the homogeneity which the British national myth, with its claims to a uniquely long history, requires. We may also note that war itself has a particular significance for the British. Cesarani has argued, for example:

The resonances of war in British national identity continue to divide the population along racial lines. Thousands of West Indians and Indians served in the British armed forces in 1939–45, but this fact hardly registers in public memory of the war. . . . The war is taken to evoke the British at their best, the qualities of Churchill's 'island race'. . . . It helps construct a sense of nation and nationality that excludes the bulk of post-1945 immigrants. (Cesarani, 1996: 69)

The problem, then, with Britain's minority ethnic citizens is that they are intractably *different*. Their difference marginalizes them in the context of a national origin myth that emphasizes the antiquity of the group. In the context of a historical tradition that draws heavily on the heritage of empire, the problem for Britain's minority ethnic citizens is establishing a right to participation at all rather than laying claim to an extension of roles. As in some of the other areas of social life that we have reviewed in this volume, the implication would appear to be that they can be admitted only to the extent that they can conform. The question is not simply, 'Can they pass Mr Tebbit's cricket test?' but 'Would they be allowed to try?'

The alternative would be a reconceptualization of the boundaries of the nation and, critically, of its origin myths. That this is a difficult project is exemplified by the way in which even the highly individualistic conceptions of citizenship emerging in Britain in the late 1980s and early 1990s had difficulty in coping with ethnic differences which manifested themselves in the assertion of rights to distinctive cultural forms (see the discussions in Jewson and Mason, 1993: 15, 28; Mason and Jewson, 1992: 109–11).[7] On the one hand, the burden of history and tradition described above creates a situation in which the armed forces are seen, and to some extent see themselves, as symbolically representative of a political community superseded by the multi-cultural country Britain has become. On the other hand, it may be that the armed forces have a potentially unique opportunity to lead the way because of their centrality to notions of citizenship. If they could overcome the contradictions of citizenship and nationality in the 1990s, the way might be open for progress towards genuine equity.

One important initiative might be explicitly to recover and celebrate the historical contribution of the forebears of Britain's minority ethnic citizens to its military history including a much more visible public celebration of the contribution of Britain's imperial dependencies to past military successes, as for example in both World Wars. This would entail no less than creating a new version of military heritage more symbolically representative of a diverse political community and a reassessment of what it means to be British in the twenty-first century. (For a fuller discussion of these issues see Dandeker and Mason, 1999.)

Conclusion

In this chapter we have seen how the concept of citizenship can illuminate issues of equality and inequality. Its utility is not restricted to formal differences between legal citizens and non-citizens but extends to the question of whether formally available rights can be exercised in practice. Nevertheless, the formal legal framework is of crucial, contextualizing significance. This is because the concept of citizenship is a product of a world of nation-states and citizenship is exercised in the context of rights granted or guaranteed by the state. The implication of this is that universal citizenship is not possible. The very notion of citizenship entails inclusion, and hence, exclusion. If there are citizens, there must be non-citizens. While it might be possible to devise 'fair', rational, and universalistic criteria for inclusion, there is no way of avoiding the fact that citizenship implies that there are 'outsiders'. If rights are available to everyone they cease to be citizenship rights, with their location in the world of nation-states, and become human rights (Bauböck, 1991).

The intersection of citizenship and human rights provides, however, interesting terrain for further consideration of issues of equity. As we have seen, citizenship is a concept that embodies principles of equality, demanding just treatment for those who qualify for membership. Human rights define certain minimum standards that should be available to all. While universal citizenship may not be a plausible aspiration in the world of nation-states, it may not be too much to expect that there could be equitable and non-racial procedures for deciding who has legitimate access to the citizenship of any given nation-state. Were such a combination to be possible, it would represent another way in which diversity might be celebrated. It suggests that, shorn of racist and ethnocentric encumbrances, the idea of nation might return to something more closely approximating the ideals of its post-French Revolutionary proponents. In the context of this basically democratic vision, nationalism would become not the vehicle of oppression but an aspiration to join an international family of nations, each with its own valued traditions and characteristics, from which all might learn and benefit (Smith, 1971: 158–60).

Further reading

Race and Racism in Britain by John Solomos (1993), The Politics of Immigration by Zig Layton-Henry (1992), and Race and Politics in Britain by Shamit Saggar (1992) all contain a wealth of information on the various matters which are discussed in this chapter.

Racialized Boundaries by Floya Anthias and Nira Yuval-Davis (1992) makes an attempt to relate race, ethnicity, and gender to issues of citizenship and nationality.

There Ain't No Black in the Union Jack by Paul Gilroy (1987) also focuses on the relationship of race, nation, and citizenship while Frontiers of Identity: The British and the Others by Robin Cohen (1994) provides a detailed historical analysis.

Chapter 11

Conclusion: Trends, Threats, and Opportunities

Introduction

WE have, in this volume, reviewed a variety of aspects of contemporary social life, placing them in the context of the rich pattern of ethnic diversity that is modern Britain. We have, in the process, revealed persistent patterns of ethnic disadvantage and racial oppression. Yet, as well as charting those features that appear resistant to change, we have also identified areas in which significant changes appear to be under way. Not the least important aspect of those developments is the role of minority ethnic communities themselves in pressing their claim for full and effective citizenship.

In this final chapter, I want to venture a few reflections on the prospects for the future. Any such attempt is fraught with difficulties and what follows can be no more than informed speculation. Most significantly, I suggest that most social developments are Janus faced in their potential—holding out both opportunities and pitfalls. This is no less true of the issues I have chosen to highlight below. The final outcome will depend both on the political will of the powerful and on the way ordinary people of all ethnic groups respond to the challenges of the future.

The European context

In Chapter 9 we reviewed the concept of citizenship and considered the potential of new conceptualizations emerging in the 1990s to deliver greater equality of opportunity. In the light of this discussion, it is important to consider a major contextualizing factor to developing conceptions of citizenship—Britain's membership of the European Union.

In considering citizenship, we saw that it entailed more than simply a formal badge of membership in a national community. Rather it conferred a variety of benefits and duties that were seen as rightfully accruing to citizens. In this sense, the extension of the rights available to British citizens to include those guaranteed by the European Union has the potential greatly to enhance citizenship at all levels. Thus we may note that the Social Chapter, which the British government finally acceded to in late 1997, extends and guarantees a range of rights at the workplace which amount to an additional aspect of citizenship: industrial citizenship.

Perhaps of more immediate significance has been the impact of European law on the rights available to British citizens. In a series of judgments the European Court, for example, has won for British women significant extensions of benefit under equal opportunities law. Indeed, it is no exaggeration to say that pressure from Europe has been a major driving force in pushing the cause of equal opportunities for women forward. Similar developments are now in train with respect to sexual orientation and the rights of gays and lesbians.

These examples suggest, then, that membership of the European Union has the potential greatly to enhance the citizenship rights of the British people. On the other hand, there are counter-forces that may be particularly threatening to the substantive citizenship of British people of minority ethnic origin. Taking first the issue of equal opportunities, we may note that there has not been comparable pressure to enhance opportunities for minority ethnic citizens. Moreover, few other EU countries have race relations legislation which is as extensive or developed as that in Britain (Forbes and Mead, 1992) although there is evidence of pressure to tighten legislation in these areas (Commission of the European Communities, 1992; MacEwen, 1995). In addition, we should also note that in some other states of the EU, a substantial number of long-term residents of minority ethnic origin do not enjoy formal, legal citizenship (Wilpert, 1991).

This last point is also of significance given the concern that has been growing across Europe about levels of illegal immigration. In this context, proposals have been developed to tighten controls on entry, constructing what some have called 'Fortress Europe' (Gordon, 1989; Waever et al., 1993). Given that in some countries of the Union there are large populations of non-citizens, it is not difficult to see how appearing to be different, and particularly having a darker skin, could be taken as prima-facie evidence of non-citizen status—or even of illegal entry (Birmingham City Council, Race Relations Unit, 1991). Were such a situation to develop, it could seriously undermine the freedom of movement of British citizens of the EU who are of minority ethnic origin. Given the potential benefits of the right to free movement of labour within the Union, the questioning of status and harassment that could ensue would constitute a significant denial of substantive citizenship rights.

The 1990s have also seen another development that has posed a serious threat to European citizens of minority ethnic origin. In the wake of the break-up of the Soviet empire and the reunification of Germany, large-scale migrations of people began to generate serious social strains in a number of EU states. These developments coincided with a period of economic downturn and with rising unemployment. In this context, much of Western Europe has seen an upsurge in the fortunes of parties of the right, the re-emergence of neo-fascist movements, and serious outbreaks of murderous racial violence (Björgo and Witte, 1993; Cheles *et al.*, 1991; Ford, 1992; Joly, 1998). Some of the most serious of these episodes have taken place in Germany but they have been commonplace across the continent (Virdee, 1995: 6–10). These developments have raised further concerns about the dangers to Britain's minority ethnic citizens in Europe and generated speculation that pan-European forms of organization might emerge among extreme right, racist political movements (cf. Ford, 1992). More recently still, increasing numbers of people seeking political asylum in the countries of the EU, including Britain, have generated new challenges and tensions (see the discussions in Favell, 1998; Joly, 1996).

None of these dangers should be underestimated, nor should their conse-quences for individuals and groups be minimized. Nevertheless, it is important also to recall that those in Britain who have sought to promote and perpetrate racist violence have rarely required pan-European encouragement. Although events in Britain have rarely reached the scale of some of the most serious incidents recently reported from Germany, racial violence and harassment has a long history in Britain (Commission for Racial Equality, 1987; Panayi, 1993; 1994; Virdee, 1997). Indeed, in some parts of the country, it has become so routine as to be only intermittently newsworthy (see also the discussion in Chapter 9).

More generally Miles (1994) has argued that the pervasiveness of racism in contemporary Europe does not necessarily justify some of the more doomsday-like scenarios which see the rise of a hegemonic pan-European racism. So far from being expressive of a qualitative increase in levels of racism, then, devel-opments over the last decade may be seen as expressive of a continuing thread of racism and ethnocentrism in European politics. As we have seen in this volume, such a thread has been well represented in the modern history of Britain. Moreover, Miles makes another point of considerable importance. This is that efflorescences of racism in Europe have typically been accompanied by counter political movements dedicated to anti-racism and resistance. This reminds us that people make their own history and that human beings are rarely wholly powerless. Failure to recognize this means that we may unwittingly absolve oppressors from responsibility for their actions and treat the oppressed as nothing more than passive, hapless victims (Gilroy, 1990).

Social mobility

It is not only in the relationship between Britain and the rest of the EU that both challenges and opportunities may be discerned. These may also be found in processes that are more clearly domestic. An area of particular importance is that of social mobility.

The Census data reviewed in Chapter 5, the Policy Studies Institute (PSI) analysis of Labour Force Survey data (Jones, 1993) and the fourth PSI survey of ethnic minorities (Modood et al., 1997) have all provided evidence of an increasing differentiation of labour market experiences among Britain's ethnic minority citizens. The growth of a middle class of professional and managerial workers among at least some minority ethnic communities has led some to suggest that there is under-way an increasing convergence in the class structures of some groups towards that of the white population. However, the patterns are complex and should be approached with some degree of caution. In particular we should be wary of concluding, as have some on the political right, that the success of members of some groups gives the lie to the claim that discrimination lies at the root of differences in achievement and opportunity between groups (Honeyford, 1993). This is particularly important given that such progress as has been made has occurred alongside continuing evidence of discriminatory practices by employers.

There are several points that we should note. The first is that there remain marked differences in the situations of members of different ethnic groups. The evidence reviewed in Chapter 5 highlighted the particular plight of those of Pakistani and Bangladeshi descent who occupy the lowest positions in the labour market and also experience much higher levels of unemployment than other groups. Indeed continuing disparities in rates of exclusion from the labour market altogether must be borne in mind when considering the evidence of success of those in work, as must the differences between the experiences of women and men.

We also saw in Chapter 5 that, as well as differences between ethnic groups, there is also evidence of patterns of polarization occurring within ethnic categories. Thus, Jones (1993: 70) suggested that there was evidence that among groups such as those of Indian origin, apparently experiencing high rates of upward mobility, there may be a corresponding polarization under way with others in work entering an equally narrow band of jobs at the bottom of the labour market. There is, indeed, some evidence that similar processes may have characterized the experience of all groups in the 1980s (Field, 1987), with the result that it is difficult to unravel with any certainty the potential future implications. Moreover, there are also indications that the nature of both manual and non-manual occupations may be changing such that the clear-cut distinctions of the past may be becoming more uncertain (Modood, 1997b: 100). This, too, has implications for how we interpret the evidence on occupational mobility.

Finally, we should remind ourselves that upward mobility is not incompatible with continued occupational segregation. Not only may there be differences of level within broad occupational categories—such as those between senior and middle management[1]—but the kinds of enterprises in which people work have great significance. In this context, it is worth recalling that members of all minority ethnic groups are under-represented among managers of large enterprises.

New forms of exclusion

The title of this subsection may be misleading, reflecting not new *forms* of exclusion but newly *recognized*, but long-established, patterns. It may nevertheless help to make a critical point. As we have seen, at various points in this volume, the way in which things are measured exercises a decisive influence over the patterns that are discovered. Thus as long as official data worked with ethnic categories which relied upon the birthplace of heads of household, they were able to reveal little about the situation of UK born citizens of minority ethnic descent. Similarly, as long as crude distinctions were made between 'Asians' and 'West Indians', the true situation of those of Pakistani and Bangladeshi descent remained concealed.

Tariq Modood (1992: 27–45) has trenchantly attacked this kind of 'racial dualism' and has, in the process, drawn attention to an alternative way of conceptualizing the patterns of advantage and disadvantage experienced by Britain's minority ethnic citizens. Modood argues that what appears to be 'Asian' economic success in Britain is, in fact, success for those of Indian descent. In this respect, Modood's argument parallels other evidence emerging from the Labour Force Survey and the Census. However, Modood goes further, arguing that if we disaggregate groups in a different way, we find an alternative perspective on advantage and disadvantage. Thus, he argues, not all Indians are successful. Despite the economic advances made by many Indians, including many Gujeratis, those of rural Gujerati origin have been, relatively speaking, left behind. An important characteristic of this subgroup is that they are Muslims.[2] Moreover, they share not only religious affiliation but also a rural, educationally and economically deprived, background with Pakistanis and Bangladeshis. Modood's conclusion, then, is that 'by most socio-economic measures there is a major divide between Sunni Muslims on the one hand and the other Asians, and that this divide is as great as between Asian [sic] and whites, or between Asians and blacks' (1992: 33).

Modood's argument is an interesting and important one. In point of fact, since census data have not hitherto been collected using the categories he proposes, it is difficult to demonstrate with any precision. (However we should note that the 2001 Census will collect data on religious affiliation as well as ethnicity.) It is nevertheless highly plausible. Most significantly, it highlights a general problem which has run throughout the account in this book. This is that the patterns revealed by data are in part a product of prior decisions about how to categorize people. These in turn reflect political judgements about which patterns are likely to be important and which groups are deserving of attention (Mason, 1992). Thus, despite a concern to represent the ethnic diversity of modern Britain, we have for much of the time been constrained, by the prior judgements and decisions of others, to focus on only a limited range of that diversity.

That political decision making is crucial to this process is revealed by the fact that there has been a growing recognition of the distinctive patterns of exclusion experienced by British Muslims. To a large extent, this has proceeded not from analyses such as Modood's but from a growing stigmatization of Muslims as unique and self-chosen outsiders. This process has characterized not only Britain but also other parts of Europe (Joly, 1995; see also the discussion in Abedin and Sardar, 1995). Thus in Germany the outsider status of Turks is not unrelated to their Muslim religion (Wilpert, 1991), while in France demands for religious recognition by Muslims have been characterized as a direct challenge to the secular principles of the constitution (Lloyd and Waters, 1991: 49–50). In Britain, a major influence upon developing anti-Muslim sentiment was the controversy surrounding the publication of Salman Rushdie's *The Satanic Verses* (Modood, 1990b). Across the West, Islamic revivalism and events such as the Gulf War have served to revitalize old Christian–Muslim rivalries and provided a focus for inter-ethnic hostility in countries such as Britain.

In these circumstances several outcomes are possible. One is that Muslims could become a focus for continued racist scapegoating, replacing earlier stigmatized groups, such as young African-Caribbean men, as the objects of popular and press demonology. The second is that the demand to be heard, initially over *The Satanic Verses*, could become the basis for an increasing self-assertion that might provide a vehicle for effective collective political organization. Such a development would no doubt arouse fears of all kinds in the population at large and would be characterized as a commitment to conflict rather than democratic participation. However the history of systems of racial and ethnic domination in Western societies suggests that it is often only when the oppressed organize to challenge prevailing patterns that change in their situation occurs. The civil rights movement in the United States, the history of the struggle against apartheid in South Africa, and the effect of the urban riots of the 1980s in Britain all suggest that, from the point of view of the disadvantaged, conflict can sometimes be productive.

In these circumstances, wresting the power to define oneself may be a key to turning policy in the direction of one's own benefit. Reconstituting the policy process in terms of the definitions chosen by citizens, including ethnic self-identities, may not easily give rise to harmony. Indeed, we would expect it to involve a sharpened and more explicit struggle for resources. At the same time it may be a test of a mature democracy that it can harness the potential inherent in the diversity that characterizes a modern, multi-ethnic society like Britain.

Changing ethnic identities? Challenging exclusion?

What evidence is there that ethnic identities in modern Britain are changing in these kinds of ways? We have seen that ethnicity is both a matter of self-identity ('we' statements) and of categorization ('they' statements). In practice, a variety of different characteristics go to make up the identities of all of us. Evidence from the fourth PSI survey shows that Britain's minority ethnic citizens call on a wide variety of cultural and other characteristics in defining their ethnic identities (Modood, 1997c: 290–338. See also Jacobson, 1997). However, identity and categorization do not proceed entirely independently of one another. In most societies some groups and individuals have a greater capacity than others to define the terms under which categorizations are made. As a consequence, self-identification takes place in contexts where others' categorizations to some extent constrain the choices that can realistically be made. In other words, if others do not accept one's identity choices it may, in practice, be difficult, if not impossible, to act out the implications of those choices.

These kinds of constraints may take the form of subtle social cues and messages that constrain behaviour. They may, however, take much more concrete forms as in the examples of the persistence of high levels of racial violence and the operation of immigration law. The result of these experiences is frequently that, notwithstanding their formal entitlement to full citizenship rights, many members of Britain's minority ethnic communities experience a sense of exclusion from the identity 'British'.

Having said this, it would equally be a mistake to believe that identities are static or that Britain's minority ethnic citizens are simply passive victims in the face of exclusion and racism. There are myriad examples ranging from self-help community organizations, through various forms of political mobilization, to the exemplary courage and persistence of the Lawrence family, of Britain's minority citizens challenging their exclusion. More subtly there is considerable evidence of a process of continuous change in the ways the identities of Britain's varied citizens are constructed and negotiated. Modood has attempted to capture the ways in which, for second and third generation members of minority ethnic groups in Britain, subtle and complex changes in patterns of ethnic identification have occurred. His analysis suggests that there is no straightforward relationship between 'the cultural content of an ethnicity and strategies of ethnic self-definition' (Modood, 1997c: 337). The result is a shift from what Modood calls 'behavioural difference' to an emphasis on 'associational identity'.

for many the strength of their ethnic identity was owed to a group pride in response to perceptions of racial exclusion and ethnic stereotyping by the white majority. The consequent sense of rejection and insecurity was instrumental in assertions of ethnic identities, often in forms susceptible to forging new anti-racist solidarities (such as 'black') and hyphenated (such as British-Pakistani) or even multiple identities. (Modood, 1997c: 337)

Modood is at pains to argue that the resultant identifications are not weaker than those of the first generation but differently constructed. They are, he suggests, much less taken for granted (based on shared cultural values) and more consciously chosen. They are publicly celebrated and debated and enter into a contested arena of identity politics. They are, as a result, potentially fluid and may change with political and other circumstances. They may, in the process, either revive old cultural practices or generate new ones (Modood, 1997c: 337).

It is appropriate, at this point, to note that much recent work in sociology has argued that, in the modern world, *all* identities are more fluid, provisional, and multi-faceted than some more traditional characterizations of cultural difference would suggest. We may identify two broad bodies of literature from which these kinds of arguments have developed.

One of the earliest challenges came from feminist scholars and activists who, from the early 1980s onwards began to challenge what were described as essentialized conceptions of woman. Some of these challenges came from black feminists who challenged what they saw as the dominance of white middle-class perspectives and argued that patriarchal oppression was mediated by racism in ways which made the experience and opportunities of black and white women quite different. More recently, other writers in the feminist tradition have challenged the essentialization of ethnic difference, arguing that ethnicity is gendered in ways which both differentiate the experience of men and women but which are also constitutive of ethnic difference. Anthias and Yuval-Davis have argued, for example, that women play a vital role not only in the physical and cultural reproduction of ethnicities but also in marking their symbolic boundaries (1992: 113–15).

A second source for the recognition of the provisionality and negotiability of identity is to be found in post-modernist and post-structuralist writing. According to this view the pace of change in the (post)modern world, together with an ever-expanding array of choices and possibilities, creates conditions in which individuals are increasingly freed to make multiple identity choices which match the purposes (or even the whims) of the moment. (For a useful discussion of these issues see Bradley, 1999: 21–7; see also Rattansi and Westwood, 1994.)

It will be apparent from what is said above about the relationship between choice and constraint that I am sceptical about the more extreme versions of this kind of perspective. Nevertheless, as we have seen, there is some evidence that Britain's young minority ethnic citizens do perceive a wider range of identity options than some of the more rigid characterizations of ethnic difference may suggest. (For an historical analysis of the changing patterning of identity among Britain's minority ethnic citizens see Luthra, 1997: 9–64. See also Jacobson, 1997.)

It is difficult to deny the power of accounts that recognize the dynamism of ethnic identity in modern Britain. They are, after all, consistent with the conception of ethnicity (discussed above) that recognizes the significance of the boundary process. Moreover they also challenge the simplistic victimology which has all too frequently characterized discussions of ethnic inequalities in Britain. On the other hand they also present a potential problem. When we take these insights together with the evidence reviewed above about increasing social mobility, it is all too easy to make the mistake of assuming that social divisions based on ethnicity are, if not a thing of the past, at least on the way to solution. As the evidence above demonstrates, however, measured by material inequalities and differences of treatment, this is far from yet being the case.

The difficulty arises not simply because of a debate about the meaning of the evidence, or even the pace of change. There is a more fundamental difficulty arising from the clash of modernist and postmodernist perspectives. Concern with social divisions based on material inequalities is firmly located within a modernist world view. From whatever theoretical perspective it is approached, there is an implicit acceptance that social divisions are problematic. This may be because they are thought to undermine some minimum common standard—expressed in such notions as equality, citizenship, or human rights. Alternatively, it may be because they are perceived to threaten social cohesion either by undermining shared value systems (anomie) or by encouraging political dissent. Thus whether inequalities are to be challenged or justified, there is a common belief that solutions are available in the form of political and social action.

By contrast, for postmodernist writers the old theoretical and political per-spectives underpinning these traditional approaches are no longer tenable in a world characterized by diversity, fluidity, and fragmentation. Abandoning faith in such certainties, postmodernism is more likely to move to a celebration of difference rather than to detect in it signs of social decay. In its extreme forms, postmodernism represents a celebration of choice and the triumph of style. Even in its less triumphalist guise, however, it identifies in the diverse identity options open to individuals in the modern world, the opportunity to challenge the stereotyping and categorization all too often characteristic of the behaviour of 'ethnic majorities' (see the discussion in Jenkins, 1997: 29–30). It thus celebrates rather than problematizing difference.

The difficulty with this is that while it may be easy to agree that ethnic diversity in modern Britain should be viewed positively—as something con-tributing to the richness of the lives of all citizens—all too often difference has been seen as problematic. Indeed, as we have seen, even when it gives rise to positive assertions of identity, 'difference' has frequently been a product of exclusionary processes and practices. Thus challenges to the essentialization of the ethnic categories can also become challenges to the processes of monitor-ing and measurement which have been central to tracking inequalities between ethnic groups and, hence, providing the evidential base for challenging them.

Is there a solution to this apparent impasse? Tariq Modood has suggested that the way forward lies with a conception of equality that recognizes:

the right to have one's 'difference' recognized and supported in both the public and the private spheres. (1997c: 358)

It implies, he argues, common rights and responsibilities and, in the end, a renewal of concepts of Britishness within which currently negative views of difference are framed. We need, he argues:

to develop a more plural approach to racial disadvantage, and to formulate an explicit ideal of multicultural citizenship appropriate to Britain in the next decade and beyond. (1997c: 359).

But herein lies the dilemma. Without the capacity to measure the patterning of material inequalities and differences of treatment among Britain's minority ethnic groups, how will it be possible to know whether progress has been made in reducing disadvantage? Such measurement must, by definition, use some set of categories in terms of which data can be collected. However sensitive we seek to be to people's self-definitions, any category system runs the risk of failing to capture the richness and complexity of people's identity choices. There is, then, a danger that we may reproduce the very divisions we seek to problematize.

Conclusion

My overall conclusion, then, has not changed significantly since the first edition of this volume. It is that there lie ahead a variety of trends, challenges, and opportunities for all Britain's citizens. They are all potentially Janus faced in their implications. Ultimately the choice is stark. Difference can continue to be seen as a problem, imposing costs and demanding choices of allegiance. Alternatively, diversity can be embraced as a positive contribution to the well-being and citizenship of all. Both courses involve meeting challenges. However, as events in Bosnia-Herzogovina, and more recently in Kosovo, show with tragic clarity, the failure to choose wisely may lead to an abyss from which no one returns unscathed.

Further reading

Not Easy Being British by Tariq Modood (1992) poses a number of challenges to some orthodox positions and assumptions. He is particularly concerned to emphasize the distinctiveness of the experience of British Muslims. His arguments raise difficult questions about how we conceptualize change and how we comprehend the commonalities and differences in the experiences of members of different groups.

Ethnic Minorities in Britain (1997) by Tariq Modood *et al.* provides evidence of change in both material circumstances and identity choices. Modood's analysis in chapters 9 and 10 offers an interpretation of the patterns revealed.

Britain's Black Population (1997) by Mohan Luthra offers an alternative perspective on some of these developments.

Notes

Notes to Chapter 2

1. Domestic influences were also important. See Lorimer (1978).

2. The systematic racialized divisions embodied in the apartheid system constructed in South Africa after 1948 are probably the most striking demonstration.

3. Looked at in this way, then, there can be no such thing as 'good race relations' since racism is intrinsic to the social relationship 'race'. Indeed the very term 'race relations' is problematic (though not merely for the reason that Miles argues—see 1982: 22–43). This is because, if race is a social relationship, the notion of race relations is a tautology.

4. There are, in fact, a number of different formulations of the idea of a 'new racism'. Thus Barker (1981) is concerned with the development of sociobiological notions which stress the alleged naturalness of group exclusiveness. This usage of the concept has been well criticized by Miles (1989). Balibar (1991), by contrast, emphasizes notions of cultural incompatibility. I am more concerned here with the latter. Nevertheless, this diversity in usage of what is intended to be a subtype of the generic concept of racism should alert us to a potential problem.

5. For more extended discussions of this term see Mason (1991) and (1992).

6. An example of this kind of reasoning in a British context can be found in an observation made, some years ago, by the British Conservative politician Enoch Powell: 'Ministers have increasingly of late permitted themselves to place in the sovereign's mouth speeches which suggest that . . . she is more concerned for the susceptibilities and prejudices of a vociferous minority of newcomers than for the great mass of her subjects whose stake and title in their kingdom is coeval with her own' (*The Times*, 21 January 1984: 3).

7. Again for more extended discussions see Mason, 1990a; 1991; and 1992.

8. I am conscious of the objection that this usage can itself be seen as part of a negative valuation of all that is not white. It is for precisely this reason that I prefer to avoid the more common formulation 'non-whites' and to use instead a term which emphasizes that we are speaking of people with rights and needs. Moreover, I contend that it is only appropriate to use this formulation on those limited occasions where the focus is on exclusionary practices and structures. On other occasions I prefer terms which emphasize diversity as a positive, and multi-faceted, feature of the demography of modern Britain. For a discussion of the rationale for this usage see Mason (1990a).

9. For an attempt to problematize the concept 'white' see Bonnett (1993).

10. For an extended discussion of the concept 'white' see Gabriel (1998). For a discussion of the limitations of the category in capturing variations in experience among those so designated, see Aspinal (1998).

Notes to Chapter 3

1. Fryer notes, however, that there were Africans in Britain before the English, 'a division of Moors' having served with the Roman army of occupation (Fryer, 1984: 1)

2. It should be noted that although the 1991 Census contained a question about ethnic origin for the first time, 'Irish' did not feature among the categories offered. This was a source of some controversy among sectors of the Irish-descended population and a campaign was launched to change the policy. As a result 1991 Census data are capable of providing information only on those born in, or who live in households headed by someone who was born in, the Irish Republic. These data are discussed in Chapter 4. Following a review of the Census questions, a decision has been taken to include 'Irish' as a category in the 2001 Census.

3. The term New Commonwealth is a euphemism for the countries of the former British empire populated by people whose skin colour is not white. The New Commonwealth is thus distinguished from the Old Commonwealth, the countries comprising which are thought of as having predominantly white populations. The term 'New' is justified largely on the grounds that the countries so designated attained independence after the Second World War, in contrast to Australia, Canada, and New Zealand, which had been granted effective self-government much earlier. The convolutions entailed in this usage are well illustrated by the fact that when Pakistan left the Commonwealth in 1972, it was necessary to revise the term to 'New Commonwealth and Pakistan'. This is often rendered as NCWP.

4. Good discussions of the politics of immigration control are to be found in Holmes (1988), Layton-Henry (1992), Saggar (1992), and (Spencer, 1997).

5. The Act may be seen as a product of a number of impulses, including the desire to tap sources of labour and a continuing romantic attachment to the idea of empire as a family of people sharing common rights.

6. For a discussion of the circumstances surrounding this episode, see Twaddle (1975).

7. It has, in fact, been the subject of detailed amendment by the Immigration Act of 1988. This introduced a number of changes which, it has been argued (Platt, 1990) were generally disadvantageous to members of minority ethnic groups.

8. Limited concessions were offered to wealthier members of the Hong Kong Chinese community in the wake of the agreement to return the territory to Chinese jurisdiction.

Notes to Chapter 4

1. In the analysis of the data derived from the 1991 Census, it became clear that there were problems with the categories used. In particular, they did not adequately allow those with 'mixed' ethnic origins to identify themselves, they made no explicit provision for those who wished to embrace both a British and another identity (as, for example, Black British) and they did not permit a

disaggregation of the white category. Proposed revisions to the categories for the 2001 Census are intended to address these problems. It would be an illusion, however, to imagine that other issues will not then arise. See the discussion in Dale and Holdsworth (1997).

2. The discussion of 1991 Census data which follows is largely derived from the analyses by Dr David Owen published as Census Statistical Papers by the Centre for Research in Ethnic Relations (see Owen, 1992; 1993*a*, *b*, *c*, *d*; 1994). The data themselves are Crown copyright and are made available to the academic community through the ESRC purchase.

3. At the same time, we should note that these people represented less than half the total population of those classified as members of New Commonwealth descended ethnic minorities. Moreover some 15 per cent of those born in the New Commonwealth were white (Owen, 1993*d*: 2 and 19).

4. We should also note that nothing has been said here about those long-standing national and ethnic differences within the British population which are associated with Scots, Welsh, English, and Cornish origins and identities. Nor have we addressed the situation of Gypsies who some would argue are one of the most excluded minority groups in Britain (see Hawes and Perez, 1995).

Notes to Chapter 5

1. Citizenship is discussed at more length in Chapter 10.

2. In this table the percentages of economically active and inactive persons do not sum to 100 because they are calculated using different bases. Thus the economically active are expressed as a percentage of those aged 16–64 for men or 16–59 for women. The economically inactive are expressed as a percentage of all those over 16. This procedure has been adopted to avoid distortions of the comparison of white with minority ethnic inactivity rates that would otherwise arise from the radically different age structures of the respective populations. Given the very substantial proportion of economically inactive white people who are retired, restricting the calculation to those of working age would artificially depress the white inactivity rate.

3. It is not possible in the course of a brief discussion of this kind to deal adequately with a subject as complex as homeworking. Not only is the range of activity that the term covers large and diverse but people—men and women—undertake it for a variety of reasons. Moreover, key issues distinguishing different kinds and conditions of homeworking are the economic circumstances and relative profitability of the industries and firms employing it. In focusing here on the potentially exploitative character of homeworking there is no intention to characterize those undertaking it as merely, and always, hapless victims. Nor is it intended to suggest that homeworking is identified in some simplistic way with 'ethnic minorities'. For detailed discussions of these issues see Allen and Wolkowitz (1987), especially chapter 3, and Felstead and Jewson (1996 and 1999).

4. In this connection we should note that recent research has indicated that Asian minorities are significantly underrepresented among applicants for, and entrants to, nurse and midwifery education (Iganski *et al.* 1998).

Notes to Chapter 6

1. Note that the data used by the PSI analysis differ somewhat from Jones's in terms of their coverage.

2. Until recently, the British higher education system was divided between polytechnics and universities. In 1992 polytechnics acquired the right to become universities and almost all dropped the designation 'polytechnic'. Since this date there has been considerable convergence within the sector but there also remain differences of organization, tradition, and resourcing which coincide to a considerable degree with the old binary divide. Perhaps more significantly, there are clear differences of prestige between pre- and post-1992 universities that are reflected in their attractiveness to potential students and in public estimations of the worth of their awards.

3. It is important to note that the size of the differences in qualification level between members of different groups depends to some degree on how they are measured. The Youth Cohort Study for example (Drew *et al.*, 1992) found a larger disparity than the LFS. For a discussion of the reasons for these differences see Jones, 1993: 36–7.

4. Drew has argued that the variables traditionally interrogated in studies of underachievement, ethnicity, gender, and socio-economic group, together explain relatively little (just over ten per cent) of the overall variation in examination performance.

5. The question of school effects has been one that has been vigorously debated. See, for example, Gillborn and Drew (1992), Drew (1995), and Hammersley and Gomm (1993).

6. See the special issue of *New Community* on the Education Reform Act, 16(3), April 1990.

7. A number of commentators have suggested that this initiative was born more out of concern to boost the numbers of schools applying for grant maintained status than out of concern for the needs of minority ethnic groups. Nevertheless, it does indicate the extent to which the reforms have at least the potential to offer new forms of response to community needs.

8. Interestingly, the fourth PSI survey found that fewer than half (48 per cent) of Muslim respondents supported the existence of religious schools within the state sector (Modood, 1997c: 325).

Notes to Chapter 7

1. For a general discussion of the political economy of housing in the post-war period see Dunleavy (1981).

2. For a more sophisticated and complex account see Ratcliffe (1981).

3. To some extent these variations may reflect culturally determined housing preferences as well as market conditions and the availability of capital (Robinson, 1989: 262).

4. In some cases, families purchased and shared property in order to meet the special needs posed by large families. It should also be noted that not all of those

who purchased property in this way were seeking to satisfy their own housing need. Some were entrepreneurs 'whose actions may be grounded almost solely in the profit motive' (Ratcliffe, 1981: 147).

5. It should be not be assumed that relatively lower levels of owner-occupation among African-Caribbean people are simply a matter of preference. There has long been evidence of a strong aspiration for home ownership among members of this group (Ratcliffe, 1981: 158).

6. Leaving aside the fact that such policies are intrinsically discriminatory, distinguishing between people as they do on grounds of skin colour or ethnicity, a potentially serious additional consequence is that they may make people particularly vulnerable to racial harassment and attacks.

7. The fourth PSI survey also produced data on housing circumstances which confirms many of the observations below and which provides a more detailed analysis (Lakey, 1997. See also the analyses in Karn, 1997).

8. It might, of course, be argued that this difference is largely a product of the different relative sizes of the groups involved in the two societies (Smith, 1989: 38).

9. For general discussions see Edwards and Batley (1978); McGregor and Pimlott (1990); Robson (1987); Prestwich and Taylor (1990); Smith (1989: 67–77).

Notes to Chapter 8

1. It is no accident that one of the first areas in which citizens' charters were developed was that of the National Health Service, while possession of the formal status of a British citizen is a prerequisite of access to National Health Service care.

2. In this connection it also worth noting how influential have been culturalist explanations of class differences in health (Townsend and Davidson, 1982).

3. At the height of the campaign for immigration control in the 1960s, it was frequently claimed that New Commonwealth immigrants were introducing diseases such as leprosy, tuberculosis (Foot, 1965: 9 and 16), and smallpox (Holmes, 1988: 261).

4. Publicity surrounding the high rates of schizophrenia apparently diagnosed among people of African-Caribbean descent may be a case in point here.

5. Oppenheim (1993) notes that the social security system also operates to reinforce poverty among members of minority ethnic groups. See also Storey (1986) and Collins and Storey (1983).

6. For a useful review of these issues see Parsons et al. (1993)

7. I have used this phrase to cover a potentially complex range of patterns that cannot be fully explored here. However, medical science distinguishes four different phenomena in this connection. Thus 'infant mortality' refers to death in the first year of life, 'perinatal mortality' refers to stillbirth or death in the first week of life, 'neonatal mortality' refers to death in the first 28 days of life and 'postneonatal mortality' refers to death between 28 days and a year.

8. Vitamin D is known to be synthesized in the body as a result of exposure to ultra-violet light.

9. For useful reviews, see Bhat *et al.* (1988: 194–200); Donovan (1986: 56–9); Pilgrim and Rogers (1993); Sashidharan and Francis (1993); Smaje (1995); and Westwood *et al.* (1989).

10. The authors also offer a critique of the quality of currently available data and ethnic monitoring categories and suggest alternative measures which may be more sensitive to the complexity of illness causation.

11. For useful discussions, see McNaught (1988, chapter 2) and Ward (1993).

Notes to Chapter 9

1. It is important to note that there may be significant weaknesses in the quality of the data relied upon by the Home Office. Thus, much police data is dependent on decisions about whether and how to record events of various kinds. Moreover, ethnic comparisons are made unreliable by different procedures adopted in different parts of the criminal justice system for recording ethnic origin. Thus the police are more likely to utilize classification based on appearance, the Probation Service to use self-classifications, and the prison service a mixture of these methods. This has obvious implications for the comparability of data (see Fitzgerald and Sibbitt, 1997; Home Office, 1998).

2. For a discussion of the particular problems encountered by black women in the criminal justice system see Agozino (1997).

3. See Cashmore and McLaughlin (1991).

4. Concerns about the number of deaths of minority ethnic prisoners in custody probably represent the most dramatic examples. See Institute of Race Relations (1991).

Notes to Chapter 10

1. We should also note that some of the rights available to citizens may also be available, either *de jure* or *de facto*, to non-citizens. Thus aliens may be entitled to civil rights in the form of a fair trial. Such rights may be guaranteed by provisions such as the United Nations Convention on Human Rights. Citizens of other states, perhaps as result of bilateral or other arrangements, may have reciprocal access to some social rights such as health care. This last situation characterizes the position in Britain of citizens of other states of the European Union. For a discussion of some of these issues, see Bauböck (1991).

2. For a fuller discussion of the political and economic context of these developments see Jewson and Mason (1994); Layton-Henry (1992); Saggar (1992: 172–96).

3. See, for example, Mrs Thatcher's comments in 1978 about people's fears of 'swamping' (Layton-Henry, 1992: 184). Sally Tomlinson also quotes a Conservative Education Minister saying, in a speech to HMI in 1986: 'I believe that in areas where there are few or no members of ethnic minority groups, there is a genuine and not dishonourable fear that British values and

traditions—the very stuff of school education—are likely to be put at risk if too much allowance is made for the cultural backgrounds and attitudes of ethnic minorities' (1990: 27).

4. For discussions of the ways in which conceptions of British nationality exclude those defined as 'ethnic minorities' see Anthias and Yuval Davis (1992, especially chapter 2) and Gilroy (1987).

5. For a discussion of the potentials and pitfalls of these trends see Mason and Jewson (1992); Jewson and Mason (1994). See also the discussion in Chapter 11.

6. Nobody who has visited UK military establishments, such as the Royal Military Academy at Sandhurst, can be unimpressed by the weight of history and tradition to be found there.

7. The debate surrounding the publication of Salman Rushdie's *The Satanic Verses* is a good example of the problems posed.

Notes to Chapter 11

1. Compare the experience of women in this connection (Cockburn, 1991).

2. More precisely, Modood argues they are Sunni Muslims (the majority sect) as against Shia Muslims who, he argues, have experienced greater success.

Bibliography

ABEDIN, SYED Z., and SARDAR, ZIAUDDIN (eds.) (1995), *Muslim Minorities in the West*, London, Grey Seal.

AGOZINO, BIKO (1997), *Black Women and the Criminal Justice System*, Aldershot, Avebury.

AHMAD, W. I. U. (1992), 'The maligned healer: the "hakim" and western medicine', *New Community*, 18(4): 521–36.

—— (1993a), 'Introduction', in Ahmad (1993b).

—— (ed.) (1993b), *'Race' and Health in Contemporary Britain*, Buckingham, Open University Press.

ALLEN, S., and WOLKOWITZ, C. (1987), *Homeworking: Myths and Realities*, Basingstoke, Macmillan.

ANDREWS, A., and JEWSON, N. (1993), 'Ethnicity and infant deaths: the implications of recent statistical evidence for materialist explanations', *Sociology of Health and Illness*, 15(2): 137–56.

ANIONWU, E. (1993), 'Sickle cell and thalassaemia: community experiences and official response', in Ahmad (1993b).

—— (1996), 'Ethnic origin of sickle cell and thalassaemia counsellors', in Kelleher and Hillier (1996).

ANTHIAS, F. (1990), 'Race and class revisited: conceptualising race and racisms', *Sociological Review*, 38(1): 19–42.

—— (1992), 'Connecting "race" and ethnic phenomena', *Sociology*, 26(3): 421–38.

—— and YUVAL-DAVIS, N. (1992), *Racialized Boundaries: Race, Nation, Gender, Colour and Class and the Anti-racist Struggle*, London, Routledge.

ASPINAL, PETER J. (1998), 'Describing the "white" ethnic group and its composition in medical research', *Social Science and Medicine*, 47(11): 1797–1808.

BALIBAR, E. (1991), 'Is there a "neo-racism"?', in Etienne Balibar and Immanuel Wallerstein, *Race, Nation, Class: Ambiguous Identities*, London, Verso.

BALLARD, R. (1992), 'New clothes for the Emperor? The conceptual nakedness of the race relations industry in Britain', *New Community*, 18(3): 481–92.

BANDARANYAKE, R. (1986), 'Ethnic differences in health: an epidemiological perspective', in Rathwell and Phillips (1986).

BANTON, MICHAEL (1959), *White and Coloured*, London, Cape.

—— (1967), *Race Relations*, London, Tavistock.

—— (1970), 'The concept of racism', in Sami Zubaida (ed.), *Race and Racialism*, London, Tavistock.

—— (1977), *The Idea of Race*, London, Tavistock.

—— (1987), *Racial Theories*, Cambridge, Cambridge University Press.

—— (1988), *Racial Consciousness*, London, Longman.

—— and HARWOOD, J. (1975), *The Race Concept*, Newton Abbot, David & Charles.

BARKER, M. (1981), *The New Racism*, London, Junction Books.

BARRETT, GILES A. (1999), 'Overcoming the obstacles? Access to bank finance for African-Caribbean enterprise', *Journal of Ethnic and Migration Studies*, 25(2): 303–22.

BARRITT, D. P., and CARTER, C. F. (1972), *The Northern Ireland Problem: A Study in Group Relations*, Oxford, Oxford University Press.

BARTH, F. (ed.) (1969), *Ethnic Groups and Boundaries*, Bergen, Universitetsforlaget.

BAXTER, CAROL (1997), *Race Equality in Health Care and Education*, London, Baillière Tindall.

BAUBÖCK, R. (1991), 'Migration and citizenship', *New Community*, 18(1): 27–48.

BEISHON, SHARON, VIRDEE, SATNAM, and HAGELL, ANN (1995), *Nursing in a Multi-Ethnic NHS*, London, Policy Studies Institute.

BENYON, J. (1986), *A Tale of Failure: Race and Policing*, University of Warwick, Centre for Research in Ethnic Relations.

—— and SOLOMOS, J. (1990), 'Race, Injustice and Disorder', in McGregor and Pimlott (1990).

BERTHOUD, R. (1997), 'Income and Standards of Living', in Modood *et al.* (1997).

—— (1998), *The Incomes of Ethnic Minorities*, ISER Report 98–1, Colchester, University of Essex, Institute for Social and Economic Research.

BHAT, A., CARR-HILL, R., and OHRI, S. (1988), *Britain's Black Population: A New Perspective*, 2nd edn., Radical Statistics Race Group, Aldershot, Gower.

Birmingham City Council, Race Relations Unit (1991), *1992 and Race Equality: Fact Pack*, Birmingham, Birmingham City Council, Race Relations Unit.

BISSET, L., and HUWS, U. (n.d.), *Sweated Labour: Homeworking in Britain Today*, London, Low Pay Unit.

BJÖRGO, T., and WITTE, R. (1993), *Racist Violence in Europe*, Basingstoke, Macmillan.

BLACKBURN, CLARE (1991), *Poverty and Health: Working with Families*, Milton Keynes, Open University Press.

BOHPAL, R., and WHITE, M. (1993), 'Health promotion for ethnic minorities: past, present and future', in Ahmad (1993*b*).

BONNETT, ALASTAIR (1993), 'Forever "white"? Challenge and alternative to a "racial" monolith', *New Community*, 20(1): 173–80.

BOURNE, JENNY, BRIDGES, LEE, and SEARLE, CHRIS (1994) *Outcast England: How Schools Exclude Black Children*, London, Institute of Race Relations.

BOWES, ALISON, McCLUSKEY, JACQUI, and SIM, DUNCAN (1991), 'Ethnic minorities and housing in Glasgow: from research to action', in Bowes and Sim (1991).

BOWES, ALISON, and SIM, DUNCAN (eds.) (1991), *Ethnic Minorities and Social Services in Scotland*, Edinburgh, Scottish Council for Voluntary Organizations.

—— —— (1997), *Perspectives on Welfare: The Experience of Minority Ethnic Groups in Scotland*, Aldershot, Ashgate.

BOWLER, I. (1993), ' "They're not the same as us": Midwives' stereotypes of South Asian descent maternity patients', *Sociology of Health and Illness*, 15(2): 157–78.

BRADLEY, H. (1996), *Fractured Identities*, Oxford, Polity Press.

BRAHAM, P., RATTANSI, A., and SKELLINGTON, R. (eds.) (1992), *Racism and Anti-racism: Inequalities, Opportunities and Policies*, London, Sage.

BREWER, C. (1992), 'Sushi and sake but no pickled brains', *Independent*, 24 August: 11.

British Broadcasting Corporation (BBC) (1997), *Election 97: Constituency Guide 1997*, London, BBC Political Research Unit.

British Military Studies Group (BMSG) (1991), *Women in the Armed Forces: Britain in Comparative Perspective*, London, BMSG

BROOKS, D. (1975), *Race and Labour in London Transport*, London, Oxford University Press.

—— and SINGH, K. (1979), 'Pivots and Presents', in Wallman (ed.) (1979a).

BROWN, COLIN (1984), *Black and White Britain: The Third PSI Survey*, Aldershot, Gower.

—— and GAY, P. (1985), *Racial Discrimination: 17 Years after the Act*, London, Policy Studies Institute.

BUTLER, DAVID, and KAVANAGH, DENNIS (1997), *The British General Election of 1997*, Basingstoke, Macmillan

CARBY, HAZEL (1982), 'Schooling in Babylon', in Centre for Contemporary Cultural Studies (1982).

CARMICHAEL, S., and HAMILTON, C. V. (1968), *Black Power: The Politics of Liberation in America*, London, Jonathan Cape.

CARTER, B., and WILLIAMS, J. (1987), 'Attacking racism in education', in Troyna (1987).

CARTER, E., *et al.* (1990), 'Material deprivation and its association with childhood hospital admission in the East End of London', *Community Medicine*, 15(6).

CARTER, JOHN, FENTON, STEVE, and MODOOD, TARIQ (1999), *Ethnicity and Employment in Higher Education*, London, Policy Studies Institute.

CASHMORE, E., and MCLAUGHLIN, E. (eds.) (1991), *Out of Order? Policing Black People*, London, Routledge.

CASTLES, S. (1984), *Here for Good: Western Europe's New Ethnic Minorities*, London, Pluto Press (with Heather Booth and Tina Wallace).

—— and MILLER, M. J. (1993), *The Age of Migration: International Populations Movements in the Modern World*, Basingstoke, Macmillan.

Centre for Contemporary Cultural Studies (1982), *The Empire Strikes Back*, London, Hutchinson.

CESARANI, DAVID (1996), 'The changing character of nationality and citizenship in Britain', in Cesarani and Fulbrook (1996).

—— and FULBROOK, MARY (eds.) (1996), *Citizenship, Nationality and Migration in Europe*, London, Routledge

CHELES, L., FERGUSSON, R., and VAUGHAN, M. (eds.) (1991), *Neo-Fascism in Europe*, London, Longman.

CHEVANNES, M., and REEVES, F. (1987), 'The black voluntary school movement: definition, context, and prospects', in Troyna (1987).

CHIVERS, T. S. (ed.) (1987), *Race and Culture in Education: Issues Arising from the Swann Committee Report*, Windsor, NFER-NELSON Publishing Company.

COARD, B. (1971), *How the West Indian Child is Made Educationally Sub-normal in Our Schools*, London, New Beacon Books.

COCKBURN, C. (1991), *In the Way of Women*, Basingstoke, Macmillan.

COHEN, P., and GARDNER, C. (1982), *It Ain't Half Racist Mum: Fighting Racism in the Media*, London, Comedia.

COHEN, ROBIN (1994), *Frontiers of Identity: the British and the Others*, London, Longman.

COLEMAN, D., and SALT, J. (eds.) (1996), *Ethnicity in the 1991 Census, i: Demographic Characteristics of the Ethnic Minority Populations*, London, HMSO.

COLLEY, L. (1992), *Britons: Forging the Nation 1701–1837*, New Haven, Conn.: Yale University Press.

COLLINS, W., and STOREY, H. (1983), *Immigrants and the Welfare State*, London, NACAB.

Commission of the European Communities (1992), *Legal Instruments to Combat Racism and Xenophobia*, Brussels, Commission of the European Communities.

Commission for Racial Equality (1982), *Massey Fergusson Perkins Ltd.: Report of a Formal Investigation*, London, CRE.

—— (1984), *Race and Council Housing in Hackney*, London, CRE.

—— (1985), *Immigration Control Procedures: The Report of a Formal Investigation*, London, CRE.

—— (1986), *Race and Housing in Liverpool: A Research Report*, London, CRE (revised edition).

—— (1987), *Racial Attacks: A Survey in Eight Areas of Britain*, London, CRE.

—— (1988a), *Learning in Terror: A Survey of Racial Harassment in Schools and Colleges*, London, CRE.

—— (1988b), *Report of a Formal Investigation into St George's Hospital Medical School*, London, CRE.

—— (1990), *Sorry, It's Gone: Testing for Racial Discrimination in the Private Rented Housing Sector*, London, CRE.

—— (1991), *NHS Contracts and Racial Equality: A Guide*, London, CRE.

—— (1996) *Report of a formal investigation into the Ministry of Defence (Household Cavalry)*, London: CRE.

CROSS, C. (1978), *Ethnic Minorities in the Inner City: The Ethnic Dimension in Urban Deprivation in England*, London, CRE.

CROSS, M., WRENCH, J., and BARNETT, S. (1990), *Ethnic Minorities and the Careers Service: An Investigation into Processes of Assessment and Placement*, London, Department of Employment Research Paper, No. 73.

CURTICE, JOHN, and STEED, MICHAEL (1997), 'Appendix 2. The Results Analysed', in Butler and Kavanagh (1997).

CURTIS, L. P. (1971), *Apes and Angels: The Irishman in Victorian Caricature*, London, David & Charles.

DALE, ANGELA, and MARSH, CATHERINE (eds.) (1993), *The 1991 Census Users' Handbook*, London, HMSO.

—— and HOLDSWORTH, CLARE (1997), 'Issues in the analysis of ethnicity in the 1991 British Census', *Ethnic and Racial Studies*, 20(1): 160–81

DALTON, MIKE (1991), 'Housing access: achieving racial equality', in Bowes and Sim (1991).

DANDEKER, CHRISTOPHER, and MASON, DAVID (1999) 'Diversity in the UK Armed Forces: The Debate About the Representation of Women and Minority Ethnic Groups', in Joseph Soeters and Jan van der Meulen (eds.) *Managing Diversity in the Armed Forces*, Tilburg, University of Tilburg Press.

—— and SEGAL, M. W. (1996), 'Gender Integration in Armed Forces: Recent Policy Developments in the United Kingdom', *Armed Forces and Society*, 23 (1): 29–47.

DANIEL, W. W. (1968), *Racial Discrimination in England*, Harmondsworth, Penguin.

DARBY, J. (ed.) (1983), *Northern Ireland: The Background to the Conflict*, Belfast, Appletree Press.

DAVY-SMITH, G., BARTLEY, M., and BLAKE, D. (1990), 'The Black Report on socioeconomic inequalities in health 10 years on', *British Medical Journal*, 301: 373–7.

DEEM, ROSEMARY (1978), *Women and Schooling*, London, Routledge & Kegan Paul.

—— (ed.) (1980), *Schooling for Women's Work*, London, Routledge & Kegan Paul.

—— BREHONY, K., and HEMMINGS, S. (1992), 'Social justice, social divisions and the governing of schools', in Gill *et al.* (1992).

—— and HEATH, S. (1995) *Active Citizenship and the Governing of Schools*, Buckingham, Open University Press.

Defence Analytical Services Agency (DASA) (1999), *Ethnic Monitoring Quarterly Pocket Brief*, January.

Department of Education and Science (1985), *Education for All: The Report of a Committee of Inquiry in the Education of Children from Ethnic Minority Groups*, Cmnd 9453, London, HMSO.

Department of Health (1992), *The Health of the Nation: A Strategy for Health in England*, Cmnd 1523, London, HMSO, pp. 34–5, para 4.4–4.7.

DEX, S. (1978/9), 'Job search methods and ethnic discrimination', *New Community*, 7(1): 1–22.

DHOOGE, Y. (1981), *Ethnic Difference and Industrial Conflicts*, Birmingham, SSRC Research Unit on Ethnic Relations, Working Papers on Ethnic Relations, No. 13.

DONOVAN, J. (1986), *We don't Buy Sickness, It Just Comes*, Aldershot, Gower.

DOWNES, D. (ed.) (1992), *Unravelling Criminal Justice*, Basingstoke, Macmillan.

DREW, D. (1995), *'Race', Education and Work: The Statistics of Inequality*, Aldershot, Avebury

—— GRAY, J., and SIME, N. (1992), *Against the Odds: The Education and Labour Market Experiences of Black Young People*, Youth Cohort Study, London, Department of Employment.

DUFFIELD, MARK (1985), 'Rationalization and the Politics of Segregation: Indian Workers in Britain's Foundry Industry, 1945–62', in Lunn (ed.) (1985).

DUMMETT, A. (ed.) (1986), *Towards a Just Immigration Policy*, London, Cobden Trust.

DUNLEAVY, P. (1981), *The Politics of Mass Housing in Britain 1945–75*, Oxford, The Clarendon Press.

EDWARDS, J. (1987), *Positive Discrimination, Social Justice and Social Policy*, London, Tavistock.

—— and BATLEY, R. (1978), *The Politics of Positive Discrimination: An Evaluation of the Urban Programme, 1967–77*, London, Tavistock.

EDWARDS, O. D. (1970), *The Sins of our Fathers: Roots of Conflict in Northern Ireland*, Dublin, Gill & Macmillan.

Employment Department (1991), *Equal Opportunities Ten Point Plan for Employers*, London, ED.

Equal Opportunities Review (1999), 'A war on racism in the Armed Forces', *EOR* 84, March/April: 21–5.

FANON, F. (1967), *Black Skin White Masks*, New York, Grove Press.

FARREL, M. (1976), *Northern Ireland: The Orange State*, London, Pluto Press.

FAULKS, KEITH (1998), *Citizenship in Modern Britain*, Edinburgh, Edinburgh University Press.

FAVELL ADRIAN (ed.) (1998), *The European Union: Immigration, Asylum and Citizenship*, *Journal of Ethnic and Migration Studies*, Special issue, 24(4).

FELSTEAD, ALAN, and JEWSON, NICK (1996), *Homeworkers in Britain*, London, HMSO

—— (1999), *In Work, At Home*, London, Routledge.

FEVRE, RALPH (1984), *Cheap Labour and Racial Discrimination*, Aldershot, Gower.

FIELD, S. (1987), 'The changing nature of racial discrimination', *New Community*, 14 (1/2): 118–22 .

FIELDING, STEPHEN, and GEDDES, ANDREW (1998), 'The British Labour Party and "ethnic entryism", participation, integration and the Party context', *Journal of Ethnic and Migration Studies*, 24 (1): 57–72.

FITZGERALD, MARIAN (1993), *Ethnic Minorities and the Criminal Justice System*, Home Office Research Study 20, The Royal Commission on Criminal Justice, London, HMSO.

—— and SIBBITT, RAE (1997), *Ethnic Monitoring in Police Forces: A Beginning*, Home Office Research Study 173, London, Home Office.

FOOT, P. (1965), *Immigration and Race in British Politics*, Harmondsworth, Penguin.

FORBES, I., and MEAD, G. (1992), *Measure for Measure: A Comparative Analysis of Measures to Combat Racial Discrimination in the Member Countries of the European Community*, Sheffield, Employment Department Research Series No. 1.

FORD, G. (1992), *Fascist Europe: The Rise of Racism and Xenophobia*, London, Pluto Press.

FREIDSON, ELIOT (1970), *Professional Dominance: The Social Structure of Medical Care*, New York, Aldine.

FRYER, PETER (1984), *Staying Power: The History of Black People in Britain*, London, Pluto Press.

GABRIEL, JOHN (1998), *Whitewash: Racialized Politics and the Media*, London, Routledge.

GAINE, CHRIS (1995), *Still No Problem Here*, Stoke on Trent, Trentham Books.

GEDDES, ANDREW (1993), 'Asian and Afro-Caribbean representation in elected local government in England and Wales', *New Community*, 20(1): 43–57.

GEERTZ, C, (1963), 'The integrative revolution: primordial sentiments and civil politics in the new states', in Geertz, C. (ed.), *Old Societies and New States*, New York, Free Press.

GENOVESE, E. (1968), 'On being a socialist and a historian', in *In Red and Black: Marxian Explorations in Southern and Afro-American History*, New York, Vintage Books.

GERRISH, KATE, HUSBAND, CHARLES, and MACKENZIE, JENNIFER (1996), *Nursing for a Multi-racial Society*, Buckingham, Open University Press.

GIBSON, D. (1987), 'Hearing and listening: a case study of the "consultation" process undertaken by a local education department and black groups', in Troyna (1987).

GILL, D., MAYOR, B., and BLAIR, M. (eds.) (1992), *Racism and Education: Structures and Strategies*, London, Sage.

GILLBORN, D. (1990), *'Race', Ethnicity and Education*, London, Unwin Hyman.

—— (1995) *Racism and Antiracism in Real Schools*, Buckingham, Open University Press.

—— and DREW, D. (1992), ' "Race", class and school effects', *New Community*, 18(4): 551–65.

GILLESPIE, JIM (1992), 'Legal decisions', *New Community*, 18(2): 326–31.

GILROY, P. (1987), *There Ain't No Black in the Union Jack*, London, Hutchinson.

—— (1990), 'The end of anti-racism', *New Community*, 17(1): 71–83.

GORDON, PAUL (1983), *White Law*, London Pluto Press.

—— (1985), *Policing Immigration; Britain's Internal Controls*, London, Pluto Press.

—— (1989), *Fortress Europe? The Meaning of 1992*, London, Runnymede Trust.

—— and NEWNHAM, ANNE (1985), *Passport to Benefits*, London, Child Poverty Action Group.

—— and ROSENBERG, DAVID (1989), *Daily Racism: The Press and Black People in Britain*, London, Runnymede Trust.

GRAY, PATRICK, ELGAR, JANE, and BALLY, SATYA (1993), *Access to Training and Employment for Asian Women in Coventry*, Coventry City Council, Economic Development Unit, Research Paper.

GREEN, ANNE, (1997) 'Patterns of ethnic minority employment in the context of industrial and occupational growth and decline', in Karn (ed.) (1997).

GROSVENOR, IAN (1997), *Assimilating Identities: Racism and Educational Policy in Post–1945 Britain*, London, Lawrence & Wishart.

GROVER, CHRIS, and SOOTHILL, KEITH (1996), 'Ethnicity, the search for rapists and the press', *Ethnic and Racial Studies*, 19(3): 567–84.

HAINSWORTH, P. (1998), *Divided Society: Ethnic Minorities and Racism in Northern Ireland*, London, Pluto Press.

HALL, S., CRITCHER, C., JEFFERSON, T., CLARKE, J., and ROBERTS, B. (1978), *Policing the Crisis*, London, Macmillan.

HAMMERSLEY, M., and GOMM, R. (1993), 'A reply to Gillborn and Drew on "race", class and school effects', *New Community*, 19(2): 348–53.

HARRISON, M. L. (1995), *Housing, 'Race', Social Policy and Empowerment*, Aldershot, Avebury.

HARTMAN, P., and HUSBAND, C. (1974), *Racism and the Media*, London, Davis-Poynter.

HAWES, DEREK, and PEREZ, BARBARA (1995), *The Gypsy and the State*, Bristol, SAUS.

HERBERT, D. T., and SMITH, D. J. (1989), *Social Problems and the City: New Perspectives*, Oxford, Oxford University Press.

HICKMAN, MARY J., and WALTER, Bronwen (1997), *Discrimination and the Irish Community in Britain*, London, Commission for Racial Equality.

HOLDAWAY, SIMON (1996), *The Racialization of British Policing*, Basingstoke, Macmillan.

—— (1997a), 'Constructing and sustaining "race" within the police workforce', *British Journal of Sociology*, 48(1): 19–34.

—— (1997b), 'Responding to racialized divisions with the workforce: the experience of black and Asian police officers in England', *Ethnic and Racial Studies*, 20(1): 69–90.

—— and BARRON, ANNE-MARIE (1997), *Resigners? The Experience of Black and Asian Police Officers*, Basingstoke, Macmillan.

HOLMES, COLIN (ed.) (1978), *Immigrants and Minorities in British Society*, London, George Allen & Unwin.

—— (1988), *John Bull's Island: Immigration and British Society, 1871–1971*, London, Macmillan.

Home Office (1998), *Statistics on Race and the Criminal Justice System*, London, Home Office.

—— (1999), *Race Equality—The Home Secretary's Employment Targets: Staff Targets for the Home Office, the Prison, the Police, the Fire and the Probation Services*, London, Home Office.

HONEYFORD, RAY (1993), 'Why are we still fed the myth that Britain is a racist society?', *Daily Mail*, 14 April.

HOOD, ROGER (1992), *Race and Sentencing*, Oxford, The Clarendon Press.

House of Commons (1982–83), *Second Report from the Home Affairs Committee, Session 1982–83, Ethnic and Racial Questions in the Census*, HC33-I—HC33-III.

HUBBOCK, JIM, and CARTER, SIMON (1980), *Half a Chance? A Report on Job Discrimination against Young Blacks in Nottingham*, London, CRE.

IGANSKI, P., MASON, D., SPONG, A. HUMPHREYS, A. and WATKINS, M. (1998), *Recruiting Minority Ethnic Groups into Nursing, Midwifery and Health Visiting*, London, English National Board for Nursing, Midwifery and Health Visiting, Researching Professional Education series, No. 7

—— and PAYNE, G. (1996),'Declining racial disadvantage in the British labour market', *Ethnic and Racial Studies*, 19(1): 113–34.

—— —— (1999), 'Socio-economic re-structuring and employment: the case of minority ethnic groups', *British Journal of Sociology*, 50(2): 195–216

INEICHEN, B. (1993), *Homes and Health: How Housing and Health Interact*, London, Spon.

Information on Ireland (1984), *Nothing but the Same Old Story: The Roots of Anti-Irish Racism*, London, Information on Ireland.

Institute of Race Relations (1991), *Deadly Silence: Black Deaths in Custody*, London, Institute of Race Relations.

JACOBSON, JESSICA (1997), 'Religion and ethnicity: dual and alternative sources of identity among young British Pakistanis', *Ethnic and Racial Studies*, 20(2): 238–56.

JEFFERSON, T., WALKER, M., and SENEVIRATNE, M. (1992), 'Ethnic minorities, crime and criminal justice: a study in a provincial city', in Downes (1992).

JENKINS R. (1986), *Racism and Recruitment*, Cambridge, Cambridge University Press.

—— (1997), *Rethinking Ethnicity*, London, Sage Publications.

JENNINGS, SHARON (1996), *Creating Solutions: Developing Alternatives in Black Mental Health*, London, King's Fund Publishing.

JEWSON, NICK (1990),' Inner city riots', *Social Studies Review*, 5(5): 170–4.

—— and MASON, DAVID (1992), 'The theory and practice of equal opportunities policies: liberal and radical perspectives', in Braham *et al.* (1992).

—— —— (1993), *Equal Employment Opportunities in the 1990s: A Policy Principle Come of Age?*, University of Leicester, Faculty of the Social Sciences Discussion Papers in Sociology, No. 593/1.

—— —— (1994), ' "Race", employment and equal opportunities: towards a political economy and an agenda for the 1990s', *Sociological Review*, 42(4): 591–617.

—— —— WATERS, S., and HARVEY, J. (1990), *Ethnic Minorities and Employment Practice: A Study of Six Employers*, Department of Employment Research Paper, No. 76, London, DE.

—— —— BOWEN, R., MULVANEY, K., and PARMAR, S. (1991), 'Universities and ethnic minorities: the public face', *New Community*, 17(2): 183–99.

—— —— BOURKE, H., BRACEBRIDGE, C., BROSNAN, F., and MILTON, K. (1993*a*), 'Changes in ethnic minority membership of health authorities, 1989–1992', *British Medical Journal*, 307: 604–5, September.

—— *et al.* (1993*b*), *Health Authority Membership and the Representation of Community Interests: The Case of Ethnicity*, University of Leicester, Faculty of the Social Sciences, Discussion Papers in Sociology, No. S93/5.

JOHNSON, M. R. D. (1993), 'Equal opportunities in service delivery: responses to a changing population', in Ahmad (1993*b*).

JOLY, DANIELE (1995), *Britannia's Crescent: Making a Place for Muslims in British Society*, Aldershot, Avebury, 1995.

—— (1996), *Haven or Hell: Asylum, Minorities and Citizenship*, Basingstoke, Macmillan

—— (ed.) (1998), *Scapegoats and Social Actors : The Exclusion and Integration of Minorities in Western and Eastern Europe*, Basingstoke, Macmillan.

JONES, T. (1993), *Britain's Ethnic Minorities*, London, PSI.

JORDAN, WINTHROP D. (1974), *The White Man's Burden*, Oxford, Oxford University Press.

KALUNTA-CRUMPTON, ANITA (1999), *Race and Drug Trials: The Social Construction of Guilt and Innocence*, Aldershot, Ashgate.

KARN, VALERIE (ed.) (1997), *Ethnicity in the 1991 Census, iv: Employment, Education and Housing among the Ethnic Minority Populations of Britain*, London, HMSO.

—— KEMENY, J., and WILLIAMS, P. (1985), *Home Ownership in the Inner City: Salvation or Despair*, Aldershot, Gower.

KELLEHER, DAVID, and HILLIER, SHEILA (eds.) (1996), *Researching Cultural Differences in Health*, London, Routledge.

KETTLE, M., and HODGES, LUCY (1982), *Uprising! The Police, the People and the Riots in Britain's Cities*, London, Pan.

KIERNAN, V. G. (1978), 'Britons Old and New', in Holmes (1978).

King Edward's Hospital Fund for London (1989), *Ethnic Minority Health Authority Membership: A Survey*, Equal Opportunities Task Force, Occasional Paper No. 5, London, King's Fund Publishing Office.

KIRK, BRUCE (1996), *Negative Images: A Simple Matter of Black and White?*, Aldershot, Avebury.

KUMAR, K. (1978), *Prophecy and Progress*, Harmondsworth, Penguin Books.

LAKEY, JANE (1997), 'Neighbourhoods and Housing', in Modood *et al.* (1997).

LARKIN, GERALD (1983), *Occupational Monopoly and Modern Medicine*, London, Tavistock.

LAYTON-HENRY, Z. (1992), *The Politics of Immigration: Immigration, 'Race' and 'Race' relations in Post-war Britain*, Oxford, Blackwell.

LEAPER, R. A. B. (ed.) (1980), *Health, Wealth and Housing*, Oxford, Oxford University Press.

LEE, G., and WRENCH, J. (1981), *In Search of a Skill*, London, CRE.

Leicester City Council (1990), *Earnings and Ethnicity*, Leicester, Leicester City Council.

LISTER, RUTH (1997), *Citizenship: Feminist Perspectives*, Basingstoke, Macmillan.

LLOYD, CATHIE, and WATERS, HAZEL (1991), 'France: one culture, one people?', *Race and Class*, 32(3): 49–65.

LORIMER, D. (1978), *Colour, Class and the Victorians*, Leicester, Leicester University Press.

LOWRY, STELLA (1991), *Housing and Health*, London, British Medical Journal.

LUNN, KENNETH (ed.) (1985), *Race and Labour in Twentieth Century Britain*, London, Frank Cass.

LUTHRA, M. (1997), *Britain's Black Population*, Aldershot, Ashgate Publishing.

MAC AN GHAILL, M. (1988), *Young, Gifted and Black: Student–Teacher Relations in the Schooling of Black Youth*, Milton Keynes, Open University Press.

—— (1992), 'Coming of age in 1980s England: reconceptualising black students' schooling experiences', in Gill *et al.* (1992).

MACDONALD, I., BHAVNANI, T., KHAN, L., and JOHN, G. (1989), *Murder in the Playground: The Report of the Macdonald Inquiry into Racism and Racial Violence in Manchester Schools*, London, Longsight Press.

MACEWEN, M. (1991a), *Housing, Race and Law*, London, Routledge.

—— (1991b), 'Housing allocations and the law: ethnic minorities in Edinburgh', in Bowes and Sim (1991).

—— (1995), *Tackling Racism in Europe: An Examination of Anti-discrimination Law in Practice*, Oxford, Berg.

MACPHERSON, W. (1999), *The Stephen Lawrence Inquiry: Report of an Inquiry by Sir William Macpherson of Cluny*, London, Home Office, Cm 4262-I.

McCORMICK, B. (1986), 'Evidence about the comparative earnings of Asian and West Indian workers in Britain', *Scottish Journal of Political Economy*, 33(2).

McGREGOR, S., and PIMLOTT, B. (1990), *Tackling the Inner Cities: The 1980s Reviewed, Prospects for the 1990s*, Oxford, Oxford University Press.

McKAY, DAVID H. (1977), *Housing and Race in Industrial Society: Civil Rights and Urban Policy in Britain and the United States*, London, Croom Helm.

McMANUS, I. C. (1998), 'Factors affecting likelihood of applicants being offered a place in medical schools in the United Kingdom in 1996 and 1997: retrospective study', *British Medical Journal*, 317(7166): 1111–17.

McNAUGHT, A. (1988), *Race and Health Policy*, London, Croom Helm.

MALIK, KENAN (1996), *The Meaning of Race: Race, History and Culture in Western Society*, Basingstoke, Macmillan.

MANN, M. (1987), 'Ruling class strategies and citizenship', *Sociology*, 21(3): 339–54.

MARSH, Catherine (1993), 'Privacy, confidentiality and anonymity in the 1991 Census', in Dale and Marsh (1993).

MARSHALL, T. H. (1950), *Citizenship and Social Class and Other Essays*, Cambridge, Cambridge University Press.

—— (1964), *Class, Citizenship and Social Development*, London, Doubleday.

MASON, DAVID (1982), 'After Scarman: a note on the concept of institutional racism', *New Community*, 10(1): 38–45.

—— (1986), 'Controversies and continuities in race and ethnic relations theory', in Rex and Mason (1986).

—— (1990a), 'A rose by any other name . . . ? Categorisation, identity and social science', *New Community*, 17(1): 123–33.

—— (1990b), 'Competing conceptions of "fairness" and the formulation and implementation of equal opportunities policies', in Wendy Ball and John Solomos (eds.), *Race and Local Politics*, London, Macmillan.

—— (1991), 'The concept of ethnic minority: conceptual dilemmas and policy implications', *Innovation*, Vienna, 4(2): 191–209.

—— (1992), 'Categories, identities and change: ethnic monitoring and the social scientist', *European Journal of Intercultural Studies*, 2(2): 41–52.

—— (1994a), 'Employment and the labour market', *New Community*, 20(2): 301–8.

—— (1994b), 'Employment and the labour market', *New Community*, 20(4): 673–7.

—— (1994c), 'On the dangers of disconnecting race and racism', *Sociology*, 28(4): 845–58.

—— and JEWSON, NICK (1992), ' "Race", equal opportunities policies and employment practice: reflections on the 1980s, prospects for the 1990s', *New Community*, 19(1): 99–112.

MAY, STEPHEN (ed.) (1999), *Critical Multiculturalism: Rethinking Multicultural and Antiracist Education*, London, Falmer Press.

MEMMI, ALBERT (1965), *The Colonizer and the Colonized*, London, Souvenir Press.

MHLANGA, BONNY (1997), *The Colour of English Justice: A Multivariate Analysis*, Aldershot, Avebury.

MILES, R. (1982), *Racism and Migrant Labour*, London, Routledge & Kegan Paul.

—— (1989), *Racism*, London, Routledge.

—— (1993), *Racism after 'Race Relations'*, London, Routledge.

—— (1994), 'A rise of racism and fascism in contemporary Europe? Some skeptical reflections on its nature and extent', *New Community*, 20(4): 547–62.

Ministry of Defence (MOD) (1998), *The Strategic Defence Review*, Cm. 3999, July.

MIRZA, HEIDI SAFIA (1992), *Young, Female and Black*, London, Routledge.

—— (1998), 'Black Women in Education: A collective movement for social change', in Modood and Ackland (1998).

MODOOD, T. (1988), ' "Black", racial equality and Asian identity', *New Community*, 14(3): 397–404.

—— (1990a), 'Catching up with Jesse Jackson: on being oppressed and on being somebody', *New Community*, 17(1): 85–96.

—— (1990b), 'British Asian Muslims and the Salman Rushdie Affair', *Political Quarterly*, 61(2): 143–60.

—— (1992), *Not Easy Being British*, Stoke-on-Trent, Trentham Books.

—— (1997a), 'Qualifications and English Language' in Modood, *et al.* (1997).

—— (1997b), 'Employment', in Modood *et al.* (1997).

—— (1997c), 'Culture and Identity', in Modood *et al.* (1997).

—— (1998), 'Ethnic minorities' drive for qualifications', in Modood and Ackland (1998).

—— and ACKLAND, T. (1998), *Race and Higher Education*, London, Policy Studies Institute.

—— and BERTHOUD, RICHARD, LAKEY, JANE, NAZROO, JAMES, SMITH, PATLER, VIRDEE, SATNAM, BEISHON, SHARON (1997), *Ethnic Minorities in Britain*, London: Policy Studies Institute.

—— and SHINER, M. (1994), *Ethnic Minorities and Higher Education: Why are there Differential Rates of Admission?*, London, Policy Studies Institute.

MONTAGUE, A. (1964), *The Concept of Race*, New York, Free Press.

—— (1974), *Man's Most Dangerous Myth: The Fallacy of Race*, New York, Oxford University Press.

MOORE, R., and WALLACE, T. (1975), *Slamming the Door: The Administration of Immigration Control*, London, Martin Robertson.

MURRAY, CHARLES (1990), *The Emerging British Underclass*, London, The IEA Health and Welfare Unit.

National Association of Citizen's Advice Bureaux (1984), *Unequal Opportunities: CAB Evidence on Racial Discrimination*, London, NACAB.

—— (1991), *Barriers to Benefit: Black Claimants and Social Security*, London, NACAB.

National Association for the Care and Resettlement of Offenders (NACRO) (1986), *Black People and the Criminal Justice System*, London, NACRO Race Issues Advisory Committee.

NAZOO, JAMES (1997), 'Health and Health Services', in Modood *et al.* (1997).

New Community (1990), Special issue on the Education Reform Act, 16(3), April 1990.

NOON, M. (1993), 'Racial discrimination in speculative applications: evidence from the UK's top one hundred firms', *Human Resource Management Journal*, 3(4): 35–47.

OAKLEY, R. (1988), *Employment in Police Forces*, London, Commission for Racial Equality.

O'CONNOR, KEVIN (1972), *The Irish in Britain*, London, Sidgwick & Jackson.

O'LEARY, BRENDAN (1993), *The Politics of Antagonism: Understanding Northern Ireland*, London, Athlone Press.

Office of Public Service and Science (1994), *Equal Opportunities in the Civil Service for People of Ethnic Minority Origin: Third Progress Report 1992–1993*, London, HMSO.

OMI, M., and WINANT, H. (1986), *Racial Formation in the United States*, New York, Routledge & Kegan Paul.

OPPENHEIM, C. (1993), *Poverty: The Facts* (Revised and updated edition), London, Child Poverty Action Group (CPAG).

OSLER, AUDREY (1997), *The Education and Careers of Black Teachers: Changing Identities, Changing Lives*, Buckingham, Open University Press.

OWEN D. (1992), *Ethnic Minorities in Britain: Settlement Patterns*, University of Warwick, Centre for Research in Ethnic Relations, National Ethnic Minority Data Archive, 1991 Census Statistical Paper No. 1.

—— (1993a), *Ethnic Minorities in Britain: Age and Gender Structure*, University of Warwick, Centre for Research in Ethnic Relations, National Ethnic Minority Data Archive, 1991 Census Statistical Paper No. 2.

—— (1993b), *Ethnic Minorities in Britain: Economic Characteristics*, University of Warwick, Centre for Research in Ethnic Relations, National Ethnic Minority Data Archive, 1991 Census Statistical Paper No. 3.

—— (1993c), *Ethnic Minorities in Britain: Housing and Family Characteristics*, University of Warwick, Centre for Research in Ethnic Relations, National Ethnic Minority Data Archive, 1991 Census Statistical Paper No. 4.

—— (1993d), *Country of Birth: Settlement Patterns*, University of Warwick, Centre for Research in Ethnic Relations, National Ethnic Minority Data Archive, 1991 Census Statistical Paper No. 5.

—— (1994), *Black People in Great Britain: Social and Economic Circumstances*, University of Warwick, Centre for Research in Ethnic Relations, National Ethnic Minority Data Archive, 1991 Census Statistical Paper No. 6.

—— and GREEN, A. (1992), 'Occupational change among ethnic groups in Great Britain', *New Community*, 19(1): 7–29.

PAHL, R. E. (ed.) (1968), *Readings in Urban Sociology*, London, Pergamon Press.

PANAYI, PANIKOS (ed.) (1993), *Racial Violence in Britain, 1840–1950*, Leicester, Leicester University Press.

—— (1994), *Immigration, Ethnicity and Racism in Britain, 1815–1945*, Manchester, Manchester University Press.

PAOR, LIAM DE (1971), *Divided Ulster*, Harmondsworth, Penguin.

PARSONS, L., MACFARLANE, A., and GOLDING, J. (1993), 'Pregnancy, birth and maternity care', in Ahmad (1993b).

PATTERSON, SHEILA (1963), *Dark Strangers*, London, Tavistock Publications.

PAYNE, SARAH (1991), *Women, Health and Poverty: An Introduction*, London, Harvester Wheatsheaf.

PEACH, C. (1968), *West Indian Migration to Britain: A Social Geography*, London, Oxford University Press.

—— (ed.) (1996), *Ethnicity in the 1991 Census, ii: The Ethnic Minority Populations of Great Britain*, London, HMSO.

—— and BYRON, M (1993), 'Caribbean tenants in council housing: "Race", class and gender', *New Community*, 19(3): 407–23.

PHILLIPS, D. (1985), *What Price Equality? A Report on the Allocation of GLC Housing in Tower Hamlets*, London, GLC Housing Research and Policy Report No. 9.

PHIZACKLEA, ANNIE (ed.) (1983), *One-way Ticket: Migration and Female Labour*, London, Routledge & Kegan Paul.

PILGRIM, DAVID, and ROGERS, ANNE (1993), *A Sociology of Mental Health and Illness*, Buckingham, Open University Press.

PIRANI, M., YOLLES, M., and BASSA, E. (1992), 'Ethnic pay differentials', *New Community*, 19(1): 31–42.

PLATT, CHRIS (1990), *The Immigration Act 1988: A Discussion of its Effects and Implications*, University of Warwick, ESRC Centre for Research in Ethnic Relations, Policy Papers in Ethnic Relations No. 16.

Polytechnics and Colleges Funding Council (PCFC) (1989–90), *Statistical Supplement, 1989–90*.

PRESTWICH, R., and TAYLOR, P. (1990), *Introduction to Regional and Urban Policy in the UK*, London, Longman.

RAM, MONDER (1992), 'Coping with racism: Asian employers in the inner city', *Work, Employment and Society*, 6(4): 601–18.

RATCLIFFE, P. (1981), *Racism and Reaction*, London, Routledge & Kegan Paul.

—— (1991), 'Paradigms in conflict: "Racial" and "ethnic" inequality in contemporary Britain', *Innovation*, 4(2): 211–33.

RATHWELL, T., and PHILLIPS, D. (eds.) (1986), *Health, Race and Ethnicity*, London, Croom Helm.

RATTANSI, A., and WESTWOOD, S. (1994), *Racism, Modernity and Identity on the Western Front*, Oxford, Polity Press.

REAY, D., and MIRZA, H. (1997), 'Uncovering genealogies of the margins: Black supplementary schools' *British Journal of the Sociology of Education*, 18(4): 477–99.

REES, TERESA (1992), *Women and the Labour Market*, London, Routledge.

REES, TOM (1982), 'Immigration policies in the United Kingdom', in C. Husband (ed.), *'Race' in Britain: Continuity and Change*, London, Hutchinson University Library.

REINER, R. (1978), *The Blue Coated Worker*, Cambridge, Cambridge University Press.

—— (1992), *The Politics of the Police*, 2nd edn., London, Harvester Wheatsheaf.

REX, J. (1968), 'The Sociology of a Zone of Transition', in Pahl (ed.) (1968).

—— (1970), *Race Relations in Sociological Theory*, London, Weidenfeld & Nicolson.

—— (1973), *Race, Colonialism and the City*, London, Routledge & Kegan Paul.

REX, J. (1981), 'A working paradigm for race relations research', *Ethnic and Racial Studies*, 4(1): 1–25.

—— (1982), 'The 1981 Urban Riots in Britain' *International Journal of Urban and Regional Research*, 6(1): 99–113.

—— (1987), 'Multi-culturalism, anti-racism and equality of opportunity in the Swann Report', in Chivers (1987).

—— and MASON, DAVID (eds.) (1986), *Theories of Race and Ethnic Relations*, Cambridge, Cambridge University Press.

—— and MOORE, R. (1967), *Race, Community and Conflict: A Study of Sparkbrook*, London, Oxford University Press.

RICH, P. (1994) *Prospero's Return: Historical Essays on Race, Culture and British Society*, London: Hansib Publishing.

ROBINSON, VAUGHAN (1989), 'Economic Restructuring and the Black Population', in Herbert and Smith (1989).

ROBSON, BRIAN (ed.) (1987), *Managing the City*, London, Croom Helm.

SAGGAR, SHAMIT (1992), *Race and Politics in Britain*, London, Harvester Wheatsheaf.

—— (1993), 'Black political participation and the transformation of the "race issue" in British politics', *New Community*, 20(1): 27–41.

—— (1998), 'Smoking guns and magic bullets: the "race card" debate revisited in 1997', *Immigrants and Minorities*, 17(3): 1–21.

—— and HEATH, ANTHONY (1999), 'Race: Towards a multicultural electorate', in Geoffrey Evans and Pippa Norris (eds.) (1999), *Critical Elections: British Parties and Voters in Long-Term Perspective*, London, Sage publications.

SAIFULLAH KHAN, VERITY (1979), 'Work and network: South-Asian women in South London', in Wallman (1979a).

SARRE, P., PHILLIPS, D., and SKELLINGTON, R. (1989), *Ethnic Minority Housing: Explanations and Policies*, Aldershot, Gower.

SASHIDHARAN, S. P., and FRANCIS, E. (1993), 'Epidemiology, ethnicity and schizophrenia', in Ahmad (1993b).

SAUNDERS, P. (1990), *A Nation of Home Owners*, London, Unwin Hyman.

SCARMAN, RT. HON. THE LORD (1981), *The Brixton Disorders 10–12 April, 1981*, Cmnd 8427, London, HMSO.

SCHWEFEL, D. SVENSSON, P.-G., and ZOLLNER (eds.) (1987), *Unemployment, Social Vulnerability and Health in Europe*, Berlin, Springer Verlag.

SHALLICE, ANDY, and GORDON, PAUL (1990), *Black People, White Justice? Race and the Criminal Justice System*, London, Runnymede Trust.

SHARPE, Sue (1976), *Just Like a Girl*, Harmondsworth, Penguin.

SILLS, A., TARPEY, M., and GOLDING, P. (1983/4), 'Asians in an inner city', *New Community*, 11(1/2): 34–41.

SIMPSON, ALAN (1981), *Stacking the Decks: A Study of Race, Inequality and Council Housing in Nottingham*, Nottingham, Nottingham and District Community Relations Council.

SIMPSON, G., and YINGER, M. (1965), *Racial and Cultural Minorities*, New York, Harper & Row.

SIVANANDAN, A. (1982), *A Different Hunger: Writings on Black Resistance*, London, Pluto Press.

SKELLINGTON, R. (1992), *'Race' in Britain Today*, London, Sage Publications.

SMAJE, CHRIS (1995), *Health, 'Race' and Ethnicity: Making Sense of the Evidence*, London, King's Fund Institute.

SMALL, S. (1991), 'Racialised relations in Liverpool: a contemporary anomaly', *New Community*, 17(4): 511–37.

SMITH, A. D. (1971), *Theories of Nationalism*, London, Duckworth.

SMITH, D. J. (1976), *The Facts of Racial Disadvantage*, London, Political and Economic Planning.

—— (1981), *Unemployment and Racial Minorities*, London, Policy Studies Institute.

—— and GRAY, J. (1983), *Police and People in London, iv: The Police in Action*, London, Policy Studies Institute.

—— and TOMLINSON, S. (1989), *The School Effect: A Study of Multi-Racial Comprehensives*, London, Policy Studies Institute.

SMITH, M. G. (1986), 'Pluralism, race and ethnicity in selected African countries', in Rex and Mason (1986).

SMITH, R. (1987), *Unemployment and Health: A Disaster and a Challenge*, Oxford, Oxford University Press.

—— (1993), 'Deception in research and racial discrimination in medicine', *British Medical Journal*, 306: 668–9 (13 March).

SMITH, S. J. (1989), *The Politics of 'Race' and Residence*, Cambridge, Polity Press.

SOLOMOS, J. (1986), *Riots, Urban Protest and Social Policy: The Interplay of Reform and Social Control*, University of Warwick, Centre for Research in Ethnic Relations, Policy Papers in Ethnic Relations, No. 7.

—— (1988), *Black Youth, Racism and the State*, Cambridge, Cambridge University Press.

—— (1993), *Race and Racism in Britain*, Basingstoke, Macmillan.

SPENCER, IAN R. G. (1997), *British Immigration Policy Since 1939: The Making of Multi-racial Britain*, London, Routledge.

STACEY, T. (1970), *Immigration and Enoch Powell*, London, Tom Stacey Ltd.

STEPAN, NANCY (1982), *The Idea of Race in Science*, London, Macmillan.

STONE, M. (1981), *The Education of the Black Child in Britain*, London, Fontana.

STOREY, H. (1986), 'UK Immigration Controls and the Welfare State', in Dummett (1986).

SZASZ, THOMAS (1971), *The Manufacture of Madness: A Comparison of the Inquisition and the Mental Health Movement*, London, Routledge & Kegan Paul.

—— (1972), *The Myth of Mental Illness*, London, Paladin.

THIRD, HILARY and MACEWEN, MARTIN (1997), 'The housing experience of minority ethnic groups in Scotland', in Bowes and Sim (1997).

TIZZARD, B., BLATCHFORD, P., BURKE, J. FARQUAR, C., and PLEWIS, I. (1988), *Young Children at School in the Inner City*, Hove, Lawrence Earlbaum Associates.

—— and PHOENIX, A. (1993), *Black, White or Mixed Race?*, London, Routledge.

TOMLINSON S. (1984), *Home and School in Multicultural Britain*, London, Batsford.

—— (1987), 'Curriculum option choices in multi-ethnic schools', in Troyna (1987).

—— (1990), *Multicultural Education in White Schools*, London, Batsford.

TORKINGTON, N. P. K. (1991), *Black Health: A Political Issue*, Catholic Association for Racial Justice and Liverpool Institute of Higher Education.

TOWNSEND, P. (1990), 'Living Standards and Health in the Inner Cities', in McGregor and Pimlott (1990).

—— and DAVIDSON, N. (eds.) (1982), *Inequalities in Health: The Black Report*, Harmondsworth, Penguin.

TROWLER, PAUL (1991), *Investigating Health, Welfare and Poverty*, London, Collins Educational.

TROYNA, B. (1984), 'Fact or artifact? The "educational underachievement" of black pupils', *British Journal of the Sociology of Education*, 5(2): 153–66.

—— (ed.) (1987), *Racial Inequality in Education*, London, Tavistock.

—— (1992), 'Can you see the join? An historical analysis of multicultural and antiracist education policies', in Gill *et al.* (1992).

—— and CARRINGTON, B. (1990), *Education, Racism and Reform*, London, Routledge.

—— and SMITH, D. (eds.) (1983), *Racism, School and the Labour Market*, Leicester, National Youth Bureau.

—— and WILLIAMS, J. (1986), *Racism, Education and the State*, London, Croom Helm.

TURNER, B. S. (1986), *Citizenship and Capitalism: The Debate over Reformism*, London, Allen & Unwin.

—— (ed.) (1993), *Citizenship and Social Theory*, London, Sage Publications.

TWADDLE, MICHAEL (ed.) (1975), *Expulsion of a Minority: Essays on Ugandan Asians*, London, The Athlone Press.

TWITCHEN, J. (1990), *The Black and White Media Book: A Handbook for the Study of Racism and Television*, Stoke on Trent, Trentham.

Universities Central Council on Admissions (UCCA) (1989–90), *Statistical Supplement to the Twenty-eighth Annual Report, 1989–90*.

VAN DEN BERGHE, P. L. (1967), *Race and Racism*, New York, Wiley.

—— (1981), *The Ethnic Phenomenon*, New York, Elsevier Press.

VAN DIJK, TEUN (1991), *Racism and the Press*, London, Routledge.

VIRDEE, SATNAM (1995) *Racial Violence and Harassment*, London, Policy Studies Institute.

—— (1997), 'Racial Harassment', in Modood *et al.* (1997).

WAEVER, OLE *et al.* (1993) *Identity, Migration and the New Security Agenda in Europe*, London; Pinter Publishers.

WALBY, SYLVIA (1992), 'Woman and nation', *International Journal of Comparative Sociology*, 33(1–2): 81–100.

—— (1994), 'Is citizenship gendered?', *Sociology*, 28(2): 379–95.

WALLMAN, SANDRA (ed.) (1979a), *Ethnicity at Work*, London, Macmillan.

—— (1979b), 'Introduction: the scope for ethnicity', in Wallman (1979a).

—— (1986), 'Ethnicity and the boundary process in context', in Rex and Mason (1986).

WARD, L. (1993), 'Race equality and employment in the National Health Service', in Ahmad (1993*b*).

WARD, R., and JENKINS, R. (eds.) (1984), *Ethnic Communities in Business*, Cambridge, Cambridge University Press.

WARR, PETER (1987), *Work, Unemployment and Mental Health*, Oxford, The Clarendon Press.

WATERS, R. (1990), *Ethnic Minorities and the Criminal Justice System*, Aldershot, Avebury.

WEIR, STUART and BEETHAM, DAVID (1999), *Political Power and Democratic Control in Britain*, London, Routledge.

WESTWOOD, S., COULOUTE, J., DESAI, S., MATHEW, P., and POPER, A. (1989), *Sadness in my Heart: Racism and Mental Health*, Leicester, Leicester Black Mental Health Group.

WILLIAMS, J. (1985), 'Redefining institutional racism', *Ethnic and Racial Studies*, 8(3): 323–48.

—— COOKING, J., and DAVIES, L. (1989), *Words or Deeds? A Review of Equal Opportunities Policies in Higher Education*, London, CRE.

WILPERT, C. (1991), 'Migration and ethnicity in a non-immigration country: foreigners in a united Germany', *New Community*, 18(1): 49–62.

WRIGHT, C. (1987), 'Black students—white teachers', in Troyna (1987).

—— (1992), 'Early education: multiracial education in primary school classrooms', in Gill *et al.* (1992).

YINGER, M. (1986), 'Intersecting strands in the theorisation of race and ethnic relations', in Rex and Mason (1986).

YUVAL-DAVIS, NIRA (1993), 'Gender and nation', *Ethnic and Racial Studies*, 16(4): 621–32.

—— and ANTHIAS, FLOYA (eds.) (1989), *Woman-Nation-State*, London, Macmillan.

Index

Bold numbers denote references to boxes and tables